His was a great sin who first invented consciousness,
Let us lose it for a few hours.

— F. SCOTT FITZGERALD

GLAMOUR
and STYLE

the beauty of

HEDY
LAMARR

STEPHEN MICHAEL SHEARER

LYONS
PRESS

Guilford, Connecticut

LYONS
PRESS

An imprint of Globe Pequot, the trade division of
The Rowman & Littlefield Publishing Group, Inc.
4501 Forbes Blvd., Ste. 200
Lanham, MD 20706
www.rowman.com

Distributed by NATIONAL BOOK NETWORK

British Library Cataloguing in Publication Information available

Library of Congress Cataloging-in-Publication Data
Names: Shearer, Stephen Michael, 1951– author.
Title: Glamour and style : the beauty of Hedy Lamarr / Stephen Michael
  Shearer.
Description: Guilford : Lyons Press, 2021. | Includes bibliographical
  references and index. | Summary: "A photographic tribute to Hedy Lamarr
  containing hundreds of personal and professional photographs, many never
  before published, along with private letters, memorabilia, ephemera,
  estate jewelry, and gowns. Features commentary by biographer Stephen
  Michael Shearer"— Provided by publisher.
Identifiers: LCCN 2021025739 (print) | LCCN 2021025740 (ebook) | ISBN
  9781493059720 (hardcover) | ISBN 9781493063802 (epub)
Subjects: LCSH: Lamarr, Hedy, 1913-2000. | Actors—United
  States—Biography.
Classification: LCC PN2287.L24 S544 2021 (print) | LCC PN2287.L24 (ebook)
  | DDC 791.4302/8092 [B]—dc23
LC record available at https://lccn.loc.gov/2021025739
LC ebook record available at https://lccn.loc.gov/2021025740

Printed in India

This book is dedicated to:

JAMES LAMARR LODER
DENISE HEDWIG LODER DE LUCA
ANTHONY JOHN LODER

CONTENTS

ACKNOWLEDGMENTS

An author never works alone. There have been many people who have given of their time, knowledge, memories, and emotions for this book, *Glamour and Style: The Beauty of Hedy Lamarr*.

First, and foremost, I would like to thank the children of Hedy Lamarr: James Lamarr Loder and his lovely wife, Ona; Denise Loder DeLuca and her husband, Vincent; and Anthony John Loder and his lovely wife, Lise Marie. Without their cooperation and approval—not only with this book, but also with *Beautiful: The Life of Hedy Lamarr* (Thomas Dunne / St. Martin's Press–Macmillan, 2010)—I could not have proceeded.

I should like to thank Tracy Christensen and Roy Windham for their generous and knowledgeable assistance regarding film fashion and history.

I also would like to thank Ned Comstock at the Cinema-TV Library of the University of California (USC) in Los Angeles, and Howard and Ronald Mandelbaum of Photofest in New York.

I wish to thank Rick Rinehart and the entire design staff at Lyons Press for seeing the vision I have for this book. And I most certainly want to thank my editor, Melissa Hayes, for her patience, guidance, and understanding. My literary agent Deborah Ritchken of the Marsal Lyon Literary Agency has been a staunch supporter of my work on Hedy Lamarr. I give her my deepest thanks for seeing me through this project.

I must acknowledge the studios of Metro-Goldwyn-Mayer, United Artists, Paramount, Warner Brothers, RKO, and Universal, etc., and their rich history of artists who costumed, made up, and photographed Hedy Lamarr in her many films. Also, for use of private photographs in this book, I wish to thank James and Ona Loder, Denise Loder De Luca, Tim Loder, Arlene Roxbury, Roy Windham, and Randolf Destaller in Austria.

My very special thanks as always to my partner Michael Wickman for dealing with me and my erratic behavior and sometimes long hours through yet another book project, and sharing all of the trials and tribulations we as writers must endure to give birth.

For his magnificent cover photograph for *Glamour and Style: The Beauty of Hedy Lamarr* I give my deepest thanks and appreciation to Victor Mascaro of Hollywood in Color on Facebook and Instagram, for the digital color restoration.

INTERVIEWER: *Was there ever a time, Valentino, when you didn't want to be in fashion?*

VALENTINO: No . . . I remember very well when I was young . . . and I was dreaming, dreaming about movie stars, dreaming about everything beautiful in the world . . . I was always attracted by magazines, by films. I had a sister. She took me for the first time to see some films and for me, the dream of my life—she was a beautiful lady of the silver screen. I remember . . . Ziegfeld Girl . . . Hedy Lamarr!

—*Valentino: The Last Emperor* (Phase 4 Films, 2009)

PREFACE

That face! It may have possessed the most fabulous brunette beauty . . .
to ever hit the silver screen . . .
The beauty of Hedy Lamarr should be seen in repose—
you tended to be distracted when she smiled.
—JOHN SPRINGER [1]

*T*he definition of the word beauty, as defined in most common dictionaries, is "the quality or aggregate of qualities in a person or thing that gives pleasure to the senses or pleasurably exalts the mind or spirit: loveliness." [2] In turn, beauty, as it is visually perceived, is relatively subjective, according to individual preference and taste.

In motion pictures, both male and female beauty is a bankable commodity. To possess that unique quality was and still is a most valuable asset in Hollywood. Motion picture glamour, in its true feminine form, most surely should be acknowledged as having originated with the immense popularity of silent screen actress Gloria Swanson, beginning in the 1920s. As the leading example of film's *femme fatale*, as well as being recognized as American cinema's first "clotheshorse" in numerous Cecil B. DeMille social dramas at Paramount, Swanson was the first American film actress to truly set the bar in films for glamour and style. The decade of the 1930s in turn glorified the blonde and brazen voluptuousness of Jean Harlow, the beauty of Greta Garbo, and the sophisticated styles of Carole Lombard, Joan Crawford, and Marlene Dietrich.

As one critic wrote in 1939, "[T]he very word *glamour* was unknown to the industry until 1914 or so." [3] In the 1910s there were many popular actresses who epitomized beauty—Mary Pickford, Lillian Gish, Irene Castle, and Elsie Ferguson, for example. However, they were considered actresses—or, more so, personalities—and they did not necessarily contribute to style until Swanson came into the public consciousness. When

MGM star Jean Harlow died prematurely in June 1937, an era ended. Still a major box-office draw, Harlow was herself in the process of evolution toward the end of her brief career. The trademark pencil-lined eyebrows, platinum-white hair, and bee-stung lips made so very popular by the glamour queen were now supplanted by a softer, warmer-looking, honey-color coiffure, thicker eyebrows, and a fuller, lipstick-lined mouth. But by the following year, 1938, Garbo, Dietrich, and Crawford were all labeled box-office poison, and Hollywood was balancing on the precipice of seeking a new style of glamour, a new allure.

When actress Hedy Lamarr burst onto American cinema screens in 1938, cinemagoers were mesmerized by her breathtaking beauty. Frank S. Nugent made a quick assessment of her impact on cinemagoers in the *New York Times*, cementing Lamarr's exclusive claim to glamour. "Of course, it might be objected that the very designation 'Glamour Girl' is in itself proof of publicity's past efforts in their behalf and that there is no point in gilding the gilded lilies. But the history we have in mind would not deal so much with the girl as with the glamour, since the glamour always has outlived the girl, just as the ripples always remain visible long after the pebble has gone to the bottom. That is the saddening realization, and we pause to drink a toast: to Hedy Lamarr, the pebble of today, the ripple of tomorrow . . . Miss Lamarr belongs to this history, anyway." [4]

Hedy Lamarr's beauty was her ticket. "Miss Lamarr doesn't have to say 'Yes,' all she has to do is yawn. . . . In her perfect will-lessness Miss Lamarr is, indeed, identified *metaphysically* with her mesmeric midnight captor, the loving male," remarked film critic Parker Tyler. [5] Everyone talked about Lamarr's unquestionable glamour and beauty. But beauty was not the only attribute Hedy possessed. Upon the release of her first Hollywood film, Hedy Lamarr's impact on style and fashion was unquestionable.

"After Hedy Lamarr first appeared on the screen in *Algiers*," wrote author Margaret J. Bailey, defining the impact Hedy Lamarr had on the fashion trade, "drugstores experienced a run on hair dyes, and soon everybody, including starlets and established luminaries like Crawford and Joan Bennett, had changed their locks from blonde or brown to jet black. The Lamarr hairdo with the part in the middle and the total Lamarr

look became the standard of glamour. Shock waves were felt not only in personal beauty, but also in the realm of fashion, in particular, the hat. Somehow that three-letter word seems inadequate when describing what Lamarr wore in her first films. Lamarr veils, snoods, turbans, and such swept the fashion world, and millinery companies worked overtime to fill the hunger for the new cinema image. Not everyone could effect the Lamarr styles, but just about everyone tried. Turbans and snoods became *the* fashion for Forties headgear." [6]

Throughout the 1940s, moviegoers were treated to the gorgeously ethereal image of Hedy Lamarr dressed exquisitely by the leading film fashion designers of the era, coiffured, made up, and photographed immaculately by the greatest photographers ever to manage a camera, in film after film. Although many leading studio fashion designers may lay claim to having created everyday style and popularity in fashion during that era, in fact, the times necessitated changes. Yet they still allowed for occasional flights of fancy and glamorous moments, which few designers successfully achieved—except for those who dressed Lamarr.

But make no mistake. Hedy Lamarr was not just a "clotheshorse." As the late Robert Osborne wrote in my biography of Lamarr, "[S]he was also a better actress than she was ever given credit for. But she had that curse that all those beautiful women had—nobody could see beyond that. . . . I think she did many interesting things, and for anyone to think that's easy, what she did, has never been in front of a camera and a whole crew and all that. And she's very, very good, and was always good. She particularly was wonderful because she did what was needed for the women she portrayed." [7]

Hedy Lamarr was a huge film star in that glittering pantheon of Hollywood's Golden Era. As legendary photographer George Hurrell commented about such luminaries, "They didn't just walk in the door . . . They arrived . . . It was as if they had internal trumpets that blew for them just as the door open[ed]." [8]

Unlike any other star in Hollywood, the legacy Hedy Lamarr has gifted us is twofold. Not only has she left behind a memorable canon of glorious motion pictures from the Golden Era of Hollywood, to be seen, examined, and studied, she has also given the world a very unique gift of scientific invention, for which she is equally noted.

Hedy Lamarr was not unintelligent. She recognized the real and the unreal. She did not suffer fools gladly, nor did she completely buy into her hype and beauty. In fact, in her most famous and often-repeated quote, she reveals her innately pragmatic and logical sensibility: "Any girl can be beautiful. All she has to do is stand still and look stupid."

chapter 1

MONSTERS, OGRES, AND KNIGHTS

What is fact? What is fiction? Fact is truth. Fiction is altered fact. If fiction is repeated often enough, it sometimes can become fact. In the 1962 Western film classic *The Man Who Shot Liberty Valance* (Paramount), directed by John Ford and written by James Warner Bellah and Willis Goldbeck, the character of Ransom Stoddard (James Stewart) asks Maxwell Scott (Carleton Young), "You're not going to use the story, Mr. Scott?" To which he replies, "No, sir . . . When the legend becomes fact, print the legend."

Sometimes fiction becomes fact, and sometimes it becomes legend.

The fiction that became the legend surrounding the life of Hedy Lamarr was created for the awaiting press even before beautiful Viennese film actress Hedwig Kiesler stepped off the French liner *Normandie* in New York in late September

Opposite page: Hedy Kiesler, Sturm im Wasserglas / Die Blumenfrau von Lindenau *(Sascha-Felsom, 1931).*

Above left: Hedy Lamarr's father, Emil Kiesler, 1924.
Above right: Five-year-old Hedy Kiesler and her father, Emil Kiesler, c. 1919.

1937. For decades that very fiction remained fact in the collective minds of filmgoers and the public. Did it really matter that she was born into an affluent family in Vienna; that she began her film career as a teenager? That she appeared nude in a foreign film in 1933, and simulated orgasm in a somewhat explicit lovemaking scene in that same picture? Should the public care that she married a wealthy industrialist in her native Austria, living a lavishly pampered and privileged life, and that her coming to America was simply a career opportunity she wanted to pursue? Her obvious beauty was immediately recognizable. That mattered. She was destined for fame and fortune in America. Her life from then on out would be perfect. Nothing else really mattered. Cut and print.

Gertrud "Trude" Lichtwitz Kiesler, c. 1921. (Denise Loder DeLuca Collection)

The Kiesler home at 12 Peter Jordan Strasse, Vienna, Austria, 2020. (Photograph courtesy of Randolf Destaller)

In the case of Hedy Lamarr, facts belie fiction in many ways. The struggle that accompanies success at any level cannot be overlooked. Nothing in life is ever "easy" or completely understandable, much less totally transparent. For a biographer or historian, finding those facts, recognizing the fiction, and then explaining the subject's existence through life transformations can be daunting and very much a challenge. The earliest interviews, contemporary reports, reviews, and articles about—or given by—the subject can bring forth hidden truths that are much more explainable and realistic than the fiction that has become fact. If it does not make chronological and personal sense, then it's possible it just is not true. The difference between the publicly acknowledged Hollywood life of Hedy Lamarr and the keenly intelligent real life of Hedwig Kiesler

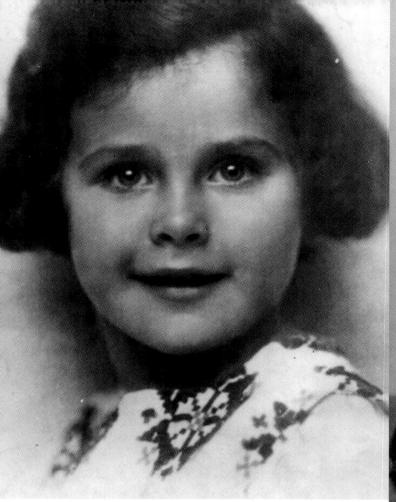

Above left: Hedwig Eva Maria Kiesler, Vienna, Austria, c. 1920.
Above right: Hedwig Eva Maria Kiesler, Vienna, Austria, c. 1925.
Right: Hedy Lamarr, c. 1940

truly borders on, even defines, historic significance and perpetuity.

As I chronicled in the opening chapter of my definitive biography of the actress's life, *Beautiful: The Life of Hedy Lamarr*, "To understand the life of Hedy Lamarr, it is important to understand the world in which she was born." [1] Hedwig Eva Maria Kiesler was born in Vienna, Austria,

Hedy's uncle and Hedy Kiesler, c. 1932.

at the very end of the Belle Époque on Sunday, November 9, 1914, just as Europe was plunged into World War I. For decades Vienna had been a melting pot of congregated European nationalities, predominantly those fleeing overwhelming religious suppression in other countries. Austria became the center of European arts, culture, and especially music. Throughout the conflict and decimation of most of the continent

Hedy Kiesler lounging, Austria, 1931.

during World War I (1914–1918), Vienna itself remained primarily unscathed. Its population of numerous assimilated European cultures was primarily Jewish by heritage, and largely Catholic by religious practice.

Emil Kiesler, born December 27, 1875, was a Ukrainian-born Jew who had immigrated to Vienna around 1900. An established well-to-do banker, he was the manager of the Creditanstalt Bankverein in Vienna. His Jewish-born wife, Gertrud Lichtwitz, part of the "Jewish haute bourgeoisie," was born on February 3, 1897, in Budapest, Hungary. She was barely seventeen years old when she gave birth to the couple's only child. Trude, as she was called, would later convert to Catholicism and raise Hedy as a Catholic.

As a toddler Hedwig could not pronounce her name, so instead called herself Hedy (pronounced "Hay-dee"). She was a beautiful and well-proportioned baby. Emil doted on her, quickly recognizing his child's innate intelligence and curiosity about the world

THE BEAUTY OF HEDY LAMARR

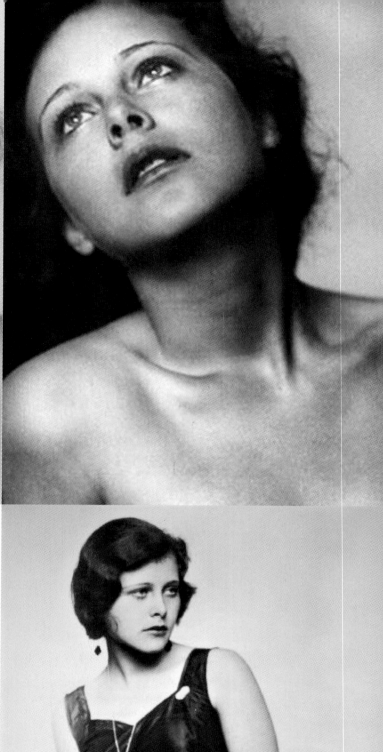

Above left: Hedwig Kiesler, Vienna, c. 1928-1929.
Above right: Hedwig Kiesler, Vienna, c. 1929.
(Photograph by Trude Fleischmann)
Right: Hedy Kiesler, Geld auf der Strasse
(Sascha-Film, 1930).

around her. He would spend hours reading to her and taking apart and explaining to her how objects such as clocks and music boxes worked. When Hedy was born the family lived at 2b Osterleitengasse in Dobling, in one of six apartments of a four-story stucco building on a narrow street in a fashionable area of Vienna. Soon after

Hedy Kiesler and Fred Döderlein while filming Die Koffer des Herrn O.F., *Vienna, Austria, 1931 (Tobis-Klang-film, 1931).*

Hedy's birth, however, the family moved to an impressive nine-room apartment in the hills, at 12 Peter Jordan Strasse in the nineteenth district, now part of Wahring.

As a Hollywood magazine reporter would later write, her father's position in Vienna "was sufficient to provide the family with many luxuries. Hedy, quite naturally, learned to love pretty things. 'It wasn't just learning to love them,' she has often said, 'but rather, I was born *feeling* them. Rich, soft fabrics, beautiful surroundings—they were there, that's all.' " [2] Her parents were quite socially active, so Hedy was reared primarily by nurses and nannies, and later, a governess named Nicolette, or Nixy, as she was affectionately called.

Above left: Sascha-Felsom Films starlet Hedy Kiesler, Austria, 1931.
Above right: Hedy Kiesler, Die Koffer des Herrn O.F. *(Tobis-Klangfilm, 1931).*

Like most children in Germany and Austria at that time, Hedy was familiar with Johanna Spyri's *Heidi*, *Grimm's Fairy Tales*, *Max und Moritz*, and the terrifying *Struwwelpeter*. These stories told of good and bad children, of frightening monsters and freaks, of magic, sentiment, and superstition. "They are first met in the nursery through haunting melodies and verses whose underlying theme is often violence," wrote author Angela Lambert. "[T]hese provide a wonderful insight to the German soul." [3] Hedy would recall that as a child, because of her fear of ugliness, she would suffer recurring nightmares with visions of her beloved dolls' faces melting before her. She would wake up screaming. This culture of such harsh good and evil left indelible marks on German children of that era.

Yet these stories also stimulated the imagination, something Hedy, a sensitive only child, struggled with her whole life. Her desire for love and romance was deeply influenced by these tales of good and evil. She always strived to be what others perceived her to be, but her innate intelligence and impatience often would not allow her to be docile.

From Hedy's earliest development, her mother taught her manners and etiquette, as well as an appreciation for fashion and beauty. Trude was a very feminine, somewhat self-absorbed young

Hedy Kiesler, Cine-Allianz Tonfilm starlet, Austria, 1932.

woman whom Hedy would study at a distance when her mother dressed and applied her makeup. Hedy too was always dressed meticulously, and she would soon come to rely upon her own natural beauty.

Not always a dutiful student, Hedy regularly attended the respected Döblinger Mädchenmittelschule, a private school in Vienna. Later, in 1929, she was sent to a private finishing school in Lucerne, Switzerland. Like most teenage girls, Hedy wanted to become a film actress and would lose herself in the glamour and fantasy of her favorite Hollywood movies, which she attended often. She would act out these screen roles in real life, naturally

Hedy Kiesler, Sascha-Felsom Studio, c. 1931.

charming adults with her wiles. But with young boys and older suitors, she often found her beauty and allure accomplished what her lack of maturity could not comprehend. She "fell in love" often, and recklessly.

When on vacation in the Swiss Alps with classmates after a school term in 1930, Hedy met a young Austrian lad who professed his love for her. She was not yet sixteen when they got engaged. He demanded she give up her dreams of becoming an actress. She would not, and legend has it he killed himself. Fact or fiction, Hedy was learning that beauty could be damning.

Home in Vienna for her fall school term in late 1930, Hedy faked a school pass from her mother without her knowledge so that she could spend two days working as an extra in what became her first film, Sascha-Film's *Geld auf der Strasse* (*Money on the Street*), the Vienna company's first sound picture. Directed by Georg Jacoby, with musical score by Stefan Weiss and cinematography by Nicolas Farkas, *Geld auf der Strasse* starred the popular Georg Alexander, Leopold Kramer (who would later play her father in *Extase*), Rosa Albach-Retty

(mother of Hedy's future lover, Wolfgang Albach-Retty), Hans Moser, and Lydia Pollman. The slight romantic comedy included a cabaret revue at "The Carlton Bar" featuring the number *"Mir ist alles einerlei ganz einerlen"* sung by Harry Payer. When the film was released in December 1930, Hedy, stunningly garbed in her own slinky dark sleeveless gown, accessorized with a jeweled brooch, necklace, and bracelet, can be spotted in a three-quarter shot with her movie escort, toasting each other during the number.

Convincing her parents to allow her to continue working in film, Hedy embarked on her second picture for the newly named Sascha-Felsom studio, as an extra in *Sturm im Wasserglas* (*Storm in a Water Glass*), also known as *Die Blumenfrau von Lindenau* (*The Flower Woman of Lindenau*), with musical score by Peter Herz, and cinematography by Guido Seeber. Yet another slight comedy-drama and again directed by Georg Jacoby, it starred Hansi Niese, the beautiful and tragic Renate Müller, Harald Paulsen, and Paul Otto. *Sturm im Wasserglas* premiered on March 31, 1931, and was released nationally in April. Hedy portrays a secretary in the film. Her two film costumes, from her own wardrobe, consisted of a long-sleeved, light-colored blouse and dark skirt for her office scene, and for the courtroom sequences, an overcoat over a blouse and tie, and on her head, a woolly beret.

Hedy enjoyed film work, and her ambition grew. Through Tobis-Klangfilm producer Alexander Ganowsky, she received an introduction to the Deutsches Theater in Berlin to study acting with the legendary theatrical impresario Max Reinhardt. The introduction led to an audition and classroom study. (Hedy never graduated, nor was she awarded a diploma from her high school academy in Vienna.) Eventually, however, she was rewarded with a role in the stage comedy *Das schwache Geschlecht* (*The Weaker Sex*) at the Theater in der Josefstadt. The comedy ran from May 8 to June 8, 1931, in Vienna. She played opposite young American actor, and later Pulitzer Prize–winning journalist, George Weller. Hedy would travel to Berlin on August 31 that year to repeat her role on the German stage.

Returning after a couple of weeks to Vienna, Hedy was given a supporting role and film buildup in the motion picture *Die Koffer des Herrn O.F.* (*The Trunks of Mr. O.F.*)

Hedy Kiesler, Cine-Allianz Tonfilm starlet, Austria, 1932.

at Tobis-Klangfilm Productions. It was filmed between September 15 and October 17, 1931. Advertised as "A Fairy Tale for Adults," the film takes place in the fictional town of Ostend (as the main theme says, "The world is so big . . . and Ostend is so small"). Directed by Alexander (Alexis) Granowsky, the picture starred actor Peter Lorre in a welcome comic departure from his recent role as a child murderer in the classic Fritz Lang drama *M*.

In *Die Koffer des Herrn O.F.*, a social musical comedy about a mysterious set of trunks delivered to a small-town hotel in care of Herr O. F. ("Oskar Flott," as Lorre's character Stix insists), Hedy portrays the mayor's daughter, Helene, in a cast that also included Alfred Abel, Harald Paulsen, Ludwig Stössel, cabaret star Margo Lion, and handsome Alfred Döderlein, who was Hedy's lover at the time. The picture was scored by Kurt Schröder, with cinematography by Reimar Kuntze and Heinrich Balasch. Hedy's performance in *Die Koffer des Herrn O.F.* is still painfully self-conscious and awkwardly amateurish, her voice shrill and a bit high-pitched. But she is noticed. Seen also in an ever-so-brief role is the equally attractive Aribert Mog, with whom Hedy would soon begin an affair. The comedy was a surprise hit when it was released on December 2, 1931, in Berlin.

Heinz Rühmann and Hedy Kiesler, Wir Brauchen kein Geld *(Cine-Allianz Tonfilm, 1932).*

For this film, Hedy's nine costumes were coordinated by Edward Suhr. More than likely, as for most modern-dress European films of the era, she was required to supply her own wardrobe, which apparently she did in at least seven of her scenes. Always stylish, these were typically traveling clothes and afternoon wear with long sleeves, berets, and proper accessories. For daytime indoor scenes, she usually sported light-colored sleeveless dresses of cotton or wool. The singular scene in which Hedy was most likely dressed by costumer Edward Suhr, who would later create costumes for the 1934 Heinz Rühmann film *So ein Flegel* (*Such a Boor*) and 1935's classic *Der Student von Prag* (*The Student of Prague*), was the wedding for the sequence where all the brides wore matching period wedding gowns. Hedy, still a teenager, was still a bit plump, typical of many European actresses of the era. But her beauty was very much apparent, despite the fact that her bare arms were a bit heavy-looking and her waist, a little thick.

Throughout this period, prior to her romance with the dashing Aribert Mog, Hedy was also escorted about Vienna by Austrian film actor Wolfgang Albach-Retty. Their

Hedy Kiesler, Cine-Allianz Tonfilm starlet, Austria, 1932.

affair was short-lived. Eventually Albach-Retty met and married actress Magda Schneider. Joining the Nazi Party in 1940, Albach-Retty became a popular film star during the Third Reich. The couple's actress daughter, Romy Schneider, born in 1938, would star in a series of romantic *Sissi* movies in the 1950s based on the life of the tragic Austrian empress Elisabeth, known lovingly by her countrymen as "Sissi."

After her breakup with Albach-Retty, Hedy then dated her handsome co-star Fred Döderlein, and the two became engaged. Hedy and Döderlein were frequently photographed together for the press and Austrian film magazines, once at Vienna's Airport Wein-Aspern with her father, Emil, greeting German aviatrix Marga von Etzdorf on August 18, 1931. An attractive couple, their engagement ended with the completion of *Die Koffer des Herrn O.F.*, when she fell in love with actor Aribert Mog, whom she had met on the set.

After the stage production of *Das schwache Geschlecht*, which she performed in during the day, Hedy was cast as Sybil in Noël Coward's *Private Lives*, again, for the Viennese stage, and yet again directed by Max Reinhardt. George Weller, cast in the role of Victor, later related an incident that would cement Hedy's destiny upon the world stage. During a rehearsal of the café scene, with reporters hanging about backstage, Herr Reinhardt casually pronounced, "Hedy Kiesler is the most beautiful girl in the world." [4] Within five minutes of that proclamation, news services throughout Europe were telephoned and the newspapers of the Innere Stadt dispatched the proclamation to other news services and press on the Continent. Hedwig Kiesler was definitely a young actress to watch.

During the run of *Private Lives*, Hedy worked in film at night. Because of her acclaimed beauty, she was cast in *Wir Brauchen kein Geld* (*We Need No Money*), also known as *Man Braucht Kein Geld* (*His Majesty, King Ballyhoo*), a clever little comedy about financial bluff, for Allianz-Tonfilm. Directed by Karl Boese with a musical score by Artur Guttmann and cinematography by Willy Goldberger and Karl Sander, Hedy was given co-star billing as Kathe Brandt opposite one of Europe's most popular comedians, Heinz Rühmann. Also appearing in the cast were the hilarious Hans Moser, delightful Ida Wüst, Ludwig Stössel, and tall, heavy film favorite Kurt Gerron, in a splendid comedic performance.

In Berlin in 1928, Kurt Gerron as Tiger Brown introduced the song "Mack the Knife" in the Bertolt Brecht / Kurt Weill stage play *Die Dreigroschenoper* (*The Threepenny Opera*). In the early 1930s Gerron was a popular film character actor, but after the rise of fascism in Germany, and because he was Jewish, he and his wife were forced to flee the country in 1933. Arrested in 1943, they were sent to the Theresienstadt concentration camp where Gerron was forced by the Nazis to direct the notorious propaganda film *Der Führer schenkt den Juden eine Stadt* (*The Führer Gives a City to the Jews*), a fictional filmed appeasement to the Red Cross to show the world the goodness of their Führer. Promised freedom once the film was completed, Gerron and his wife and most of the Theresienstadt populace were transported on the last train out and exterminated at Birkenau in late October 1944. Before he entered the gas chamber, Gerron was forced at gunpoint to sing "Mack the Knife" one last time.

Hedy's performance in the feminine lead opposite Heinz Rühmann is static and awkward at the beginning of the film, but eventually she melds into the comedic antics of the plot and is ultimately quite effective. Her wardrobe for the film, consisting of nine different outfits, is on par with the typical European couture of the era. One ensemble, a leopard-like fur coat and hat, which she sports in two different scenes, is quite becoming.

In another sequence she wears a satin sleeveless top complemented by a full tulle skirt—probably not from her own wardrobe. Costumes for this picture were credited to Margarete Scholz and Walter Schröder. It is more than likely that this latter outfit was created by them.

Photographed lovingly by Willy Goldberger and Karl Sander (the soft still photography was credited to Rudolf Brix), along with dialogue by Karoly Noti (Karl Noti) and Hans Wilhelm, with sparkling performances by the complete cast, *Wir Brauchen kein Geld* became a moderate hit, opening in Vienna on December 22, 1931. With several stylish Deco sets and at times impressive art direction by Julius von Borsody, *Wir Brauchen kein Geld* is still fresh and thoroughly

Hedy Kiesler, Vienna, 1933.

delightful. Hedy received her first critical film reviews for this picture, and for the most part they were more than favorable. "Excellent work by a cast of familiar German actors, reinforced by Hedy Kiesler, a charming Austrian girl," wrote the *New York Times* after its American premiere, adding that "fine photography and sound reproduction make the effort thoroughly enjoyable." [5]

Hedy's popularity in her native Austria was at its peak when she began yet another new stage comedy called *Intimitäten* (*Intimacies*). After its modest run, she was enticed

by Aribert Mog to journey to Prague, Czechoslovakia, and to co-star opposite him in a moody film drama titled *Extase* (*Ecstasy*), to be directed by the famed Czech film director Gustav Machaty. [6] "I went [to Prague] because I was in love with somebody," said Hedy somewhat vaguely in 1970. [7] While she may have accepted the starring role because of the gorgeously Aryan Aribert Mog, she could not have known then that her participation in this film "would define her screen image and impact her life to the end of her days." [8]

Hedy Kiesler, Extase (Elekta, 1933).

chapter 2

THE MOST
BEAUTIFUL GIRL
IN THE WORLD

*I*f there's one single film that defined Hedy Lamarr and forever embedded her in the minds of moviegoers as a film legend, it is most certainly *Extase (Ecstasy)*, also known as *Symphonie der Liebe (Symphony of Love)*. The history and the backstory of the making of this motion picture, and all of Hedy's films, are extensively detailed in *Beautiful: The Life of Hedy Lamarr*. But it bears repeating that *Extase* was conceived as a prestige film, and was directed by legendary Czech film director Gustav Machaty, who had huge successes with both *Erotikon* in 1929, and with *From Saturday to Sunday* in 1931.

The plot of *Extase* is finely drawn from a screenplay by director Machaty, Frantisek "Franz" Horky, and Vitezslav Nezval, based on the book by Robert Horky and Jacques A. Koerpel. It tells the tale of Eva, a young woman who marries a kind, older man, Emil (Zvonimir Rogoz), who has little interest in romance and affection

Foto Erich Balg, Berlin

Aribert Mog

Aribert Mog

and stubbornly maintains a fixed and dull bachelor routine. He falls asleep on their wedding night.

Eva realizes she has made a bad marriage, which inevitably leads her into the arms of a young, rugged road engineer named Adam (Aribert Mog), whom she has met by chance. She falls in love with Adam after a night of lovemaking, and when her husband discovers her infidelity, he commits suicide at the hotel where Eva and Adam rendezvous. Eva is shocked when she discovers that Emil is dead but does not tell Adam that he was her husband. They leave the hotel and wait at a train station before departing together. When Adam falls asleep, a remorseful Eva gently kisses her slumbering lover farewell and quietly departs.

Photographed by Jan Stallich and Hans Androschin, with a brilliant musical score by Dr. Josef "Guiseppe" Becce, *Extase* is told with limited dialogue, allowing the images to speak for themselves. In its near-complete, restored version today, *Extase* is a remarkably beautiful film. The acting is superb, and young Hedy Kiesler is stunning.

Two major sequences caused a great deal of discussion when an edited, truncated version of the picture hit American shores in the mid-1930s. First, there is a brief scene

40

GLAMOUR & STYLE

Hedy Kiesler and Zvonimir Rogoz, Extase *(Elekta, 1933)*.

shot from a distance of the nubile—and nude—Eva running through a wooded area and plunging into a lake, after which she chases her stray horse to gather her clothing. The scene that possibly created more controversy, however, is her love scene with Adam. As they embrace and kiss in his cabin in the woods, a storm raging outside, he lies her back on his bed, his form slipping out of view as the camera caresses Hedy's beautiful face as she responds to his lovemaking. As Eva's necklace of pearls symbolically breaks apart, we see a close-up of her face as she winces, and we know she has experienced ecstasy.

Although no costume designer is credited in the film, director Gustav Machaty preferred his actresses in contemporary films to wear light-colored dresses, which Hedy

Hedy Kiesler, Extase *(Elekta, 1933).*

does. The Czechoslovakian couturier as film fashion designer was yet to emerge in the 1930s, so actresses were expected to source their own wardrobes, with Machaty overseeing their choices. Hedy certainly knew how to complement the storyline with garments that defined the moment, and as such, her choices were superb. Just eighteen years old when filming commenced, Hedy was still a bit plump in 1932, yet her seven costume changes in this film are slimming and quite flattering.

Actresses working in the Czech film industry in the 1930s, especially those with means, would often purchase their onscreen wardrobe during their travels abroad, or through leading fashion houses in Prague. The latter included famous couturier Hana Podolská at her Adria Palace, the three-story Maison Podolská with its entire floor for

Hedy Kiesler, Extase *(Elekta, 1933).*

customers and a showroom on Jungmannova Street; the Oldrich Rosenbaum company, which specialized in dresses and robes; and Arnostka Roubickova at her Salon Roubicek.

Most likely Hedy's wedding ensemble and veil, seen at the beginning of the film, along with the three-strand pearl necklace so important to the film's plot, were obtained from Maison Podolská. Podolská also designed for film actresses Lida Baarova and Adina Mandlova. Her aesthetic in design mirrored the cultivated English style, which was highly influenced by the French.

It is of interest that Hedy Kiesler was not the first actress offered the role of Eva in *Extase*. Mexican film actress Lupita Tovar, mother of actress Susan Kohner (Oscar nominee for Universal's 1958 *Imitation of Life*), who had starred in the Spanish-language version of Universal's *Dracula* (1931), was originally offered the role. The script explicitly stated that the part would require nudity and sexual simulation. However, because of her

Leopold Kramer and Hedy Kiesler, Extase *(Elekta, 1933).*

pending marriage with Universal's European sales agent Paul Kohner, who objected to the fact his future wife would appear nude in the film, Tovar had to turn down the opportunity. Though not an issue in Europe (Tovar had worn a see-through chiffon gown in the Spanish-language *Dracula*), the nudity would have surely destroyed her burgeoning American film career. Other actresses over the course of the following decades have also claimed to have been offered the part.

When released in Europe by Slavia Films in January 1933, *Extase* was immediately heralded as a masterpiece. In London, reviews mentioned the beautiful cinematography, as well as the limited use of dialogue and the musical score, even praising the "sensitive

Hedy Kiesler and Aribert Mog, Extase *(Elekta, 1933).*

and imaginative performance" of its leading lady. [1] No mention is made of the two scenes with nudity and simulated sex. *Extase* was, however, condemned as indecent by Pope Pius XI—not for the nudity, but for the scene of Eva's ecstasy. Because of this, *Extase* was not allowed to be shown in the United States upon its initial release.

In 1934 *Extase* would win the Prague State Prize for Excellence, and it would attract the largest crowd—and second prize—at the Venice Film Festival on August 2, 1934. It gained critical acclaim and public acceptance wherever it played.

After having completed *Extase*, Hedy returned to Vienna, not expecting that her world would change dramatically.

Pierre Nay and Hedy Kiesler, Extase *(Elekta, 1933).*

Hedy Kiesler and Aribert Mog, Extase *(Elekta, 1933).*

According to Hedy's memoir, *Ecstasy and Me*, when she resumed her career in Vienna she *immediately* was cast in the Theatre an der Wien stage production of Fritz Kreisler's musical operetta *Sissy, the Rose of Bavaria*. This operetta was based on the comedy play *Sissy Brautfahrt* (*Sissy's Engagement*), which had opened in Vienna on December 23, 1932, starring legendary actress Paula Wessely and directed by Otto Langer.

While this is the legend as it was created, it was not that simple.

In her memoir Hedy details her parents' response to the Vienna premiere of *Extase* on February 14, 1933. According to the oft-repeated story, Emil Kiesler was incensed by Hedy's brief nudity (although this may not have been the case, as nudity did not cause

the embarrassment in Europe that it did in the United States at the time). With Trude and daughter Hedy in tow, Emil allegedly stormed out of the cinema in anger, disgust, and humiliation, forbidding his daughter to ever appear on the screen again. This may have been because the Kieslers were a prominent family in Vienna.

Hedy and her lover, the handsome and romantic Aribert Mog, had ended their affair soon after completing *Extase*, after which it is possible that Hedy may have suffered a physical and/or emotional breakdown. She had lost an immense amount of weight, which was credited to "poisoning." She did not stay with her parents at this time, but with film director Joe May and his wife Mia. May's family name was Mandl; he was the cousin of Austrian munitions czar Fritz Mandl. (According to FBI records, Hedy reportedly said she'd first met Fritz Mandl in 1931, possibly through Joe and Mia May.)

During these weeks in late 1932 and early 1933, Hedy was looking for film work. It was reported that she desperately wanted to portray Caroline Esterhaz in the film musical

Hedy Kiesler and Aribert Mog, Extase *(Elekta, 1933).*

Hedy Kiesler, Extase *(Elekta, 1933).*

Leise flehen meine Lieder (*Unfinished Symphony*), co-produced by the Austrian Cine-Al-lianz Tonfilmproduktions and the Gaumont-British Picture Corporation. The picture was written by Willi Forst, along with Benn W. Levy and Walter Reisch, directed by Anthony Asquith, and filmed by legendary cinematographer Franz Planer. [2] The sumptuous cos-tumes for the film were by fashion designer Gerdago, the "Edith Head of Austrian film." The cast included Hans Jaray and American actress Helen Chandler. Though screen-writer Reisch championed Hedy Kiesler for the starring role, she could not sing, and the part she was seeking was ultimately assigned to Marta Eggerth, who handed in a career-making performance.

Nonetheless, Hedy *was* offered a film contract by the American film company Para-mount, as she joyfully advised the press. It was also announced that she'd been offered a contract with MGM, but this is unlikely, as she wouldn't meet the studio's chief executive,

Louis B. Mayer, until 1935, at Max Reinhardt's white castle, the Schloss Leopoldskron. (He would have remembered her.)

On January 20, 1933, it was announced that Hedy was replacing actress Rose Stradner (who would later come to Hollywood and marry Joseph L. Mankiewicz). Stradner had been serving as understudy for Paula Wessely in the stage hit *Sissy*, but left to play in *Fanny* (and would later return to replace Hedy before abandoning her European career).

When Paula Wessely left the production, Hedy replaced her in the role. Though she could *not* sing well, Hedy's appearance on the Vienna stage as Austria's beautiful and tragic Sissy/Sissi proved to be a sensational hit in no small part because of her radiant beauty.

Photographs of her in the role show that Hedy's weight loss was so drastic she appeared almost skeletal. Nonetheless, she was stunning as she stepped out onto the stage in March of 1933, in nineteenth-century period Viennese costumes and gowns designed by theatrical fashion consultant "Lillian" for this production. Fritz Kreisler himself conducted the orchestra for this Theater an der Wien stage production of *Sissy*,

Aribert Mog and Hedy Kiesler, Extase *(Elekta, 1933).*

his second musical theatrical production. His first was *Apple Blossoms*, produced on Broadway with Fred and Adele Astaire in 1919.

In *Sissy*, the story revolves around the young, beautiful Elisabeth of Austria and her fairy-tale romance with the equally revered young Prince Franz Josef (Hans Jaray). Because of her untimely death by an assassin in September 1898, the much-beloved then-empress Elisabeth had become a tragic legendary figure in the minds of Austrians. The freshness of her young life and the much-loved lilting music of old Vienna were deliciously captured in this play, despite Hedy's limited musical abilities.

Hedy Kiesler, Extase *(Elekta, 1933).*

Hedy's personal life was rich with romance during this period of popularity. She was admired from afar by no less than Austria's Archduke Max, brother of Kaiser Karl, who likened her to a "porcelain doll." She was squired about Vienna by the new head of the Theater in der Josefstadt, young Otto Preminger, who had succeeded Max Reinhardt as its director. She was also involved with film producer Sam Spiegel, who would flee Berlin along with Peter Lorre and Otto Preminger, in mid-May. The three of them, Spiegel, Preminger, and Hedy, could be seen about town at this time in Spiegel's limo.

As spring turned into summer in 1933, Hedy was continuously bombarded by suitors, one of whom sent her expensive bouquets accompanied by small expensive gifts, which she could not overlook. Each gift came with a card that read simply "Fritz Mandl." Hedy knew who he was. When he eventually presented himself to her backstage, he said, " 'I suppose you have heard a lot about me?' To which she was reported to have replied, 'Yes,

but nothing good.' " [3] She would soon learn a great deal more about Fritz, herself, and the reality of the world around her.

There is no doubt that young, beautiful Hedy Kiesler fell in love with Fritz Mandl at their first meeting backstage at the Theater in der Josefstadt. Though not typically handsome, the thirty-three-year-old *bon vivant* was nevertheless a most sensually appealing, enigmatic, and sexually desirable man. His wealth and notoriety preceded him everywhere he went in pre–Nazi era Austria.

Fritz was born Friedrich Alexander Maria Mandl on February 9, 1900, to Jewish industrialist Dr. Alexander Mandl, whose father had established the great Hirtenberg cartridge factory in 1870, near the Vienna forest on the banks of the Triesting River. Fritz's mother, like Hedy's, had converted to Catholicism, and raised him in her faith.

At age twenty-one Fritz married his first wife, actress Helene "Hella" Strauss, but the couple divorced two years later in 1923. His chiseled looks and dashing personality attracted many young women, pretty actresses and society mavens both, whom he escorted and squired about Vienna for the next decade. One of those beauties was beautiful film actress Eva May, born in 1902, daughter of his first cousin, director Joe May. Eva's infatuation with Fritz would prove fatal. When Fritz rejected her desires to marry, she committed suicide by shooting herself on September 8, 1924, at the Hotel Herzoghof at Baden.

Resigning himself to concentrating on the company factory works, Fritz successfully made the most of his situation, uniting the Hirtenberg factory with the cartridge factory of Lichtenworth and the Grünbacher Steinkohlenbergbau coal mine, creating the vast Hirtenberger-Patronen-Fabrik. By the mid-1930s, Fritz Mandl would become the third-wealthiest man in Austria. He allied himself with two important figures—Count Ernst Rüdiger Camillo Maria von Starhemberg (also spelled Stahremberg) and Italian fascist dictator Benito Mussolini. "An Austro-Fascist himself," I wrote in *Beautiful: The Life of Hedy Lamarr*, "Mandl was prominent in European political circles, making both public and secretive munitions deals." [4]

Hedy's subsequent marriage to Fritz Mandl prolonged her time in Austria, a country quickly realizing the impending threat of European annihilation. In Adolf Hitler's

manifesto *Mein Kampf*, written during his 1925 imprisonment for a failed putsch in Munich in 1923, the Austrian-born leader of the Nazi Party clearly defined his intentions toward Austrian Jews. The fall of the Weimer Republic and the rise of Nazi Germany had been propelled by the Nazi Party coming to power in January 1933.

Hedy Kiesler in the stage production of Sissy, *Vienna, 1933. Costumes by Lillian.*

Fritz's own participation leading to Austria's eventual fall into totalitarian power cannot be understated. Mandl was a leading manufacturer of military munitions and armaments for fascist powers. In 1932 a railroad shipment of Hirtenberg armaments traveling through Austria and destined for foreign borders was diverted and exposed by militant railway workers. Known as the *Hirtenberger Waffenaffare*, according to one historian, "the Hirtenberg scandal led indirectly to the dissolution of the Austrian National Council in March 1933 and to Austria's transformation into an authoritative state." [5]

With blood on his hands, Fritz Mandl had become a power to be dealt with—and on his terms. His friendship with the vice chancellor of Austria, Ernst von Starhemberg, commander of the Heimwehr (the Austrian nationalist militia), guaranteed him authority as long as von Starhemberg remained in power. Fritz's friendship with Mussolini gave him the wherewithal to make munitions deals with the German socialist Nazis as well.

Hedy knew little of this political manipulation. Her life had been a fairy tale, part of which included a wealthy and handsome prince.

Her marriage to Fritz Mandl would have lasting consequences.

THE BEAUTY OF HEDY LAMARR

Mme. Fritz Mandl, c. 1936.

chapter 3

MADAME MANDL AND THE GATHERING STORM

War clouds began accumulating over Europe throughout the 1930s, after Adolf Hitler's rise to power in Germany. Hedy's father Emil could clearly read the signs. His fears and worries for his wife and only child increased as news of what was happening within Germany filtered into neighboring Austria. Jews' freedoms were being restricted, and Jewish-owned businesses were being targeted with destruction.

With her parents' blessing Hedy accepted Fritz's proposal in May of 1933. Her last performance in *Sissy* was May 16. Per Fritz's wishes, she not only turned down the Paramount film contract—she left her career. Hedy Kiesler and Fritz Mandl were wed on Thursday, August 10, 1933, in the tiny chapel of the elaborately baroque Karlskirche in Vienna, a ceremony attended by over two hundred guests. Hedy was dressed in black and white and carried a bouquet of white

Fritz Mandl, c. 1940. (Photofest)

orchids. The couple honeymooned extensively for the rest of the year, visiting the Italian Lido, Venice, Capri, Cannes, Nice, Biarritz, Lake Como, and Paris, returning to Vienna in January 1934.

Hedy soon became quite comfortable with their lush lifestyle. Early in the marriage Fritz started referring to Hedy as his little "Hansi," or Bunny, drenching his beautiful bride in jewels and expensive perfumes created by the likes of Schiaparelli. In Paris on their honeymoon they strolled by Cartier's on the Place Vendôme, its display windows rich with precious diamonds, emeralds, and rubies set in platinum and gold. Fritz asked Hedy if she saw anything in the window that she particularly favored. Overwhelmed, Hedy could not decide, so he grandly purchased the complete jewelry display for his Bunny. Fritz's beautiful trophy wife was also gowned in sumptuous fashions designed by some of the best couturiers in Europe, such as Hubert de Givenchy, Pierre Balmain, and Cristobal Balenciaga.

Hedy also enjoyed the experience of meeting some of Austria's and Europe's most powerful and influential people. Among the illustrious guests at the frequent Mandl dinner parties were Fritz's closest friend, Count Ernst von Starhemberg, who was not actually a count but a hereditary prince, along with his then-wife, Countess Marie-Elizabeth von Salm-Reifferscheidt-Raitz. Also frequently present were Austria's two federal chancellors, Engelbert Dollfuss and Kurt von Schuschnigg. Other dinner guests included Madame Schiaparelli; Prince Nicolas of Greece; Prince Gustav of Denmark; Albrecht the Prince of Bavaria and his wife Maria, and their niece Dorothea Theresa (later, Archduchess Gottfried of Austria); writer Fritz Werfel and his wife, the widow of Gustav Mahler; Sigmund Freud; and painter Georg Kirsta.

Many of the Mandl dinner parties were primarily attended by Fritz's business associates and colleagues and their wives. After dinner the women—except for Hedy—would be excused, as the men, deep in cigars and digestifs, would discuss armaments around the table. At one Mandl soiree Hedy was introduced to Italian dictator Benito Mussolini, who became enamored with her beauty. He caused quite an embarrassing scene when he demanded to be seated next to her at dinner. It should be clarified that as an "Honorary

Aryan," Fritz Mandl was quite indomitable in 1933. However, as Jews, Fritz and Hedy would *never* have been introduced to Adolf Hitler. His hatred of Jews was so strong that a direct meeting would never have taken place.

The Mandls owned several homes, including a luxurious ten-room apartment at 15 Schwarzenbergplatz in Vienna; the Schloss Schwarzenau chateau, located in remote Waldviertel near the Czechoslovakian border; and the hunting lodge estate, Villa Fegenberg, each boasting numerous maids and staff. Fritz also owned a fleet of limousines, which were at his disposal night and day, along with a handful of chauffeurs. One of his prized cars, a 1935 Mercedes, sold at auction in the 2000s at over US $200,000, and their 1937 Rolls-Royce Phantom III Drophead Coupe, the last vehicle the couple purchased, sold at auction at Bonham's in 2015 for nearly US $700,000.

Hedy would often remain at her husband's side of an evening, looking beautiful and bored as Fritz and his cronies spoke of coming political conflicts and military armaments. Although she remained apart and distant, and did not participate in discussion, Hedy slowly began to comprehend what they were talking about, including the possible invention of some kind of wireless communication to secure their weaponry. The uncomfortable feeling of the inevitability of European conflict with the ever-threatening

Hedwig and Fritz Mandl, c. 1934. (Author's Collection)

fascist powers was tangible. Socialist agitation was blamed for the insurgent crimes now being committed by Nazi activism on one border, as Italy's Il Duce, Benito Mussolini, made firm alliances with Hitler's Germany.

Fritz's own concerns were making themselves known by the very actions he took to protect his wife and his fortune. In Germany in 1932, for instance, Hedy's comedy *Die Koffer des Herrn O.F.* (*The Trunks of Mr. O.F.*), retitled *Bauen und Heiraten* (*Building and Marriages*), was edited down by almost a half simply because most of the cast and crew were Jewish. With the Nazi Party now in control of German government, *Extase* was banned there not because of the nudity or the simulated sex scene, but simply because Hedy was *not* Aryan. After viewing the motion picture himself, Fritz set about to purchase every existing copy of the film, even the one privately owned by

Hedy Kiesler, c. 1933 , before she married Fritz Mandel

Mussolini, spending up to $60,000 per print to do so. (Of course, that only encouraged the film distribution company to print even more copies.)

In November of 1934, the US distribution rights for *Extase* (*Ecstasy* in the United States) were purchased by entrepreneur and film exporter Samuel Cummings. Because of the two key scenes of nudity and simulated sex, in puritan America the film was considered "pornographic," and it was banned for American distribution. Attempting to release the film in a truncated format, Cummings fought with the US Treasury for almost two years before the ban was lifted. This, after *Ecstasy* had been secretly shown in tents, "smokers," and carnival side shows for two years, promising much, delivering less, and making Cummings quite a lot of money. After being legally released in America

Hedy Kiesler Mandl, c. 1935.

as *Ecstasy* in 1936, the unwarranted yet notorious history of the film would follow Hedy for the rest of her life.

In July 1934, on an invited stay at Herr Reinhardt's castle home in Salzburg, Hedy and Fritz were introduced at a dinner party to MGM film mogul Louis B. Mayer. [1] Mayer, his ailing wife Margaret, and his entourage were winding up his annual trip to Europe to sign up artists for Metro and to bring them under contract to Hollywood. Not necessarily a religious or politically minded man, a Jew himself, in hindsight Mayer's benevolent annual act literally and effectively saved the lives of many artists as they fled their native European countries.

Mayer had seen *Extase* and condemned it as a "dirty" picture. Nonetheless, over dessert Reinhardt asked Mayer what he thought of Hedy, dressed elegantly and looking ravishing, signing with MGM and coming to Hollywood. Mayer's exact remarks then, crude as they surely were, are somewhat lost in the shadows of time. However, he did state that it would be difficult to make a star out of Hedy, as she could not speak English well; moreover, he felt American audiences would not warm to an actress who ran about in the raw on film.

Furious that he had been "set up" by Herr Reinhardt (and possibly by Hedy as well), Fritz restrained his comments about the conversation until he and Hedy were behind closed doors. The marriage was strained already by this time, as Hedy was beginning to become restless and bored as a trophy wife. On several occasions she had begun responding to the glances of admiring men, one of whom was Fritz's best friend, Count Ernst von Starhemberg.

Von Starhemberg's marriage to Countess Marie-Elizabeth was a sham. For many years his mistress had been Austro-Hungarian film actress Nora Gregor. Born in 1901, Gregor had starred in German-language films made in Hollywood during the transition to sound. In 1932 she had co-starred opposite Robert Montgomery in MGM's *But the Flesh Is Weak*. Returning to Europe, Nora Gregor starred in *Was Frauen tramen* (Tobis-Klangfilm, 1933), written by Billy Wilder and co-starring Gustav Fröhlich and Peter Lorre.

The following year Gregor divorced her first husband, Mitja Nikisch, son of famed orchestral leader Arthur Nikisch, and bore an illegitimate son, Heinrich, to Ernst. On December 2, 1937, just five days after his marriage to Marie-Elizabeth was officially annulled, Ernst and Gregor wed. They would eventually flee Austria to France, through

Mme. Fritz Mandl, c. 1934.

Switzerland, where Nora Gregor would star in Jean Renoir's classic film *La Règle du Jeu* (*The Rules of the Game*). Despite his romantic entanglements, Vice Chancellor Ernst von Starhemberg remained a very powerful man in Austria. With Hedy's marriage to his best friend in trouble, Ernst pursued Hedy in private.

The pressures of political unrest and growing financial restrictions were weighing heavily on the minds and hearts of many assimilated Jews in Vienna and Austria during

Hedy and friend, Europe, 1937.

this time. Hedy's father Emil died of a heart attack on February 14, 1935, brought on by anxiety over this changing political scene. Grief-stricken Hedy did not attend the funeral service. Although she knew Fritz would take care of her and her mother Trude—he was more concerned about her safety and welfare than ever before—at the same time, Hedy was taking chances.

Hedy felt trapped in what she considered a loveless marriage, and would make several futile attempts to leave Fritz during the next two years. He in turn required their servants to advise him of Hedy's comings and goings. Hedy wrote in her memoir that she had once attempted to escape Fritz by confiding with a Colonel Richter, with whom she felt safe. Unfortunately, he turned out to be Fritz's employee.

Changes were brewing in Austria. On May 21, 1936, Dr. Kurt von Schuschnigg declared himself sole dictator of Austria. Count Ernst von Starhemberg was no longer vice chancellor. Ernst and Hedy began a dangerous and explosive affair that would culminate in a plan for Hedy to flee Vienna with Ernst, who had promised to introduce her to theatrical producers. With Fritz on business in Italy, the lovers boarded the Vienna–Budapest train, and were met by Fritz as they stepped off the platform in Budapest. Fritz had been notified in Rome by his spies in Vienna and had taken a plane to Budapest.

"His voice was soft and silky, but his eyes were blazing in anger," Hedy recalled in a 1939 magazine article. "You will return home with me, my Hedy. Then of course there will be no scandal." [2] In firm and continual control, Fritz's comment to Ernst was brief: "If this keeps up, our friendship ends here." [3]

In a possible attempt to appease Hedy, Fritz contracted Viennese architect Walter Sobtka that fall to design a $25,000 addition, a projected nursery, to add on to their hunting lodge in the Alps. But time was closing in on the Mandl marriage. They were at a stalemate. Hedy's restlessness and growing concern over the unstable Austrian government, combined with the buildup for war, which was fast approaching, preyed on her mind. She realized that her own immediate peril had to be addressed as the couple attended the 1937 Salzburg Music Festival together. At that point Fritz and Hedy were barely speaking to each other. The festival, the last to be held until after the war, was

highly attended. Its director was Herbert von Karajan, and under the capable conducting of Bruno Walter, audiences experienced the singing of such brilliant artists as Ezio Pinza, Esther Rethy, Giuseppe Nessi, and Mariano Stabile.

Fritz and Hedy had planned to vacation later that fall in the Antibes, but before they did so they again stayed at the Schloss Leopoldskron, the home of Herr Reinhardt and his wife, actress Helene Thimig. After Fritz had retired one evening, Hedy confided her concerns to her mentor. Reinhardt talked with her about the impending war, and the fact that her very existence was threatened if she did not leave Europe. Her mind made up, Hedy returned with Fritz to Vienna for the final act.

Fritz began taking important business trips, leaving Hedy alone and fearful. Understanding the true reason for her husband being referred to as an "Honorary Aryan," "a special status created by Goebbels for Jewish people who served Hitler personally," [4] Hedy feared the consequences of prolonging her inevitable departure.

Recklessly she began a brief, very public affair with athlete and mountain climber Count Max Hardegg. When Fritz discovered it, it was not only the end of Hedy's affair, but of their marriage as well. Carefully explaining the dire situation they both faced, Fritz plotted Hedy's escape. For years, he told her, he had been funneling his fortune to banks in Switzerland and South America. For the time being he was in control of his destiny, but not Hedy's. Fritz explained that Hedy would make what would appear to be a desperate "escape" from her controlling husband, stealing away in the night and traveling to France, and eventually England, where Hedy's family had friends. She would pack a limited amount of clothing, as if leaving on a brief holiday with just a couple of pieces of luggage. She would hide her most precious jewels within the linings of her dresses and two couture gowns. She would leave alone.

It's possible there was no love lost between them at this critical juncture in their doomed marriage. But that love would resurface in later years. Surely Hedy understood the dire necessity of this "play." They would both perform their roles brilliantly.

The myth that Hedy escaped in the dead of night after drugging her look-alike maid (no one looked like Hedy), then jumping out a window so the other servants wouldn't notice, racing to the train station, and hopping a Paris-bound train would make a good plot in a bad MGM movie. But it was not that simple, or logical.

After her arrival in Hollywood, the MGM biographers—particularly Mayer's right-hand man, Howard Strickling—took over inventing Hedy's story. It was repeated endlessly, even by Hedy herself, perhaps to emphasize her peril while also exonerating herself. But contemporary stories, news releases, and even interviews of the time present a different story.

On a Thursday evening in late August (major events in Hedy's life always seemed to happen on a Thursday), while Fritz was either on a hunting trip or away on business, Hedy, with the assistance of her faithful maid, Laura, dressed inconspicuously, and with luggage and passport listing her as "Hedwig Mandl" drove to the Hauptbahnhof on the Mariahilfer Strasse. After bidding farewell to Laura, Hedy boarded the Trans-Europe Express to Paris.

Count Ernst Rüdiger von Starhemberg, vice chancellor of Austria, c. 1935.

Arriving in Paris, Hedy hadn't even unpacked her suitcases at the hotel when a cable arrived from Laura, warning that Fritz had returned and was on his way to France. Perhaps Fritz had second thoughts, or perhaps this did not happen exactly as was told, as Fritz was under surveillance by this time, as well. But the fact is that after arriving in France, Fritz did not pursue Hedy to England. Hedy continued on to London alone,

THE BEAUTY OF HEDY LAMARR

Hedy Mandl, two unidentified women, and Fritz Mandl arriving at the Salzburg Music Festival, summer of 1937.

having repacked quickly and catching a train to Calais. There she boarded a channel ferry to England that very afternoon. Fritz did not pursue Hedy across the Channel. They had said their good-byes.

On September 18 it was reported in the papers that Fritz and Hedy had filed a mutual divorce action. Within a week, she would be on her way to America.

True to his threat, Hitler made the *Anschluss* of Austria the first casualty of the Nazi Party, on March 12, 1938. Faced with increasing anti-Semitic hostility and threats, Fritz resigned his position as general manager of his own company on March 27, and escaped

arrest to neutral Switzerland, refuting his Jewish heritage there by denying his blood relation to his own father. He then fled to France. The Hirtenberger-Patronen-Fabrik munitions works was absorbed by the Nazi Party.

Their friendship remaining intact, in 1940 Fritz brought former prince Ernst von Starhemberg, along with his wife Nora and their son, to France after von Starhemberg had had a threatening personal quarrel with Nazi minister Hermann Göring and was forced out of Austria. Eventually in 1940, they would all be exiled to Argentina, where Fritz would reestablish himself in factory works, eventually aiding the country's dictator, Juan Perón, to gain power. Fritz would marry three more times, and father three children. His last wife was Monika Brücklmeier. Her father was German diplomat, lawyer, and freedom fighter Eduard Brücklmeier, who was convicted and hanged for being involved in the July 20, 1944, attempt to assassinate Adolf Hitler.

According to press accounts, as well as her own admission later to the FBI, Hedy and Fritz did meet by chance in New York in 1940 when they both were spotted with new mates at a nightclub in Manhattan. They would never see each other again. Even though she would take loans from Fritz after she arrived in Hollywood, as much as $10,000, Hedy would consistently refer to him in conversation as "the son-of-a-bitch." Even so, Fritz Mandl and Hedy Lamarr did keep in close touch with each other over the years by letter or by telephone, especially on their birthdays, until his death on September 8, 1977. He always addressed Hedy as "Bunny."

After arriving in London and checking safely into the Hotel Regent Palace in the center of Piccadilly Circus, Hedy reorganized her plans, which were gathering momentum. Hedy was beginning a new life, the life she had always wanted—which at that moment must have been nearly impossible for her to imagine.

chapter 4

THE POWER OF THE HOLLYWOOD STUDIO MACHINE

*I*n London, safely away from Fritz and Austria, Hedy—still called Madame Mandl—spent little time enjoying her newfound freedom. She immediately sought ways to secure her independence as well as figure out her next plan for survival. It's here in England during that fall of 1937 that the Hollywood mythology of international émigré Hedy Lamarr began.

The facts weighed heavily on the heart and mind of twenty-two-year-old Hedy Kiesler Mandl. Though her parents' friends in London tried to help her, like her, they knew that Hedy was treading on thin ice. The world was about to go to war. And Hedy was not only Jewish—she was also still the wife of a very powerful and influential fascist social figure. Hedy knew she could never return to Austria and Fritz. Her options were few.

Opposite page: Hedy Lamarr, Metro-Goldwyn-Mayer, 1938. (Photograph by Clarence Sinclair Bull)

Above left: Mme. Fritz Mandl in her purple velvet gown and signature diamond earrings, January 16, 1937, at the Vienna Opera Ball, Austria. She would bring this gown and jewelry with her on the Normandie *later that year. Above right: Mme. Fritz Mandl wearing the second couture evening gown by an unknown designer, with her Austrian diamond earrings. This was the second of only two gowns she brought with her on board the* Normandie, *September 1937. (Photographed in Austria, 1935)*

Establishing her presence with her family's friends, Hedy vigorously attacked the trade publications to learn who in the entertainment world was visiting England, specifically, London. Within days of her arrival in the city, Hedy connected with the handsome forty-year-old MGM talent scout and publicist Robert Ritchie, whose personal relationship with Metro star Jeanette MacDonald (they may have been married) could possibly guarantee Hedy a contract and career with the studio. Ritchie in turn advised

Opposite page, top: Charles Boyer and Hedy Lamarr, in the velvet gown, Hollywood, December 31, 1938. Opposite page, bottom: Hedy Lamarr in the velvet gown, Metro-Goldwyn-Mayer, 1938. (Photograph by Clarence Sinclair Bull)

Above left: Hedy Lamarr. Metro-Goldwyn-Mayer, c. 1938.
Above right: Hedy Lamarr. Metro-Goldwyn-Mayer, c. 1938.

her that Louis B. Mayer was concluding his annual—and, as it turned out, his last—
European talent-scouting tour of the Continent.

Hedy jumped at the chance to meet with Mayer again at his Claridge Hotel suite once
he'd arrived in town from Vienna. "She's not only gorgeous, but she can act," Ritchie
advised Mayer by phone. "You can make her a big star at MGM." [1]

Traveling with his ailing wife Margaret, as well as MGM studio executives Howard
Strickling and Benny Thau (known as the studio's "Fixers"), this particular year Mayer

Above left: Mme. Fritz Mandl arriving in New York aboard the Normandie, *September 30, 1937.*
Above right: Transformation: Hedy Lamarr arriving in Los Angeles, California, October 4, 1937.
Below: Hedy Lamarr in the Austrian evening gown, Metro-Goldwyn-Mayer, 1938.

Above left: Hedy Lamarr. United Artists, 1938 (possibly wearing the same earrings she wore at the Vienna Opera Ball, January 1937). (Photograph by Robert Coburn)
Above right: Hedy Lamarr. United Artists, 1938. (Photograph by Robert Coburn)

was acting on advice from his former mistress, Adeline Schulberg. Mayer had contracted on tour such renowned artists as screenwriter Walter Reisch; Polish-born opera coloratura Miliza Korjus; English actress Greer Garson, whom Mayer was most excited about; British film director Victor Saville; German actress Rose Stradner (who replaced Hedy in *Sissy*); Hungarian actress Ilona Hajmassey (last name later changed to just Massey); dancer Tilly Losch; writer-director Reinhold Schünzel; French film director Julien Duvivier, who had helmed the successful *Pépé le Moko* starring Jean Gabin the previous year; and actresses Mireille Balin, Gabin's co-star in that film, and Jacqueline Laurent. Mayer's signing of this talent to Metro, in effect, saved their lives, as many were Jewish exiles.

Above left: Hedy Lamarr. Metro-Goldwyn-Mayer, 1940.
Above right: Hedy Lamarr. United Artists, January 19, 1939. (Photograph by Robert Coburn)

Arriving at Mayer's Claridge Hotel suite at their appointed hour, Hedy was shuffled into the mogul's presence and was confronted by his entourage of executives. Dressed immaculately in her best European-designer day apparel, Hedy allegedly looked stunning. Ritchie did most of the talking, to guide the discussion in the appropriate direction. Mayer of course knew who Hedy was; Mrs. Mandl, to be sure. According to Hedy, in his abrupt and somewhat crude and vulgar manner, Mayer again voiced his sentiments about her appearance in *Ecstasy*. "You're lovely, my dear," Mayer said. "At MGM we make clean pictures. We want our stars to lead clean lives. I don't like what people would think about a girl who flits bare-assed around the screen." [2] According to later publicity, Hedy argued that she was but a child when she made *Ecstasy* and was unaware of the

THE BEAUTY OF HEDY LAMARR

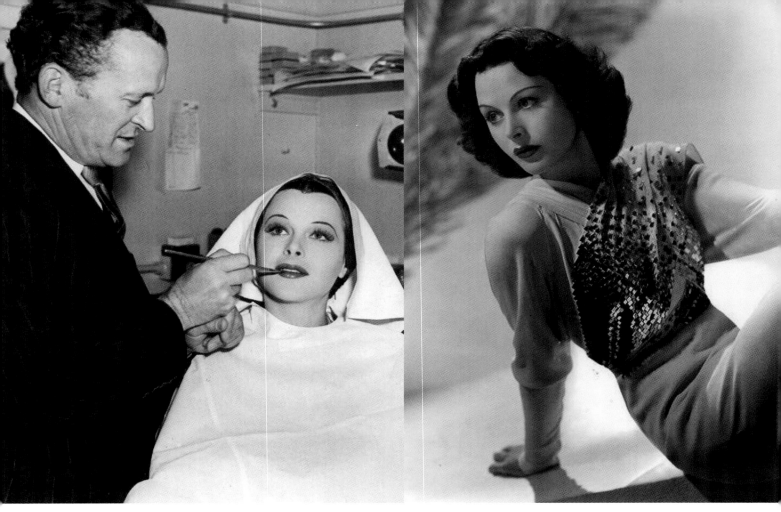

Above left: Hedy Lamarr and makeup artist Jack Dawn, I Take This Woman, *Metro-Goldwyn-Mayer, original 1938 version.*
Above right: Hedy Lamarr, Boom Town *(MGM, 1940). Costumes by Adrian*
Opposite page: Hedy Lamarr. Metro-Goldwyn-Mayer, 1939 (costume by Adrian). (Photograph by George Hurrell)

nudity involved until the day of filming. Mayer sensed her compliancy and offered her a $125-per-week standard six-month contract.

Though Mayer's rudeness and language may not have insulted her, his meager offer did. She had heard him bluff and blunder before. Hedy Kiesler had been a star on both stage and screen in Europe even before her marriage to Fritz. Coolly and calmly, she stood and addressed Mayer. "Speaking in her most precise broken English, which was horrendous at best, she refused to be intimidated or bamboozled into accepting 'a cheap contract.' " [3] As she turned and walked out, with Robert Ritchie following, thus effectively ending their meeting, Mayer was heard to say he admired her spirit.

Above: Hedy Lamarr. Metro-Goldwyn-Mayer, 1939.
Opposite page: Hedy Lamarr. Metro-Goldwyn-Mayer, 1939.

An hour later, over coffee at Sylvain's restaurant, Hedy and Ritchie discussed the uncomfortable meeting. Realizing she had best secure a contract with Mayer, Hedy chose to accept his offer after receiving sobering advice from her European lawyer, Paul Koretz, who would negotiate her eventual MGM contract and himself later come to America, in 1939.

However, later that afternoon Ritchie discovered the Mayer party had already checked out of the hotel and left for France, to board the luxurious 83,500-ton superliner *Normandie*, leaving for New York from Le Havre.

"Is it possible to fall in love with a ship?" wrote Maria Sieber (later, actress Maria Riva), the twelve-year-old daughter of Marlene Dietrich, who with her mother had sailed

Above left: Hedy Lamarr, Algiers (United Artists, 1938). (Photograph by Clarence Sinclair Bull)
Above right: Hedy at her home, Hedgerow. Metro-Goldwyn-Mayer, 1940.

to and from Europe that same year aboard the *Normandie*. "She was the greatest ocean liner of them all! Nothing could top her. Nothing ever did . . . the first moment you saw her, lounging elegantly in her berth, you caught your breath in wonderment and never breathed normally again."

The flagship of the French Line, the *Normandie* was the speed queen of the North Atlantic upon her entry into service in 1935, until the next year when she was surpassed in speed by the RMS *Queen Mary*. "[T]he *Normandie* had the most beautiful First Class dining hall, which seated seven hundred people in an area the size of a football field, festooned with rows of soaring columns [twelve in total] of light in the shape of upside-down wedding cakes of Lalique, aglitter with Christofle silver, Limoges and De Havilland

Hedy at her home, Hedgerow. Metro-Goldwyn-Mayer, 1939.

porcelain, and shimmering Baccarat . . . [e]ven the Waldorf had nothing like this . . . [t] he whole ship was a Busby Berkeley production but with *class*!" [4]

Upon checking with the French Line offices in Paris, Ritchie discovered that the ship was completely booked. Cleverly he suggested a scheme to land Hedy aboard. Ritchie represented fourteen-year-old American violinist prodigy Grisha Goluboff, who was returning to America after finishing his highly successful European concert tour and was already booked to sail on the ship. Hedy would pose as his nanny.

Packing her suitcase with her remaining jewels (she had pawned most of them in Paris and London) and her two designer gowns, probably by Vionnet and Alix, Hedy

Hedy Lamarr. Metro-Goldwyn-Mayer, 1938. (Photograph by Clarence Sinclair Bull)

was traveling light, with no steamer trunks. Crossing the Channel that very evening, the following day she secured her passage, listed as simply Hedwig Mandl, German wife, on the ship's manifest. Accompanying young Goluboff, she then boarded the liner.

Shortly after departure from Le Havre the ship lost a propeller and had to return to port overnight, the passengers remaining on board as repairs were made. During the daytime on the ship Hedy wore a simple, tailored gray jacket and skirt suit and gloves. In her handbag she carried $900. In the evening, however, Hedy dazzled everyone on board. As she casually strolled through the 20-foot-tall bronze-adorned doors (crafted by Raymond Subes) of the exquisite 305-foot-long, 28-foot-high, Art Deco dining hall, every eye in the room was riveted on her exquisite classic beauty. With her on the *Normandie* she had two formal outfits, both definitive couture gowns. Possibly created by French fashion designer Madeleine Vionnet, whom Hedy was known to have frequented in Paris during her marriage to Fritz Mandl, one was a sleeveless, floor-length, possibly dark purple (Hedy's favorite color) velvet, floor-length creation with a crossover

Hedy Lamarr and son, James Lamarr Loder. Metro-Goldwyn-Mayer, c. 1945. (James Loder Collection)

bodice. Later Hedy was photographed wearing the same gown by Clarence Sinclair Bull in Hollywood.

Hedy had been photographed earlier in the year by photographer Otto Skall sitting in a loge in this velvet creation, the night of January 16, 1937, while attending the Vienna Opera Ball. She wore with her ensemble that evening a diamond tiara and matching earrings and necklace, accessorized with jewels consisting of a large brooch and numer-ous gemstone bracelets. Everyone at the musical affair could not help but notice "Frau Generealduektorin Hedy Mandl." Her image was published in a four-page spread in the cultural and lifestyle magazine *Sie Buhne* (January 1937). Other notables attending the "From Minuet to Waltz" ball included Austrian vice chancellor Kurt von Schuschnigg, who shared a table with State Secretary Guido Schmidt, Baron Louis von Rothschild, and chamber singer Richard Tauber and his second wife, British actress Diana Napier.

After arriving in Hollywood Hedy would not only be photographed in that very gown by Clarence Sinclair Bull, but she was also seen wearing it about town, at a nightclub on New Year's Eve 1938 with Charles Boyer, and in early 1940 with Norma Shearer and her then-beau George Raft. In the latter photo Hedy sported her famous chinchilla stole.

Sailing on board the *Normandie* on that fateful voyage, along with Mayer and his entourage, Walter Reisch, Howard Strickling, Benny Thau, and lawyer Paul Koretz, was a most impressive list of film stars, international artists, and celebrities: actors Douglas Fairbanks Jr. and French star Fernand Gravet; English musical star Jack Buchanan, traveling with Cole Porter; the Olympic ice-skating and 20th Century-Fox film star, Sonja Henie; French actress Danielle Darrieux; operatic stars Mary Garden, Ezio Pinza, and Elisabeth Rethberg (having completed their European tour, which included the Salzburg Festival); the tragic Joseph Schmidt [5]; French organist Marcel Dupré; as well as CBS president William S. Paley and American ambassador to France, William C. Bullitt, who suffered a cold throughout the voyage, traveling with his thirteen-year-old daughter, Anne.

During the crossing, Louis B. Mayer, who was also suffering—in his case, from a bout of *mal de mer* (seasickness)—had witnessed Hedy's stunning effect on both the illustrious passengers and the primarily French crew. Clearly noting the impact of just her physical beauty, the mogul buckled and reconsidered his prospects with signing Hedy Kiesler to Metro. Eventually he generously offered her a substantial one-year leading-lady contract for $550 a week, with a forty-week guarantee. (He even offered a contract to young violin prodigy Grisha Goluboff, whom Mayer somewhat inaccurately kept referring to as Hedy's "protégé.")

Finding Hedy's last name Kiesler offensive to his way of thinking, Mayer claimed to have re-christened her "Hedy Lamarr" after the doomed 1920s film beauty Barbara La Marr, "the girl who was too beautiful." (Hedy always insisted that it was *she* who had selected the name Lamarr, while looking out onto the sea—*la mer*, in French—on the *Normandie* during her passage to America.) Magnanimously Mayer advised Hedy to purchase a full wardrobe and a new set of luggage on the liner's E-deck onboard Dior and Chanel boutiques. More importantly, he also suggested that Hedy lose weight, adjust

Hedy Lamarr. Metro-Goldwyn-Mayer, 1940. (Photograph by Clarence Sinclair Bull)

her makeup techniques, and learn better English. (As a girl, Hedy was taught several languages, but English was not one of them.)

Docking in New York on Thursday, September 30, 1937, the *Normandie* proceeded to unload its passengers at Pier 88, as newshounds and press, including Mayer-appointed New York publicist Howard Dietz, ran up the gangway to capture celebrities for pictures and interviews before they disembarked. Hedy signed her contract before she even touched foot on American soil. It became effective that day. As she was seated in

the ship's Winter Garden on a wicker settee surrounded by the press, Hedy Kiesler—Madame Mandl, now Hedy Lamarr, an unknown just seven days before—received the lion's share of press attention and publicity. A snubbed Sonja Henie, the other French actresses, and most of the numerous male celebrities on board were barely noticed.

Dressed in unstylish Euro-chic, a long-sleeved dark suit festooned with a large orchid corsage, wearing pearl earrings and a single-strand pearl necklace and gloves, sporting a heavy fur stole and an unattractive pair of low heels, Hedy was unfortunately heavily made up. Still, she smiled rapturously at the cameras, and with the assistance of Howard Dietz, attempted to answer the somewhat rude questions the American press asked "the *Ecstasy* girl." She stumbled her way through the Metro-produced script she'd been given, telling them she wanted to forget her unfortunate "debut" in *Ecstasy*—that she'd been but a child at the time, and never knew she would have to appear nude until the day of filming. The mythology had begun.

Disembarking the ship with her new luggage packed with a lovely new wardrobe, Hedy was driven by Dietz to the Plaza Hotel. The following day, accompanied by a studio-assigned assistant, she boarded a train at Grand Central Station, en route to California. Heeding Mayer's orders, before arriving at Los Angeles's Union Station on October 4, 1937, she would amazingly re-create her image and style. The change was as dramatic as it was defining.

Opposite page: Hedy Lamarr. Metro-Goldwyn-Mayer, 1939.

chapter 5

ALGIERS AND THE CREATION OF HEDY LAMARR

*I*t was important for all refugee exiles arriving in the United States during the height of the European exodus to assimilate into the culture as quickly as possible. They had to learn and understand English, as well, or they would soon fall behind.

Hedy was more than ready to do just this when she stepped off the train at LA's Union Station on Monday morning, October 4, 1937. She took direction well, especially from her new boss, Louis B. Mayer. On the cross-country journey, with the help of her Metro-assigned aide, she had diligently studied the language, watched her weight, worked on changing her makeup and hair, and for when the time came, selected an appropriate outfit to make her debut before the Hollywood press. Only

Opposite page: Hedy Lamarr, Algiers (United Artists, 1938). Costumes by Irene.

Above left: Charles Boyer and Hedy Lamarr, Algiers *(United Artists, 1938). Costumes by Irene (Lamarr) and Omar Kiam (Boyer). (Photograph by Robert Coburn)*
Above right: Irene Lentz-Gibbons, costume designer for Algiers, The Heavenly Body, Her Highness and the Bellboy, *and* A Lady Without Passport. *Metro-Goldwyn-Mayer.*

one MGM representative showed up at the station to pick her up. With no photograph of his assigned star to serve as a guide, he was simply told to look for "the most beautiful creature on earth." [1]

As I wrote in *Beautiful: The Life of Hedy Lamarr*, what he witnessed gracefully stepping onto the platform in search of her luggage "was a smartly dressed, attractive young woman wearing a light-colored, conservative, three-quarter-length skirt and matching jacket, bearing a small corsage of flowers. On her shoulder-length dark tresses she wore a stylish late-1930s beret. Her appearance was quite a contrast from the high-gloss, heavily made-up exotic who had descended the French Line gangway in New York just five days earlier." [2]

The difference in both the look and style of Hedy Lamarr compared to that of Hedy Kiesler was as clear as night and day. Her hair was styled off her face to emphasize her bone structure, her eyebrows were toned down and separated a bit more, and her makeup had not been applied so heavily, meaning her beautiful porcelain skin was featured, her lips glossed to a more-natural line. She was stunning.

Greeting MGM's new find with a large bouquet of red roses, the publicist helped collect her luggage. He then advised his charge that he was taking her to the studio to meet with Mayer and his executives, who had flown to Los Angeles earlier. After showing Hedy around the studio, having her meet with Mayer, and advising her once again to study English and watch her weight, the publicist drove

Hedy Lamarr on the set of Algiers *(United Artists, 1938).*

Hedy to the Chateau Marmont, where Metro had secured a suite for her initial stay. Exhausted and overwhelmed, her flowers wilting, Hedy signed the Chateau Marmont guest registry. Though she had been given her new name, she didn't yet know how to spell it, so shakily she wrote "Hedy Lamar."

Hedy had arrived.

Within the week Hedy had contacted fellow exile, Hungarian actress Ilona Hajmassey—now, Massey—who had also just arrived in Hollywood. Massey asked Hedy

Hedy Lamarr's first appearance in Algiers *(United Artists, 1938), wearing her Austrian diamond earrings, with Claudia Dell (left), Robert Grieg (behind Hedy), and Bert Roach. Costumes by Irene.*

to move in with her and share her apartment at 120 South Medio Drive (later the residence of actress Jane Powell). For weeks the two went to the movies, listened to the radio, and assimilated the culture and language. "She buried the English language after I murdered it," Hedy once humorously remarked about her roommate, Ilona Massey. [3]

The studio eventually found Hedy a lovely house in the hills at 1807 Benedict Canyon, which she decorated with Walt Disney–inspired Snow White and the Seven Dwarfs figurines scattered in her tiny garden. Hedy was cared for by Ericka Manthey, a French woman who served as housekeeper, cook, chauffeur, and companion.

And then began the wait.

Signing with Hollywood's largest, wealthiest, and most respected film studio, Metro-Goldwyn-Mayer, Hedy was in the right place at the right time. At the end of 1937, MGM's resources were boundless, yet their most important task with Hedy Lamarr was

Above left: Charles Boyer and Hedy Lamarr, Algiers (United Artists, 1938). Costumes by Irene (Lamarr) and Omar Kiam (Boyer).
Above right: Hedy Lamarr wearing her Austrian earrings, Algiers (United Artists, 1938). Costumes by Irene.
Bottom right: Hedy Lamarr and Charles Boyer, Algiers (United Artists, 1938). Costumes by Irene (Lamarr) and Omar Kiam (Boyer).

to establish her exact type and abilities. Film property after film property was discussed as possible vehicles for her American screen debut. Meanwhile, Hedy had to achieve a comprehendible command of the language as she entered the "Hollywood Star Machine," which also required her to participate wholeheartedly in the rigorous requirements mandated by

Hedy Lamarr in profile. Metro-Goldwyn-Mayer, 1938. (Photograph by Clarence Sinclair Bull)

Hedy Lamarr. Metro-Goldwyn-Mayer, 1938.

the system to make her a star. This included taking language and diction, acting, and dancing classes. Hedy was given a typical six-month option contract, though her set salary rate was guaranteed for one year. This meant that at the end of six months she could be let go. It was mandatory, then, for her to be ready when a role was determined to be right for her.

The problem with Hedy Lamarr, with her exotic beauty and European breeding, was that studio chief Louis B. Mayer did not quite know what to do

Hedy Lamarr. Metro-Goldwyn-Mayer, c. 1939. (Photofest)

THE BEAUTY OF HEDY LAMARR

with her. He could take a nobody like Lucille LeSueur, for example, a struggling hoofer from a New York chorus line, change her name to Joan Crawford, give her schooling, posture, and diction training, and make a quasi-sophisticated grand lady out of her for the screen. When director Mervyn LeRoy joined Metro in 1938, he brought with him a pretty, voluptuous, and sexy—and somewhat undisciplined—high schooler named Judy Turner, whom the studio was able to transform into the beautiful Lana Turner. Mayer and MGM could take clay and create *objets d'art*.

But rarely, if ever, would the studio and Louis B. Mayer be handed a real lady, a true porcelain vessel, and be expected to make a star out of her. Recognizing Hedy Lamarr's unique beauty, they assumed she would be able to manage this feat on her own. And to some extent, she did.

During the months that followed, Hedy kept busy, reconnecting and sharing experiences and ideas with other European exiles as the grand exodus of artists, writers, playwrights, actors, and other artisans from Europe continued. All had arrived in Hollywood to begin new lives, having escaped the tyranny of fascist domination. By the late 1930s, such respected and talented film artists as Peter Lorre, Lotte Lenya, Kurt Weill, Jean Gabin, Otto Preminger, Jean Renoir, Lilli Palmer, Fritz Lang, Billy Wilder, Richard Siodmak, and Hedy would all live within a ten-mile radius of each other. Such established European film residents as Marlene Dietrich and screenwriter Salka Viertel would entertain and shelter this wave of artisan refugees pouring into California, seeking to continue their crafts. It's no wonder that Los Angeles soon became known as "Weimar on the Pacific."

But because of this glut of talent, jobs at the studios were limited. It became imperative for these exiles to assimilate as quickly as possible in order to secure studio positions and work; if not, after their contract options expired, they would risk being exiled back to their native countries.

The studio did what it could with Hedy. Publicity was minimal, as she had yet to prove that their investment in her was viable. In accordance with time-honored Hollywood tradition, she posed for a great deal of publicity photos, including some ridiculous

There were other actresses who attempted the "Lamarr Look" allure with makeup and hairstyle.
None but Joan Bennett successfully achieved the goal.

Joan Crawford. Metro-Goldwyn-Mayer, 1939.   *Joan Bennett. United Artists, 1938.*

Lucille Ball. RKO-Radio, 1939.   *Vivien Leigh. MGM, 1940.*   *Rita Hayworth. Columbia, 1939.*

Hedy Lamarr, 1938. (Photograph by Alfred Eisenstaedt)

bathing suit–clad cheesecake shots. Before marrying Fritz, Hedy had posed during her European career for such renowned photographers as Man Ray [4]. As an unselfconscious sixteen-year-old, Hedy had posed nude for Viennese photographer Trude Fleischmann [5], who had begun her career by photographing musical and theatrical celebrities for such publications as *Die Buhne*, *Moderne Welt*, and *Uhu*.

Now in Hollywood, one of Hedy's first sittings was for legendary portrait photographer Clarence Sinclair Bull (1896–1979), for whom Hedy once made lunch in her kitchen. He was one of the first in Hollywood to photograph the dark-haired, fair-skinned young Viennese actress. Her first sitting is still iconic, as it showcased her glamour—her luxurious beauty, the lush dark shoulder-length hair, parted in the middle, her sensual eyes and lips, her neck and wrists bedecked in jewels. More importantly, he was able to capture her innate femininity and vulnerability. Bull understood that Hedy represented

something new to the cinema-going public, even though she had not yet been showcased on film.

For several agonizing months Hedy anxiously waited for Mayer to offer her a script, as the clock ticked away her ever-decreasing option time.

Hedy seldom visited the Metro lot those first few months in Hollywood except to take a development class, pose for pictures, or talk with Mayer's secretary Ida Koverman about her growing concern that her contract would soon be up, with no work yet offered to her. Most days she was left to her own devices. She soon began to date and be seen about town. Reginald Gardiner, a quite appealing, mustachioed, thirty-four-year-old actor, became her lover and constant companion.

On a rainy evening, the third week of February 1938, Hedy reluctantly agreed to accompany Reggie to a party at the home of actor Charles Boyer. French-born Boyer, under contract with Walter Wanger, was riding the crest of a wave of popularity as a romantic leading man, having been loaned out to MGM to star as Napoleon Bonaparte in *Conquest* opposite Greta Garbo. He had just been nominated for an Oscar for Best Actor of 1937 for that role. (He would lose to Spencer Tracy for his performance in Metro's *Captains Courageous*.)

Boyer was captivated by Hedy's allure and glamour, and in her presence that evening he talked with Wanger about whether she might be considered for the leading actress role in his upcoming film for United Artists, *Algiers*. This Hollywood version was not necessarily a scene-for-scene remake, but more a mood-for-mood retelling of the successful *Pépé le Moko* (1937), starring Jean Gabin and directed by Julien Duvivier (also under Metro contract, at the time directing *The Great Waltz* with Luise Rainer, Fernand Gravat, and Miliza Korjus).

Louis B. Mayer had conducted a coup of sorts by securing the US film rights to *Pépé le Moko*, directed by Duvivier, contracting him as well as the film's leading lady, Mireille Balin (whom Mayer *never* cast in an American film), then selling those rights to make the picture to UA. Louis B. Mayer had no property ready for Hedy, and to be truthful, he didn't think she was worth the investment, beautiful though she was. By lending Hedy to

Hedy Lamarr. Metro-Goldwyn-Mayer, 1938. (Photographs by Clarence Sinclair Bull)

UA for her American film debut, he had nothing to lose should she come up short with audiences. Mayer owed Wanger for his loan-out of Boyer for *Conquest*. He had to have been very pleased and smug about his deal.

Filming for *Algiers* began on April 1, and would be completed in early May of 1938. Upon its premiere on August 5, Hedy Lamarr became an international star. More than any other motion picture of her career, *Algiers* would firmly establish the breathtaking glamour and allure of Hedy Lamarr on the silver screen. In no small part this was accomplished by the competent direction of John Cromwell and the patient support of co-star Charles Boyer. The film's music, limited except for establishing mood, was scored by Vincent Scotto and Muhammed Ygner Buchen, with some lyrics supplied by Ann Ronell. The full impact Hedy had on cinemagoers around the world was most assuredly enhanced by the costuming of Irene (Lentz) and the brilliant cinematography of multi-Oscar nominee and two-time recipient James Wong Howe (1899–1976).

Because the film takes place in 1938, the costume designs had to reflect contemporary tastes and fashion dependent upon the personal history and background, for "the most exciting characters that ever thrilled you from the screen," according to ads for the film. Hedy portrayed Gabrielle, or Gaby, a young, beautiful Frenchwoman engaged to a wealthy man whom she does not love. He gives her jewels, which she gladly accepts. Upon their trip to North Africa, Gaby and her traveling companions encounter Boyer's character, the French thief Pépé le Moko, deep inside the Casbah. He is first attracted to Gaby's jewels, but he eventually falls in love with her.

Hedy Lamarr's first screen appearance comes about thirty minutes into the picture. Her key introduction to most English-speaking audiences consists of a full-length camera shot from a distance in shadow and light. As she gets closer and closer to the camera, she turns her head to the left, then to the right, and just as she is about to step off the screen, she stops and faces full front to the camera. Hedy is dressed in a floor-length, dark tapered dress with a light-colored, fur-trimmed, long-sleeved satin bolero jacket with a lower hem in back. When she steps out of the shadows into the light and

101

Hedy Lamarr. Metro-Goldwyn-Mayer, 1938. (Photographs by George Hurrell)

a three-quarter close-up, we see she is wearing a double-strand pearl necklace and earrings. Her luscious shoulder-length dark hair is parted in the middle, and her left wrist is accessorized with a large jeweled bracelet. Audiences gasped at her beauty.

Hedy's contemporary costumes for *Algiers* were designed by Irene, with whom Hedy closely collaborated. The other costumes were created by studio designer Omar Kiam. Irene Lentz-Gibbons was born on December 15, 1901. Professionally known simply as Irene, she was generally referred to in the industry as "the best-dressed designer in the country." [6] After graduating from high school she studied music theory and composition at USC before transferring to the Wolfe School of Design to study dress design, drawing, and fashion design, graduating in 1926.

Developing a style of boldly signed fashion sketches, which became her trademark, Irene opened a dress shop in Hollywood catering to such stars as Dolores del Rio and Lupe Vélez. Her first husband, Richard Jones, whom she married in 1928, died in 1930, and Irene headed to Paris to study, returning to Hollywood in 1931 to open a shop on Sunset Boulevard. In 1933 she became head of Bullocks Wilshire Costume Design Salon, where she began work for films, independently designing costumes for various studios and reaching prominence for her creations for Ginger Rogers in *Shall We Dance* (RKO, 1937). She continued her career under contract with United Artists from 1937 to 1941. Irene's second husband was author-screenwriter Eliot Gibbons, brother of Metro's chief of art design, Cedric Gibbons, whom she wed in 1935. That year she was accorded recognition and approval, including the statement that "any garment bearing an Irene label was an indication that its wearer was a person of taste, position, and means." [7]

Irene's fashions for Hedy ranged from elegantly modern, simple, clean lines to elaborate European-influenced haute couture, from an outfit of shirred black taffeta trimmed in black velvet and worn with a lace mantilla, to an intriguing three-tone lavender floor-length dinner dress, with a bizarrely styled draped waistline and flowing cape draped over the right shoulder falling into two shirred panels down the front, with a sheer lighter-colored blouse, accessorized again with simple metallic collar, jeweled necklace and earrings and large bracelet. Most of Hedy's large, Deco, gem-encrusted jewelry pieces were supplied by Hollywood's Eugene Joseff Jewelers. Hedy's character Gaby's departure outfit was a long-sleeved, bell-shaped, two-toned black and electric blue, with a black banded belt. On top of her long tresses she wore a draped electric blue silk crepe turban with trailing scarf worn over one shoulder.

103

Most costuming for lesser players and extras in the late 1930s was supplied by Abe Schnitzer and his brother Joe at Western Costume in Hollywood at their eight-story building on Melrose Avenue, which housed 250 employees. Stockings and hosiery were commonly supplied by Willy's of Hollywood and its proprietor, former amateur boxer Willy de Mond. Still photographs for *Algiers* were by Hollywood photographer Robert Coburn (1900–1990), whose iconic images of such other stars as Henry Fonda, Rita Hayworth, Carole Lombard, Katharine Hepburn, and Lucille Ball define Hollywood glamour. Coburn immortalized Hedy's luminous allure in private settings as well as studio on-set film stills. She is young, fresh, and above all, breathtakingly beautiful.

In perhaps the most-talked-about scene in the film, Pépé and Gaby reminisce about Paris, lovingly discussing their romantic city. According to film historian Jeanine Basinger, "[Gaby] reminds him of the Paris subway. (Boyer was an actor who could tell a woman she reminded him of a subway and make it the greatest compliment she'd ever received.) The two stars, gorgeous, exotic, foreign, their speech heavily accented, lean toward each other in this scene, cooing and murmuring—reciting the names of the consecutive Paris subway stops! It's awesome." [8] (Ironically, the most often repeated quote from *Algiers* is when Pépé romantically whispers to Gaby, "Come wiz me to the Casbah"—a line *not* uttered in the film.)

Possibly the most stunning garment Hedy wore in *Algiers* was a simple black, long-sleeved, street-length dress, accessorized with a large white hat and veil, white gloves, and a white bag. In a romantic love scene in close-up with Boyer, James Wong Howe's sensitive shadows play across Hedy's deeply beautiful blue-green eyes, her wavy hair parted in the center, framing her perfect face. In stunning black and white, Hedy's natural beauty is allowed to shine through. The double strand of pearls and matching earrings and the jeweled wrist prominently on display, Pépé stares at her and asks, "What did you do before?" To which Gaby asks, "Before what?" He responds, "The jewels." She answers, "I wanted them." An unforgettable cinema moment.

For American audiences coming out of the Depression, *Algiers* just seemed right. "Boyer and Lamarr were so, so beautiful, exotic, otherworldly," noted Jeanine Basinger.

"They managed to do what stars must do: provide a direct connection to what viewers felt while lifting them totally up and away from that emotional constraint." [9] Trade ads boldly heralded the excitement and thrills of *Algiers* with such taglines as "women beyond the law's reach . . . living their own lives, fighting their own game . . . each for HER MAN . . . dark, romantic Charles Boyer in the year's most intriguing melodrama." Hedy's character of Gaby was called "a woman from another world . . . cold, yet desirable . . . tempting, yet dangerous . . . she promised wonders—and he yielded."

Audiences could not resist, and lined up around the block. *Algiers* was a huge box-office success. At the Eleventh Annual Acad-

Hedy Lamarr, wearing her Austrian diamond earrings. Metro-Goldwyn-Mayer, 1938. (Photograph by Robert Coburn)

emy Awards the film was nominated for four Oscars: Best Actor (Boyer), Best Supporting Actor (Gene Lockhart), Best Art Direction (Alexander Toluboff), and Best Cinematography (James Wong Howe). Hedy's film stardom was assured. In fact, *Hollywood* magazine in their September 1938 review of *Algiers* stated, "Probably the most important thing about the film is the introduction of Hedy [Lamarr]." Countless other observers in the international press agreed, even if they had not learned her name yet. "As Gaby, the alluring Parisienne, Hetty [*sic*] is nothing short of sensational," wrote *Silver Screen* magazine in September 1938. "With the preview audience fairly gasping over her close-ups, there doesn't seem a doubt but what she will be our newest and best Glamour Girl."

It seemed impossible to imagine that just the year before, Hollywood had epitomized American glamour with the wholesome sexuality of blonde bombshell Jean Harlow. However, at age twenty-six Harlow had tragically and unexpectedly succumbed to uremic

Hedy Lamarr. Metro-Goldwyn-Mayer, 1938. (Photograph by Robert Coburn)

poisoning, in June 1937. With the coming threat of war in Europe and the Pacific, the frivolity and showy glitziness synonymous with beauty was rapidly disappearing as the 1930s were drawing to a close. A new conscience—a new seriousness, if you will—began to prevail. New sophisticated styles and a concentrated desire for radical changes were beginning to appear in films of this era, as well. When *Algiers* premiered during the first week of August 1938, it seemed the search for perfect glamour, allure, and sophistication had ended with the image and presence of Hedy Lamarr.

"Beauty means business nowadays," wrote Mildred Adams at that time in the *New York Times*. "And business demands a change in beauty almost as often as it needs a change in the style of women's clothes." [10] According to Fred E. Basten, biographer of Hollywood makeup founder Max Factor, "By the end of the 1930s, shortly after the

release of *Algiers*, the most popular name in the Factor makeup studio was Hedy Lamarr . . . Of all the letters received by the Factors, the majority requested makeup tips for 'the Lamarr look,' far outnumbering those for other such famous faces as Marlene Dietrich, Dolores del Rio, Greta Garbo, Loretta Young, Vivien Leigh, and Merle Oberon." [11]

The impact Hedy Lamarr made on the public consciousness continued. Actresses like Joan Crawford, Vivien Leigh (not yet established in Hollywood), Lucille Ball, Frances Langford, Patricia Morison, Rita Hayworth, Margaret Lockwood, and Ann Sheridan all darkened their tresses and parted their hair in the middle. The most successful of those who copied the "Lamarr look" was natural blonde Joan Bennett, recently divorced from Gene Markey and then mistress of Walter Wanger. By the end of 1938 Bennett was starring in Wanger's *Trade Winds* for UA as an alluring brunette. (Unfortunately, Joan Bennett just did not have the facial perfection of Hedy Lamarr—her nose was a bit bulbous. Even when in repose, Joan Bennett's face often appeared as if she was smelling something rancid.)

Authors Richard Griffith and Arthur Mayer wrote of Hedy Lamarr: "The only big new star to emerge at the end of the Thirties was Hedy Lamarr, introduced by Walter Wanger in *Algiers*, 1938." [12]

Returning to the MGM lot that fall a huge star, Hedy Lamarr would now immerse herself and conquer the "star machine" of the biggest and best film studio in the world. New photo sittings were ordered for Hedy, to be handled by such renowned photographers as Laszlo Willinger (1909–1989), *Life* magazine's Alfred Eisenstaedt (1898–1995), and Peter Stackpole (1885–1973).

MGM was set to develop and solidify Hedy Lamarr's film legacy. In the process they would not only define her image—they would also almost destroy her.

chapter 6

HOLLYWOOD GLAMOUR AND STYLE

When Hedy Lamarr, now Hollywood's newest movie glamour queen, returned to the MGM lot with a newly renegotiated contract in the late summer of 1938, it was by the specific demand of self-satisfied film mogul Louis B. Mayer. And, he added, for this special meeting she best be on time.

Without any idea what to do upon signing this beautiful Austrian actress, much less having developed a viable script for her, Mayer had successfully loaned her out to another studio, United Artists, to test the waters—at their expense. He'd even made a profit by doing so, charging UA and Walter Wanger $1,500 a week salary for Hedy's services (while paying her the Metro-contracted fee of $550), and in turn UA was left to publicize her and build her up to make her a star. They and the cinema-going public did just that, leaving Louis B. Mayer and MGM to profit by their deceptively uncanny stroke of luck.

Opposite page: Hedy Lamarr, Lady of the Tropics *(MGM, 1939). Costumes by Adrian.*

Now in his cavernous office at the studio, surrounded by his lackeys, "the messianic go-getter and hamming hypocrite" [1] Louis B. Mayer beckoned Hedy to appear before him to iron out the specifics of their plans for her future.

Hedy's first task was to memorize the "facts" now laid out for her in her new official studio biography, scripted by Howard Strickling, repeating the fiction until it became comfortable and real to her. She was *not* to mention her Jewish heritage. Should the distasteful subject of *Ecstasy* arise, she was to state that she was young and innocent, and had been duped into doing *those* scenes in late

Gilbert Adrian, Metro-Goldwyn-Mayer costume designer for Lady of the Tropics, I Take This Woman, Boom Town, Comrade X, Come Live with Me, *and* Ziegfeld Girl. *(Metro-Goldwyn-Mayer)*

1932, after which she should attempt to change the subject as quickly as possible. (In fact, in several contemporary magazine and newspaper interviews given out immediately after *Algiers*, Hedy suddenly stated she was only *sixteen* years old—rather than her actual age, of eighteen—when that film was shot.)

After *Algiers*, Hedy's life was no longer her own. More legend was created, and it read as follows: Louis B. Mayer, in his "first" encounter with the beautiful Hedy Lamarr on board the *Normandie*, had sensed her potential possibilities for stardom, and thus offered her a major high-paying contract on the spot. Suddenly Mayer became the "Father Savior" of the helpless starlet, and as the years progressed, he was accorded full homage as being the one who saved her from the clutches of Nazi Germany. Nice fiction, if one

Hedy Lamarr, Adrian, and his wife Janet Gaynor on the set of Lady of the Tropics *(MGM, 1939). Costumes by Adrian. (Photofest)*

believed the pulp. Even Hedy surprisingly bought into it in later years after having repeated it for decades.

Metro had already applied pressure on Hedy to relearn her history before her loan-out to UA for *Algiers*. As one journalist would later describe her transformation at MGM, "She was turned over to makeup maestros who studied her lines and rigging and gave

her an artistic paint job bearing no resemblance to the original equipment which excited Reinhardt's admiration and came in full view in *Ecstasy*. . . . She was given a diet and after she pried off excess poundage by strict observation, publicity experts took over and posed her for innumerable stills in bathing suits and slinky gowns. . . . And then they forgot about her. For the next nine months Hedy was occupied by nothing more strenuous than admiring the new superstructure Hollywood had built around her original keel, going to the movies and drawing her paycheck." [2]

Metro makeup artist Jack Dawn was assigned to help Hedy with her revamp. According to the artist, Hedy's "mouth was made over to give it that luscious curve; her hair was done in loose waves and that long bob was decreed, her eyebrows were revamped so that there was more space between them. But, he added, she had a practically perfect face to begin with. . . . Her hair was softened above the forehead, her eyebrows lifted, and her lips shortened." [3] He remarked that she had little of the allure audiences had come to expect from her when she first came to Hollywood. "Once in America," wrote publicist and agent John Springer and writer Jack Hamilton, "nobody paid much mind to . . . Hedy Lamarr. But that face! It may have possessed the most fabulous brunette beauty . . . to have ever hit the silver screen. Hollywood makeup men did their job well—the face of Hedy Kiesler was nowhere to being as entrancing, but obviously, there must have been something there in the first place." [4]

One thing was obvious to Mayer and the rest of the fanciful, fantasy directors in Hollywood: Hedy was a valuable commodity. And as such, Mayer would exert his powers to make her the biggest female star on the lot. He would personally oversee her first film for Metro, *A New York Cinderella*, a property written by Charles MacArthur, one of the most expensive screenwriters in Hollywood and the husband of actress Helen Hayes. Bankrolling it at $700,000, Hedy would star opposite the studio's hottest actor, Spencer Tracy, fresh off the heels of his film *Boys Town*, which would earn him his second Best Actor Oscar the following year.

The contemporary storyline of *A New York Cinderella* told of beautiful New York society model Georgi Gragore (Hedy), who, after an ill-fated affair with her lover Phil Mayberry

Louella Parsons and Hedy Lamarr being served canapés on the set of Lady of the Tropics *(MGM, 1939). (Photofest)*

(Walter Pidgeon / Kent Taylor), attempts suicide by trying to jump off a ship, but is saved by New York physician Dr. Karl Decker (Spencer Tracy), also on board. Once back in the city she weds the doctor, even though she does not love him. He leaves his practice downtown and joins a high-society uptown clinic, where he realizes he does not belong after the death of a young social debutante (Adrienne Ames / Laraine Day) and Georgi's assumed infidelity with her former lover. Back downtown and feeling appreciated, Dr. Decker and Georgi realize they love each other by the final scene. A contrite and seemingly ridiculous, convoluted script. Production geared up at once. Filming commenced in mid-October 1938 with director Josef von Sternberg, who had handled the early, highly stylized Paramount pictures of Marlene Dietrich.

Entering the MGM lot, where Louis B. Mayer boasted "more stars than there are in heaven," Hedy was joining the elite of all film studios. Major players at MGM in 1938 included Norma Shearer, Clark Gable, Myrna Loy, young Mickey Rooney and Judy Garland, Lana Turner, Joan Crawford, Robert Taylor, Greta Garbo, Eleanor Powell, Jeanette MacDonald and Nelson Eddy, and James Stewart. With at least fifty-two feature films in production at all times, the studio was able to supply its massive theater chain with a new film each week. To produce such an output of motion pictures, I wrote in *Beautiful: The Life of Hedy Lamarr*, "Metro had 140 different departments at its disposal on the lot, efficiently running like clockwork—a makeup department that would handle more than twelve hundred makeups an hour, costume designers, songwriters, screenwriters (with thousands of novels, plays, and short stories at their disposal), set designers, carpenters, directors, producers, musicians, contract players, electricians, medical staff, and so on." [5]

Said Metro head of makeup, Jack Dawn, "Some idea of the volume of work done may be obtained from [the] quantities of material we use. In a year we require more than 1,000 large cans of face powder, 3,000 lbs. of grease paint, 500 lbs. of false hair for beards and wigs, 20 gallons of spirit gum, and 50 lbs. of assorted waxes and plastics." [6] "What most distinguished MGM's films was their general air of unreality," wrote one Hollywood historian. "Mayer loved beauty as an aesthete did. He particularly believed, in accordance

Hedy Lamarr and Robert Taylor, Lady of the Tropics *(MGM, 1939). Costumes by Adrian.*

with his somewhat antiquated nineteenth-century view of women, in idealizing his female stars, and that became one of the benchmarks of the MGM look." [7] Said George Cukor, "Louis B. Mayer was a great believer in his movie queens 'looking right.' " [8]

Metro took particular care of their stars' appearance in each and every production, according to the specific demands of each character. "The MGM makeup department consisted of fifty-two people and was famous for the boast it could 'make any plain-looking woman beautiful in one hour and any beautiful woman hideous in four minutes,' " wrote Jeanine Basinger. "They worked in a suite filled with spirit gum, false hair, wigs, putty, fish skin, sponge rubber lips, paint, grease pencils, cotton fluffs, mortician's wax,

THE BEAUTY OF HEDY LAMARR

false teeth, aluminum powder, and a gelatin capable of changing an entire facial contour. They were the wizards in the land of Oz." [9]

In *Beautiful: The Life of Hedy Lamarr* I wrote, "Metro-Goldwyn-Mayer also had an immense photography system. Each one of their twenty-five major stars between 1937 and 1940 was extensively photographed for at least five thousand portraits every year. The top stars received an average of one portrait sitting a month. MGM sent more than 200,000 selected negatives taken on the set, in sittings, and for fashion shoots. Prints from those negatives cost Metro approximately $100,000 (in 1930s dollars) each year. For every big film MGM produced during its heyday, over six hundred stills were taken during production." [10]

Answering to the studio publicity department, the "Hollywood stills photographers were, on the whole, among the least admired or appreciated of their fraternity," wrote British film historian John Kobal. "Few of them ever even became as well known as free-lance photographers working for fashion magazines. . . . Great care went into the stills sessions; the lighting, the costume, the props and the makeup were all designed to contribute to the production of a quintessential look of personal style." [11]

"It is a curious notion that a still image could have such power on a movie star's trajectory," Vicki Goldberg wrote for the *New York Times* in 1997. "David O. Selznick declared that Hedy Lamarr 'had actually been established purely by photography.' " Yet, Goldberg continues, "In Hurrell's and other studio photographers' images, the subjects, in poses and settings as vivid as tableaux vivants, often work themselves up to a high of emotion, so that we sense a tensely compressed narrative, an excerpt from some unwritten drama." [12]

Every film studio had its own house photographer during Hollywood's Golden Age. At Paramount there were Eugene Robert Richee, William Walling, and, for a time, Otto Dyer. The top photographers at Warner Brothers included Elmer Frye, Bert Six, and Scotty Welbourne. Columbia had A. L. "Whitey" Schafer, who later went over to Paramount, Carl DeVoy, and William Fraker. Universal had Ray Jones, assisted by Roman Freulich and Bill Walling. United Artists secured freelancers John Miehle, Madison

Hedy Lamarr. Metro-Goldwyn-Mayer, c. 1939.

Lacy, and Al St. Hilaire, once assistant to George Hurrell. And 20th Century-Fox utilized Max Munn Autrey, Hal Phyfe, Frank Powolny, Gene Kornman, and Alexander Kahle.

The lead photographer at RKO Radio was Ernest A. Bachrach, with his innovative "dazzling geometric studies of the human face and form" [13], and Bob Coburn, who also worked at Columbia and UA. Coburn's photographs of Hedy on set and off during the filming of *Algiers* were some of the first to exploit her beauty. "Glamour was the key—we

117

were always trying to out-glamour the others," said Coburn about his craft. "It was a contest to see who could provide the most glamour . . . those beautiful pictures of beautiful women. We sat in from beginning to end on a movie. Our business was to sell that mystique . . . that appeal. We were painting pictures with lights." [14]

Metro-Goldwyn-Mayer led the way in proficiency and style with Clarence Sinclair Bull, who photographed all the Metro stars from the early 1920s until his retirement in 1955. They also employed Ted Allen, who went over to the radio networks in the 1930s; Eric Carpenter (1909–1976), who had begun his career as an MGM office boy in 1933 before becoming an assistant to Clarence Bull; and the versatile Laszlo Willinger, who came to MGM in 1938, and whose ability to enhance the female stars' "allure by imbuing them with thoughtful intelligence as well as obvious beauty, predictably made him very popular with Metro's high-powered, competitive female stars." [15]

Clarence Sinclair Bull had begun his career in 1918 at the old Metro Studio as an assistant cameraman who also took stills of the stars. This led to a career with Goldwyn lasting into the merger of Metro with Goldwyn Studio in 1924, when he then became head of the still department. "I never said 'Hold it' or 'Still, please,' " he once admitted. "The face did that when it matched the inner moods. All I did was light the face and wait and watch, and when I saw the reflected mood I clicked the shutter." [16] There were of course independent photographers in Hollywood throughout its history, including Gaston Longet, Russell Ball, Ruth Harriet Louise, Edward Cronenweth, Paul Hesse, George Hommel, and Irving Lippman, many of whom photographed the beauty of Hedy Lamarr.

George Hurrell (1904–1992), who came to MGM in the late 1920s and remained with the studio until 1932, when he opened up his own studio, was the man who took the most memorable of all Hedy's glamour portraits. Writing of his experience photographing Hedy Lamarr, Hurrell stated, "Although Hedy Lamarr did not have the strong bone structure of a Garbo, her beauty was so outstanding that any angle was good. She wasn't always in a sultry mood, so it was necessary to build an atmosphere around her, which I usually accomplished with music. The first time I shot her was in 1938. . . . She was quiet and introspective. . . . Her coloring, smooth white skin, and raven black hair were so

spectacular I wished I had brought along some color film . . . I realized instantly that she was one of those actresses who can wear an absolutely blank expression and yet convey an attitude of complete intrigue. They can sometimes be more expressive before a still camera than on the motion picture set." [17]

Not every photographer found Hedy Lamarr as pliable a subject. "How do you make Hedy Lamarr sexy?" Laszlo Willinger once said. "She has nothing to give. It wasn't as simple as showing legs or cleavage. She was not very adept at posing. . . . She felt if she sat there, that was enough. . . . It never occurred to me that one could wake her up." [18] Even George Hurrell had his difficulties with Hedy. "I didn't get too much out of Hedy because she was so *static*. Stunning. But it was the nature of her, she was so phlegmatic, she didn't project anything," he later told John Kobal. "It was just a mood thing. And she had just one style. It didn't vary particularly." [19] Still, the photographs of Hedy taken by both Hurrell and Willinger are perhaps the most iconic of any ever made of her.

"There was such a dramatic quality in those days," Hurrell once told John Kobal. "[W]e were all such romantics. The stars were really wonderful about stills . . . they'd cooperate. There wasn't any false pretense of 'dignity'—just a naturalness. They were electric, full of sexual qualities, alluring. Our world was a storybook—a romantic fantasy. We were talented. We were working. We were making money and assumed it would always be so. We didn't fret and worry about it like they do today. We were too busy being alive. We were the children of the gods." [20]

chapter 7

THE MACHINE
AT WORK

*P*reparations and preproduction for *A New York Cinderella* dragged on for months. Perhaps too many months. Hedy had moved again, from her then-modest home at 2727 Benedict Canyon Road to a more-spacious house further up the road. Once filming began on October 18, 1938, it was apparent there were major issues with nearly every aspect of the production. Trouble loomed ahead. As I chronicled in my biography of Hedy Lamarr, the script was bad, one of the worst ever penned by Charles MacArthur. To add more stress, director Josef von Sternberg was proving difficult as he faced insurmountable proof that he had his work cut out. Then there was Louis B. Mayer's annoying and ever too frequent presence on the set. In addition, Spencer Tracy wasn't keen on the idea of supporting

Opposite page: Hedy Lamarr, Lady of the Tropics *(MGM, 1939). Costumes by Adrian.*

Above left: Hedy Lamarr. Metro-Goldwyn-Mayer, 1940. (Photograph by Bud Graybill)
Above right: Hedy Lamarr and completed bust of her by sculptress Nina Saemundsson, for the 1939 New York
World's Fair, created during the filming of Lady of the Tropics *(MGM, 1939). (Photograph by Eric Carpenter)*

Hedy Lamarr, and he voiced his complaints frequently in the press. Filming came to an unceremonious and complete halt in early November, and von Sternberg was let go.

Of course, MGM publicists handed out this and that nonsense, reasons and non-reasons. Perhaps one of the major reasons for the shutting down of the film, then and even later, was that many of the film's players—all but Hedy, in fact—had prearranged contractual obligations for other pictures. Spencer Tracy and some of the original supporting players had to go on to other projects. Walter Pidgeon, Ina Claire, Jack Carson, Adrienne Ames, whom Hedy had championed for in her role, even Fanny Brice, were involved in the picture at one point or another. Although some of their scenes were filmed for *A New York Cinderella*, they eventually departed.

Robert Taylor and Hedy Lamarr, Lady of the Tropics *(MGM, 1939). Costumes by Adrian.*

Hope for completion of the filming came with the immediate assigning of the respected Frank Borzage, who took over as director. Now titled *I Take This Woman,* with photography by celebrated cameraman Harold Rosson, filming under Borzage's direction resumed on November 7. It was rumored that Borzage, who had once conducted romances with both Joan Crawford and Margaret Sullavan, also succumbed to a brief affair with Hedy at this time.

One key aspect Borzage had to address regarding the picture was fashion, as styles were rapidly changing. Hedy's costumes in particular were once again a problem. "In the

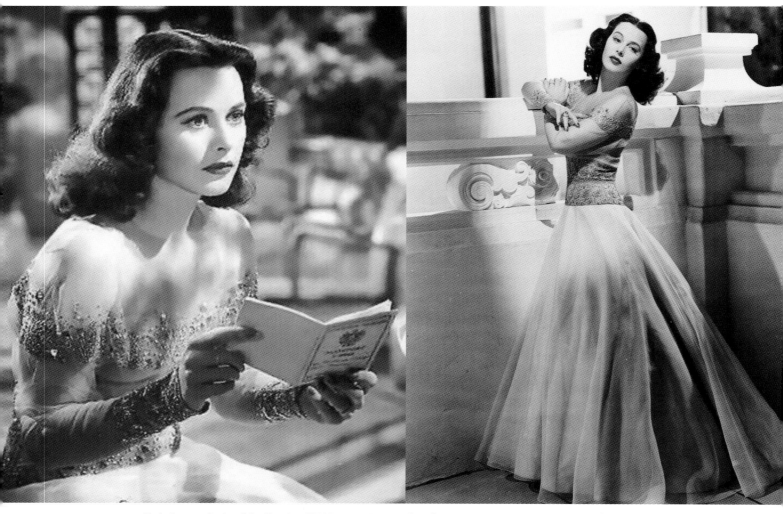

Hedy Lamarr, Lady of the Tropics (MGM, 1939). Costumes by Adrian.

first part of the 1930s there was this sort of return to conservatism, and a very feminine, soft, romantic hour-glass figure," observed Broadway fashion designer Tracy Christensen. "The hems went way down. . . . During the second part of the 1930s, the hemlines started coming up. There was a change of shape . . . to a more tailored, utility feel." [1] This complicated matters with Hedy at this time, as her figure was changing, and the previously designed costumes did not match the needs of the era. During the brief time that shooting had stopped and started, Hedy's silhouette had altered almost completely.

Hedy's costumes for *I Take This Woman* were designed by studio designer Adrian, born Adrian Adolph Greenburg (aka Gilbert), on March 3, 1903, in Naugatuck, Connecticut. By the age of eighteen Adrian was enrolled at the New York School of Fine and Applied Art (now the Parsons School of Design). Recommended by designer Robert Kalloch to Florence Cunningham, Adrian began to design for the Gloucester Playhouse during his first summer vacation from school. In the 1920s he transferred to the Place des Vosges in Paris. Later discovered by songwriter Irving Berlin, Adrian designed for a couple of *Music Box Revues*. Designer Natacha Rambova, then married to Rudolph Valentino, asked him to create the costumes for the projected film *The Hooded Falcon*, which did not happen. Adrian's first screen credits, however, were for two Valentino films, *The Eagle* and *Cobra*. After a brief stint designing for Cecil B. DeMille at DeMille

Rare off-set photo of Hedy Lamarr laughing, during filming of Lady of the Tropics *(MGM, 1939). Costumes by Adrian.*

Pictures Corporation from 1926 to 1928, Adrian became the head fashion designer at MGM from 1928 to 1942.

Designing iconic costumes for the studio's two most important actresses, Norma Shearer and Joan Crawford, Adrian established himself as a true fashion trendsetter when in 1932 he created the "Letty Lynton" dress Crawford wore in the film of the same title. "The rag trade were always interested in Joan Crawford's clothes," wrote one Hollywood

fashion historian, "and with full co-operation of the studio's vast publicity machine, would copy the clothes quickly enough to get them into the shops for the film's release." [2] As the studio's chief designer, Adrian's contract allowed him exclusive credit and billing as "Gowns by Adrian."

"When Adrian made a sketch," said John B. Scura, who was employed in the Metro wardrobe department for over four decades, "no producer or director dared to change it." [3]

Above left: Hedy Lamarr and Robert Taylor, Lady of the Tropics *(MGM, 1939). Costumes by Adrian. Above right: Adrian's temple costume from* Lady of the Tropics, *as displayed today (MGM, 1939). Costumes by Adrian.*

Adrian's designs for innumerable MGM pictures of the era set trends that would last for years. "I try and bring common sense to clothes," he said in 1935. "I admit that some of my creations may have seemed mad at first, but they all had a definite idea of personality behind them. It is the *mind* of a woman that counts." [4]

"Fashion evolves in spite of designers, and not because of them," Adrian once confessed to a fan magazine writer in the mid-1930s. "There is an evolutionary law in fashion changes, just as there is in painting or any other art. A new Hollywood mode, used consistently, does not make itself felt very quickly, and it is widely copied if it is good and right and sound." [5] As film fashion historian David Chierichetti defined, "Often, the role of the movie designer was not to create next year's fashions, but to simply guess what they would be." [6] Adrian had brought back into fashion in the early

Hedy Lamarr, Lady of the Tropics *(MGM, 1939). Costumes by Adrian.*

1930s the redingote line, a nipped-in, fitted waistline, and a full gored skirt. This trend in fashion prevailed from the late 1930s into the 1950s.

Adrian faced real and serious problems with the clothing he designed for Hedy for *I Take This Woman.* He knew it would be a challenge to dress one of the most beautiful women in Hollywood—and Mayer's newest glamour star—recognizing that Hedy's physical beauty would most likely supersede the concepts of his fashion. He would come to show great empathy for Hedy in her struggles with the making of *I Take This Woman.*

Spencer Tracy and Hedy Lamarr, I Take This Woman, *original 1938 version, Metro-Goldwyn-Mayer. Costumes by Adrian, not used in the final film. (Photograph by Laszlo Willinger)*

Scenes for most motion pictures, then as now, are rarely shot in continuity. With the demands of set designers and craftsmen, the availability of studio space, the various set-ups, even the resuming of particular scenes long after they were originally shot—there were many starts and stops. In the case of *I Take This Woman*, time was not at a premium. Metro had an investment in the picture now, and issued various reasons and possibilities for delays, all smoke and mirrors. The Hollywood gossips were spinning with speculation and rumors.

Adrian realized that Hedy Lamarr's body was changing, and it was increasingly apparent that even with ingenious direction, studio photographers, and editing, it would be hard to hide. Keen eyes would suspect there were career-threatening issues at hand. Adrian's original designs for Hedy, nine key costumes in the final cut of the picture, ranged from slinky, silky, and flowing negligees and smart suits and even a working smock, to a

Hedy Lamarr, I Take This Woman, *second 1939 version, Metro-Goldwyn-Mayer. Costumes by Adrian, not used in the final film. (Photograph by George Hurrell)*

couple of magnificent, spectacular evening gowns. One outfit was a heavy white crepe, square-shouldered blouse with stand-up collar, open long sleeves, and extreme pocket bands, tucked into a street-length black crepe skirt with a deep waistband and eight-inch vertical pockets.

As Tracy's character comments about his wife's beauty in a scene where she sports a sleek black street ensemble of ruffled jacket, short skirt, white blouse, and white gloves, "She's like something you see in a jeweler's window—a single flawless gem on a piece of black velvet. You take a long last look, and then you pass on." And in reality, in close-ups Hedy is stunning.

Filming the second time around was halted once more in January of 1939. By now the picture had cost Metro some $900,000. Throughout the Borzage months, Hedy had

129

Hedy Lamarr, I Take This Woman, second 1939 version, Metro-Goldwyn-Mayer. Costumes by Adrian. (Photograph by Laszlo Willinger)

become increasingly more difficult to photograph—not because of any unprofessionalism on her part, but rather because of her figure. Mayer was determined and ruthless in his attempts to complete the film. The script remained a major problem, and as the costumes Hedy wore were continually changing, Adrian had new hurdles to overcome daily. "I always emphasize the bad features of a woman," Adrian once commented, "to the point where they seemingly disappear. . . . Show the public your bad points and they won't notice them, particularly if another part of your dress holds their attention." [7]

Spencer Tracy and Hedy Lamarr, I Take This Woman *(MGM, 1940). Costumes by Adrian.*

Unfortunately, Hedy's weight changes could not be disguised, and they were shown in full view.

The official reason given for the second halt in the filming of what Hollywood was now calling *I Re-Take This Woman* was that Spencer Tracy had to begin work on February 1 on MGM's expensive Technicolor adventure, *Northwest Passage.* Yet speculation still abounded, and rumors began anew. Hedy had, during this period, renegotiated her contract with the studio and was receiving $750 a week. Her steady beau was still Reginald Gardiner. But, in the early months of filming *I Take This Woman*, Hedy was rumored to have had a brief affair with Spencer Tracy. These affairs may or may not have played a part in the uneven filming history of this motion picture.

According to the press, with her leading man now making another picture, there was nothing lined up for Hedy until April, when she would begin filming *Lady of the Tropics* with Robert Taylor, to be directed by Jack Conway. Surprising Hollywood even further was Hedy's sudden elopement on Saturday, March 4, 1939, the day after the declaration of World War II in Europe. Her new husband was 20th Century-Fox film producer Gene Markey, "a talented, witty author and man-about-Europe from Chicago," wrote Douglas

Fairbanks Jr., whose mother was once squired by Markey ever so briefly. "For years he was the principal love in the life of Broadway's superb comedienne Ina Claire. He was one of the few who did not marry Gloria Swanson, but they lived very happily together for quite a while. He did, however, marry such glamour girls as Joan Bennett, Hedy Lamarr, and Myrna Loy." [8]

Hedy had acquired a legal divorce from Fritz Mandl sometime in 1938. Gene and Hedy were married in Mexicali, Mexico. The wedding of Hedy, swathed in the Mexican sun in a full-length mink coat that she never took off, and the somewhat paunchy, balding, middle-aged Gene Markey raised several eyebrows. The couple did not honeymoon, Hedy stating she had to begin a picture that following Monday. (*Lady of the Tropics* would not begin filming until April.) The couple returned to Hedy's new hilltop home, called Hedgerow, located at 2707 Benedict Canyon Drive. During this period Gene was producing films at 20th Century-Fox. As a naval reservist for many years, Markey was also helping Douglas Fairbanks Jr., whose infant daughter was Markey's godchild, complete his naval exams to enlist prior to America's entry into World War II.

While MGM was left to salvage *I Take This Woman*, Hedy was summoned to Metro in April of 1939 to begin shooting *Lady of the Tropics*, cast opposite the studio's equally beautiful actor Robert Taylor. Set against the then-contemporary setting of French Indochina, the storyline was pure soap opera. On a cruise to the Orient, playboy Bill Carey (Robert Taylor) meets the beautiful, mysterious half-caste Manon DeVargnes (Hedy Lamarr), who wishes to acquire a passport and leave her native country. She is "sponsored" by wealthy plantation owner Pierre Delaroch (Joseph Schildkraut), who is jealous of Manon's affections for Bill. Manon and Bill marry, Delaroch hires Bill to work for him, and finally gives Manon her passage out of the country. But not before misunderstandings, murder, and Manon's death. All very dark and gloomy.

Many of Hedy's early scenes in the film were photographed toward the end of June by the competent George J. Folsey. The musical score was supplied by composer Franz Waxman. Designer Adrian once again was assigned the task of garbing Hedy in over a dozen outfits for the film. His costumes were meant to represent a contemporary sleek American

Above left: Hedy Lamarr, I Take This Woman *(MGM, 1940). Costumes by Adrian.*
Above right: Hedy Lamarr, I Take This Woman, *second 1939 version, Metro-Goldwyn-Mayer. Costumes by Adrian. (Photograph by Clarence Sinclair Bull)*
Bottom right: Hedy Lamarr, I Take This Woman, *second 1939 version, Metro-Goldwyn-Mayer. Costumes by Adrian. (Photograph by Laszlo Willinger)*

look combined with a somewhat fanciful Asian flair. And again, nothing was to distract from Hedy's natural beauty. Most of these costumes were long, flowing garments, cleverly camouflaging Hedy's torso, waist, and hips. This has always been a bit inexplicable, because here was one of Metro's top glamour queens now appearing in what would be her first picture for the studio, and for some reason they did *not* display her figure except in heavy shadows in the temple sequence, shot toward the very end of filming.

Nevertheless, Hedy's dozen costumes were stunning. A particular outfit—made of opulent fabric and trimmed with huge jewels—of simple straight lines in a shell pink lamé wrap with plush velvet sleeves was but one example of Adrian's tasteful, and in this case, exotic, touch. In another costume, he created a beautiful gown with long sleeves, embroidered with brilliants, silver paillettes, and emeralds, with a deep girdle that edged the cape yoke and sleeves of a beige "souffle" (a nude mesh fabric) bodice, complementing a full, floor-length skirt of white *mousseline de soie* over a crisp taffeta slip, worn toward the end of the film. Surprisingly Hedy is only seen in it briefly, in full frontal view.

In the film, there is a brief scene of her character in a white flowing street outfit, with heavy jewelry, dangling earrings, dark gloves, and white turban, Hedy's perfect face radiant in close-up. In another scene Hedy wears a light-colored, embroidered outfit, with a cap and flowing veil to and around her shoulder. Many of her scenes are shot from over the shoulder as she sits at tables dressed in black and wearing veils, or in white flowing robes full-length, seen from the back. Hedy particularly liked Adrian; the two were quite *simpatico*. He allowed her to design the one jeweled side-hat with flowing dark veil for the film, a task she enjoyed because of her study of fashion as a young girl in Vienna. Adrian in turn appreciated Hedy's enthusiasm, and privately created many of the garments for her personal wardrobe.

Adrian created one particularly stunning outfit for Hedy for this film that revealed his trademark style: an elaborate twenty-five-pound gown made entirely of jewels, which Hedy's character wears to dance in the moonlight for her betrothed at a temple in the jungle. "More than 12,000 jewels, 10 bunches of gold spangles, each numbering 2,000 strands with each strand holding 1,000 spangles to total 2,000,000, and 300 yards of gold bullion went into the making of the costume." [9] Hedy was extensively photographed during this shooting by Clarence Sinclair Bull, his portraits from the film defining Hollywood

Opposite page: Hedy Lamarr. Metro-Goldwyn-Mayer, c. 1940.

glamour photography. Filming was completed on *Lady of the Tropics* in late June of 1939.

On December 4, after Hedy was given five months off, with new schedules arranged and reconfirmed, new cast members in place, the script rewritten yet again, *I Take This Woman* resumed shooting for a third time. During those previous six months, Hedy had unsuccessfully sued MGM for breach of contract. Her renegotiated contract gave her a better salary of $1,000 per week, with a forty-week guarantee, but the dispute had initiated a bitter and contentious relationship between Hedy and her boss, Louis B. Mayer.

Avant-garde music composer George Antheil, c. 1930s.

Eager to recoup his investment with *I Take This Woman*, despite the script being insurmountably bad, Mayer started up production this time under the competent direction of W. S. "Woody" Van Dyke II, also known as "One-Take Woody." With Van Dyke at the helm, the long-awaited completion of the picture arrived at last, at the end of December. And a rush job it was, reshooting scenes, shuffling dialogue, and tweaking the script to fit new situations. Some of Adrian's costumes for Hedy were scrapped and a couple of new ones added as the wardrobe was changed yet again, multiple times.

Hedy had begun work on the film more than a year earlier. At the start of filming her makeup was a bit heavy, and her long lush hair was styled very much in the mode of 1938 glamour. When the film's title became *I Take This Woman* in November of 1938, Hedy's hair was longer, and her makeup and cosmetics had been toned down. In most of

those Borzage-directed scenes she looks heavy, and one is frustrated at never seeing her character's complete figure. Then suddenly, in interspersed and none too eloquently edited scenes, the results of the couple of weeks of shooting handled by Van Dyke in December of 1939, one is finally given full-figure shots of Hedy. In these scenes, her acting is greatly improved, her hair is much shorter, and her Adrian-designed costumes begin to take on a life of their own.

In fact, in one key scene at a nightclub, Hedy is seated at a table, her hair short in the close-ups. She is wearing a stunning black velvet and white satin evening gown with a flaring front panel of black chiffon velvet (not the long-sleeved dark original one with breast jewels, used in publicity shots). Over this she sports a short black coat trimmed with leopard, and a mandatory matching muff. Yet when she stands to leave with Tracy, her hair is suddenly longer and fuller, and she appears to be wearing a completely different coat with spotted fur collar. The scene is all very subtle, the editors having worked overtime.

Hedy Lamarr. Metro-Goldwyn-Mayer, c. 1939.

In the final analysis, despite a reasonably fine musical score by Bronislau Kaper and Artur Guttmann (now spelled Guttman), who had written the score for Hedy's *Wir Brauchen kein Geld* in 1932, it is sadly undeniable: *I Take This Woman* is a mess.

During the period Hedy was between pictures, June through December 1939, she and Gene Markey began the process of adopting a little boy the press reported she had found in a Los Angeles orphanage in October. Hollywood's powerful gossip Louella Parsons

THE BEAUTY OF HEDY LAMARR

broke the news in her daily newspaper column. The child, according to the contemporary press, had been born in Los Angeles County on March 6, 1939, his young, unwed parents having given him up. Hedy and Gene named him James Lamarr Markey, and called him Jamesie. He was not photographed until he was a toddler, and little press was released about him.

At the same time, Markey and Hedy were drifting apart, and it wouldn't be long before Hedy would file divorce proceedings against her husband, claiming that he was distant and dull.

When both *Lady of the Tropics,* which opened in August 1939, and *I Take This Woman,* which premiered the following January, garnered disastrous reviews, Hedy knew she had to do something to salvage her career. The ad lines for *Lady of the Tropics* were particularly banal: "You, too, will be 'Hedy' with delight . . . and your verdict will be '*Lamarr*vel-ous'!" The press was full of news of the failures of these two motion pictures, although surprisingly *Lady of the Tropics* was named one of the Best Films of 1939 in the March 1940 issue of *Photoplay* magazine. Nonetheless, even though it made back its $1 million cost, *I Take This Woman* ranks today as one of the worst MGM films ever to come out of Hollywood's Golden Age.

It should be noted that three of the 1939 Best Picture Oscar nominations were MGM films—*Gone with the Wind, The Wizard of Oz,* and *Ninotchka,* which "was doing subpar business because of the war-torn European market which had always been essential to the success of Garbo's pictures." [10] Most of Metro's $9.5 million in profits for that year came from the success of low-budget B-pictures and the *Andy Hardy* series, starring the number-one box-office star of 1939–1940, Mickey Rooney. At this time Louis B. Mayer was losing touch with the changing and improved market tastes of the general public as the country moved out of the Great Depression. Metro still needed to make big-bud-get pictures, but its profitability rested on its more economically produced B-films and series. As Thomas Schatz wrote, "MGM, it seems, had peaked early and now was curi-ously out of synch with Hollywood's golden age." [11]

Hedy Lamarr. Metro-Goldwyn-Mayer, c. 1940. (Photographs by Eric Carpenter)

Hedy confided in Clark Gable on the Metro lot about her failure to achieve box-office security with the studio, expressing her disappointment with how her Hollywood career was working out. According to Hedy, it was Gable who suggested she approach Mayer for a role in his upcoming picture. Heeding the affable star's advice, she did just that.

The leading female role in Gable's new film was already cast, with actress Claudette Colbert. Realizing the secondary female role was more interesting, Hedy petitioned Mayer for the supporting role of Karen Vanmeer in *Boom Town*. It was a wise decision that would alter her career, placing the glamorous Hedy Lamarr into the highest ranks of film stardom.

chapter 8

THE INDELIBLE IMAGE ON THE SILVER SCREEN

B y 1940 Hedy Lamarr's official studio biography had been rewritten and permanently set in stone by Metro-Goldwyn-Mayer and Louis B. Mayer's "fixer" publicist Howard Strickling under the title "The Life Story of Hedy Lamarr." In the sixteen-page publicity history Hedy's life up until that year is told with some truths, some lies, and many distortions. Her work as an unbilled extra in her first two Austrian films is eliminated, and her success is preordained.

Not surprisingly, her appearance in her very first leading role in *Wir Brauchen kein Geld* with Heinz Rühmann and Kurt Gerron is not mentioned at all, possibly because of the political climate at that time. Her role in *Ecstasy* is included, albeit efficiently explained away as a juvenile mistake, compounding the myth of Hedy's total lack of knowledge about the nude scene and the close-up shots. Her youthful

Opposite page: Hedy Lamarr, Ziegfeld Girl (MGM, 1941). Costumes by Adrian.

Hedy Lamarr. Metro-Goldwyn-Mayer, c. 1939.

indiscretions are fancifully explained away, years are cut off her actual age, and she is "Americanized" as much as possible. In fact, when the story comes around to her marriage to Fritz, she is but a mere sixteen years old (Hedy was in fact eighteen at the time). Strickling came up with a great deal of Hedy's likes and dislikes, some true—like her fondness for ice cream—yet all conforming considerably to the mores of young cinema-going American women of that era. It was written for publicity purposes, and it became Hedy's legend.

Publicity of any sort during Hollywood's Golden Age (the 1920s through the 1960s) was vital to the building up and sustaining of a vested studio player. Motion picture magazines had been around since the 1910s, and included publications like *Photoplay, Motion Picture, Picture-Play, Pictures and the Picturegoer*, and later, *Modern Screen, Hollywood, Silver Screen*, and more, all focused on the industry and the stars themselves. "The fan mags cooperated with the studios because movies were their main source of advertising," wrote film historian Jeanine Basinger. "Unlike the unattractive and destructive tabloids of today, these magazines specialized in beautiful layouts, color portraits, and sumptuous ads. . . . These magazines told fans everything—that is, everything the studio wanted them to know." [1] Thus, the Hollywood fictionalized hype was sold to the masses to effectively propagate the film industry.

A new decade had begun. According to film historian John Kobal, "The Forties began with a bang. A big one. Halfway through 1939 the outbreak of war slammed the door on

Hedy Lamarr. Metro-Goldwyn-Mayer, 1939. (Photographs by Clarence Sinclair Bull)

the Thirties and, with them, on the richest era of the American cinema." [2] With the out-break of war in Europe in 1939, and with America's entry in 1941, movies provided the war-weary masses with entertainment, propaganda, dreams, and escapism. It was a brief moment in time when patriotism was exalted to its highest, imagination pushed to its most plausible (and technological) limit, and the seriousness of reality could be altered at least for a couple of hours, when audiences could be swept away with the tempo, vigor, and excitement of the times.

During the brief period before the Axis attack on Pearl Harbor on December 7, 1941, America tried to avoid entering the war, backed up by a strong isolationist attitude. For the first year of the 1940s, feminine couture remained stuck in the 1930s, frothy and elaborate. But after 1941, with the imposed necessity of lifestyle change and an accep-tance of reality, a more-practical approach to fashion design was embraced.

Above left: Hedy Lamarr. Metro-Goldwyn-Mayer, 1941. (Photograph by Clarence Sinclair Bull)
Above right: Hedy Lamarr and husband Gene Markey at Hedgerow with their first Great Dane, Prince.
Metro-Goldwyn-Mayer, 1940.

Escapism was becoming necessary to distract filmgoers from the war overseas. With that in mind, filming began on March 9, 1940, on what would become Hedy Lamarr's breakthrough Metro film, *Boom Town*. Directed by Jack Conway, with a screenplay by John Lee Mahin and a magnificent, sweeping score by Franz Waxman, *Boom Town* told the story of two oil barons, Big John McMasters (Clark Gable) and John Sand (Spencer Tracy), during the Texas oil boom of the 1910s. As their fortunes rise and fall, Betsy Bartlett (Claudette Colbert) enters their lives. Betsy marries McMasters, suffering through his relationship with Karen Vanmeer (Hedy Lamarr), companion of the disreputable Harry Compton (Lionel Atwill). Hedy's glamorous character is surprisingly sympathetic, eventually bowing out of her affair with Big John when she realizes McMasters loves his wife.

Costumes for *Boom Town* were again by Adrian. Because they were contemporary to the times (1910s–1920s), they were still 1930s stylish in important ways. Hedy's seven

144

Hedy Lamarr, Boom Town *(MGM, 1940). Costumes by Adrian.*

outfits were fashioned to match her character. In her first scene, she appears in stylish black velvet lounge pajamas, with a long-sleeved, light-colored satin jacket over a dark-colored matching bow-neck under-blouse. Her ensemble is accented with tiny pearl earrings. Her luxurious hair is now four inches shorter yet still parted in the middle, styled by Sydney Guilaroff, and her porcelain-white skin completes the effect. Other costumes include a sensual misty pink floor-length

Hedy Lamarr and Spencer Tracy, Boom Town *(MGM, 1940). Costumes by Adrian.*

pleated flowing negligee with a snug bodice and wide girdle, with ostrich-feather trimmings, which Hedy complements with a single strand of pearls.

Guilaroff's cropping of the Lamarr mane was sensational news at the time. Hedy had set trends now for almost two years with her long flowing bob that boasted "a casual ease that defied waves and curls." Her new shorter cut, with the ends curled and turned under, mirrored the trend toward shorter hairstyles, which became popular for a brief time. "All of which means," wrote one newspaper journalist, "believe it or not, a revolution in several fields. Magazine illustrators, whose lovely ladies, to date, have adopted the Lamarr coiffure, are busy erasing hair-lengths to coincide with the new system, and wax models are being turned over to hairdressers for coiffures attuned to the times." [3]

Again, Adrian chose not to take away from Hedy's natural feminine beauty with his design choices. One

Hedy Lamarr, Boom Town *(MGM, 1940). Costumes by Adrian. (Ph_ graph by Laszlo Willinger)*

Above left: Clark Gable and Hedy Lamarr, Comrade X (MGM, 1940). Costumes by Adrian.
Above right: Clark Gable and Hedy Lamarr, Boom Town (MGM, 1940). Costumes by Adrian.

stunning outfit is a long-sleeved evening gown with a metallic top, over which she drapes a faux-fur cape; another is an admirable street-length dark dress, an open long-sleeved affair detailed with sparkling embroidery around the neck, sleeves, and waistline. (For her personal wardrobe Adrian would design special outfits for Hedy, as would California designer Gladys Parker.)

It is interesting to note that throughout the film, Oscar-winning actress Claudette Colbert is garbed in rather severe and boring ruffles, prints, and bows, which might have matched her own preferred style somewhat, but did *nothing* toward winning her any awards in glamour. Hedy's fashion style is cleverly reinvented in *Boom Town*, showing a more-vulnerable, womanly Lamarr and at the same time firmly placing her among the most fashionably attired stars of the new decade. Cinemagoers felt a new relatability to

147

Hedy Lamarr, Come Live with Me (MGM, 1941). Costumes by Adrian.

the alluring Hedy Lamarr with this fashion. Hedy's career was reestablished with this film, and she became a bankable star at MGM. *Boom Town*, a precursor to the epic films to come in the 1950s, was a monster hit upon its release in August 1940. *Boom Town* earned three Academy Award nominations, for Best Black-and-White Photography, Best Special Effects, and Best Sound, but did not win any of them.

Louis B. Mayer wisely saw that the chemistry between Lamarr and Gable played a major role in the picture's success. He quickly cast them together again in what many critics then considered a *Ninotchka* rip-off, the lightweight comedy *Comrade X*. In the immensely popular 1939 MGM comedy *Ninotchka*, written by Billy Wilder, Charles Brackett, and Walter Reisch, a Soviet Russian female envoy is brought to Paris to negotiate a lawsuit over stolen Russian jewels. In the process, Nina Ivanovna Yakushova—"Ninotchka"—played by Greta Garbo, falls in love with Leon (Melvyn Douglas). Brilliantly directed by Ernst Lubitsch, the film revitalized Garbo's career (though she only made one more picture, in 1942), earning her an Oscar nomination.

The key similarity between the two films is the fact that the Russian leading female role is played seriously until love enters her life. There are other parallels, however. Both pictures feature character actors Felix Bressart and Sig Rumann, and actress Eve Arden's character in *Comrade X* is played in a similar fashion as was Ina Claire's sharp-tongued and witty supporting character in *Ninotchka*. The films' plots do differ somewhat. In *Comrade X*, an American reporter, McKinley "Mac" Thompson (Clark Gable), working in the Soviet Union, is blackmailed into marriage to a streetcar conductor, Theodore Yahupitz (Hedy Lamarr), to safely get her out of the country, and she agrees to the sham. Complications ensue, political war-themed incidents occur, and after a hilarious chase across the border in a stolen military tank, all ends happily.

Directed by King Vidor, with a new story by Walter Reisch and screenplay again by Wilder and Bracket, with Charles Lederer and (uncredited) Herman J. Mankiewicz, *Comrade X* was produced by Gottfried Reinhardt, son of Max Reinhardt. Photography was handled by ten-time Oscar winner Joseph Ruttenberg, who had received the first of his four Oscars for *The Great Waltz* (MGM, 1938). He would be awarded again for *Mrs. Miniver*

149

(MGM, 1942), *Somebody Up There Likes
Me* (MGM, 1956), and *Gigi* (MGM, 1958).
Veteran cinematographer Karl Freund
captured the night scenes in *Comrade
X*, although he was not credited. The original
musical score was by Bronislau Kaper.

Costuming was again assigned to
Adrian, yet he had little to do for Lamarr
in this film. Although he apparently sought
to show her beauty again through her natural looks, according to her character and

the script, her costumes in *Comrade X* were totally unmemorable. The four basic costumes for Hedy consisted of two utilitarian outfits—one, a female streetcar conductor's uniform, and the other, a Soviet daytime outfit consisting of tight skirt, silk blouse, boots, and beret. There was also a mandatory, nondescript light-colored floor-length nightgown, which Hedy's character throws a coat over and wears for most of the film. The jaw-dropping outfit worn at a baseball game at the end of the picture is a strange white day outfit with a garishly over-done hat. It is a disaster, a definite farewell to the 1930s. When *Comrade X* was released in December 1940, it raked up gold at the box office, and would be nominated for an Oscar the following year for Best Story of 1940. (It lost to Paramount's *Arise My Love*.)

In her personal life, Hedy separated from Gene Markey early in the summer of 1940. Their divorce became final in October, with Hedy retaining custody of Jamesie. She was soon seen about town with actor John Howard.

Hedy's mother Trude had escaped Austria to live with friends in London after the *Anschluss*. Concerned for her safety as London suffered through the *Blitzkrieg*, Hedy wrote to her mother frequently as forces working through Metro successfully gained her passage to Canada, where she lived briefly before she was allowed entry into the United States.

Hedy grew increasingly worried as news reports of the war in Europe became more and more ominous.

She was also concerned about her career.

Hedy was oftentimes crudely advised by Louis B. Mayer that American male audiences preferred large-breasted women. That summer, perhaps to appease Mayer because of her own concern over her less-than-ample bosom, Hedy was introduced to eccentric music composer George Antheil at a dinner party, held at the home of designer Adrian and his wife, actress Janet Gaynor.

Born in New Jersey on July 8, 1900, Antheil was perhaps best known for his *Ballet Mécanique* (1923–1925), which had rocked the music world when it premiered in Europe. Because his music was robustly cacophonic, he was known as "The Bad Boy of Music."

But Hedy was more interested in Antheil's hobby, which was studying the endocrine system. He had written a series of articles for *Esquire* magazine purporting that glandular

Hedy Lamarr and James Stewart, Come Live with Me *(MGM, 1941). Costumes by Adrian.*

extract injections could increase the size of a woman's bosom. That evening at dinner the four discussed Antheil's theory, continuing their conversation over digestifs served in the pale blue and green living room, with its magnificent seventeenth-century over-mantel carved in fruitwood above the fireplace (a work by Grinling Gibbons). Although Hedy was drawn to the concept, she would never indulge in the injection process herself.

Hedy and Antheil's meeting under this pretense would prove to be most congenial. Their future private rendezvous together would prove to be historic.

With two major box-office hit films making money for the studio, Hedy was quickly cast in a romantic comedy opposite young actor James Stewart, then on a particular rise of popularity because of his three loan-out performances in *You Can't Take It with You* (Columbia), which had won Best Picture in 1938, *Mr. Smith Goes to Washington* (Columbia), for which he was nominated for Best Actor in 1939 (losing to Robert Donat for *Goodbye, Mr. Chips* for MGM), and the hit Western *Destry Rides Again* (Universal). Stewart had just completed *The Philadelphia Story* for Metro, for which he *would* win the Oscar, for Best Actor of 1940. The picture with Hedy and Stewart was the delightful *Come Live with Me*, directed by Clarence Brown, with cinematography by multi-Oscar-nominated George J. Folsey and romantic musical score by Herbert Stothart. Once more, costumes were created by Adrian.

The story, by Virginia Van Upp, with a screenplay by Patterson McNutt, told of refugee Johanna Janns, "Johnny Jones" (Hedy), who is having an affair with a married publisher. She offers to pay none-too-successful writer Bill Smith (Stewart) to marry her, with certain caveats: He cannot ask any questions, and they will divorce soon after the wedding. Bill begins writing a fictitious story about his relationship with Johnny and her involvement with the publisher. By accident, Johnny submits the completed manuscript to her married lover, Barton Kendrick (Ian Hunter), who recognizes that the story is about him. Through various misunderstandings, the three rendezvous at a farmhouse. Bill realizes it is Kendrick who has shown an interest in his book and is the other man in Johnny's life. In the end Johnny and Bill fall in love—trite, but nonetheless a moneymaker.

Adrian's designs for Hedy in this picture were contemporary and extremely feminine in approach. Her half-dozen outfits include a long-sleeved, square-shouldered dark

Above: Hedy Lamarr, Comrade X (MGM, 1940). Costumes by Adrian.
Bottom right: Hedy Lamarr. Metro-Goldwyn-Mayer, c. 1941. (Photograph by Clarence Sinclair Bull)

velvet ensemble with layer-collared neck-line jacket and floor-length tapered skirt, accessorized with one large jeweled bracelet. Another costume is a fur-trimmed, light-colored, ruffle-collared, full-skirted satin gown and matching overcoat. Hedy's day apparel is contemporary and street-length, with one outfit sporting a puritan collar, with a stunningly brief, gratuitous close-up shot of Hedy trying on a white turban.

Now sporting a trim figure, Hedy's confidence in wearing fashion was unparalleled on celluloid in part because of her self-assured awareness of her own beauty. Her changing image, plus her new figure, had

thankfully eliminated showy, heavy costumes. By late 1940 her style had given way to a contemporary vibe and feel. More importantly, she wears these fashions in a relaxed style. "[Y]ou see the amazing shift in perspective," states costume designer Tracy Christensen in her clear observations of 1940s fashion. About Hedy herself and the style she represents, Christensen says, "[She has a] very unselfconscious way about her. She was at ease with herself and was not confused between herself and 'the symbol,' which was for other people. She made that work for her—really feminine but strong." [4]

During this defining era in Hollywood fashion history, Hedy is flashed back into an alluringly glamorous fantasy world. For *Ziegfeld Girl*, her next film—and a musical at that—costumes were created, for the last time on film for her, by Adrian. This was the second of the MGM films based on the life of theatrical impresario Florenz Ziegfeld. The studio's *The Great Ziegfeld* in 1936 had won Best Picture. *Ziegfeld Girl* follows the tradition of the first. *The Ziegfeld Follies* in 1946 was the last, and least successful, of the trilogy. The musical score was under the direction of Herbert Stothart, and the expansive musical numbers and choreography were handled by Busby Berkeley.

Filming commenced in October of 1940. Adrian's over-the-top designs were on display, allowing the costumer to take flights of fantasy and whimsy as he had done in such early Metro talkie musicals as DeMille's 1930 box-office dud, *Madam Satan*. In this film Adrian was given free rein to display the female form in as much glitter and sequins, jewels and fur, and feathers and flesh as the moral code would allow, possibly representing the height of the costumer's voyeuristic ideology. While there may not have been much actual flesh shown in *Ziegfeld Girl*, there was more than enough—cleverly exposed and ingeniously disguised—to allow the moviegoer to imagine the rest.

Adrian was challenged with creating both fantasy and modern contemporary costumes for not only the three leading ladies—Hedy Lamarr, Lana Turner, and Judy Garland—but also the cast of leading men—James Stewart, Tony Martin, Jackie Cooper, and Ian Hunter. He was also challenged to create costumes for the supporting players, as well as the couple of dozen showgirls, dancers, and numerous extras required in the huge production numbers.

Above: Hedy Lamarr, Judy Garland, and Lana Turner, Ziegfeld Girl (MGM, 1941). Costumes by Adrian.
Bottom right: Judy Garland, Hedy Lamarr, and Lana Turner, Ziegfeld Girl (MGM, 1941). Costumes by Adrian.

The plot of *Ziegfeld Girl* revolves around the rise and fall, and the fall and rise, of three showgirls who are discovered and star in *The Ziegfeld Follies*. Of course, it also follows their romances as they win and lose, and lose and win, the men in their lives. Not much on storyline, but *Ziegfeld Girl* still offers up a cornucopia of music, glitz, romance, spectacle, and show.

Hedy's character is dressed in a dozen outfits, which range from minimal, again showcasing her natural beauty, to the two elaborate Ziegfeld costumes in the two production numbers in which

Above left: Hedy Lamarr, Ziegfeld Girl (MGM, 1941). Costumes by Adrian.
Above right: Tony Martin and Hedy Lamarr, Ziegfeld Girl (MGM, 1941). Costumes by Adrian. (Photofest)

she is featured as a showgirl. In the scene preceding the "You Stepped Out of a Dream" sequence backstage, Hedy is seen in her dressing gown wearing a bandanna around her hair. She is nervously trying to apply lipstick and says to the showgirls' attendant, "Oh Jenny, I can't even put on my lipstick," to which Jenny (Mae Busch) replies, "Relax, honey. They won't be looking at your mouth."

For the subsequent "You Stepped Out of a Dream" number, which introduces Hedy's showgirl character onto the stage, Lamarr's startling costume is spectacular. Adrian drapes yards of soft silk tulle covered with small glittery-sequined star appliqués over a stylish long-sleeved, light-colored silk gown, which Hedy holds with arms out in Ziegfeld style for the trailing camera as she ascends (in heels) some sixteen smaller and smaller steps, stepping in time to the music. Tony Martin serenades her as she eventually comes to a stop at the pinnacle. Strapped to her back, highlighting her head and torso and out of

157

Above left: Judy Garland, Hedy Lamarr, and Lana Turner, Ziegfeld Girl (MGM, 1941). Costumes by Adrian.
Above right: Hedy Lamarr, Ziegfeld Girl (MGM, 1941). Costumes by Adrian.

camera view, is a starburst halo of sparkling glittery stars surrounding her beautiful face in repose, resulting in one of the most remarkable and iconic images in cinema musicals.

The second showgirl costume Hedy wears in *Ziegfeld Girl* is a bit of a disaster. For the "Minnie from Trinidad" production number, sung by Garland, the showgirls are dressed in tropical-inspired creations meant to express a lot about very little. Constructed to show as much flesh as possible (through the overuse of mesh netting, required by the moral code of the time), Hedy is garbed again in a long-sleeved, sequined, netted outfit with faux flowers over her breasts. The mesh over her midriff is "bare," with a hip-to-floor glittering skirt, and massive feathers attached to her left thigh. Topped off by a towering, strange faux-flower headdress, the whole ensemble looks hideously inappropriate. It was as "nude" as Adrian dared to go with Lamarr.

In *Ziegfeld Girl*, Judy Garland came of age, and Lana Turner, far too short to be a showgirl, but dressed in cleverly designed gowns showcasing her gams, became a star. Of the three female stars of *Ziegfeld Girl*, Hedy Lamarr is the only one who truly looks like a showgirl.

Thankfully, most of Hedy's clothes in the picture are contemporary in design, again sticking with the tried-and-true formula of dark- or light-colored, long-sleeved blouses,

knee-length daywear skirts, dresses, and coats, all showcasing Hedy's remarkable face and her trademark shoulder-length hair, parted in the middle. One outfit Adrian called "Clean Cut" was a black-and-white henna wool with unusual stripes. In a confrontational scene with actress Rose Hobart, Hedy is dressed in a smart black-and-white, long-sleeved day dress, subtle in its understated elegance, giving in to the squared-shoulders trend of the era.

Of course, *glamour* is the key word in this film, and scenes were designed to showcase Hedy Lamarr in evening gowns. One gown featured a floor-length flowing satin skirt with a long dark coat adding a dramatic line. Hedy's face is accentuated with long dangling jeweled earrings. The other formal gown she wears is in a scene that takes place in Palm Beach. Adrian called it "Summer Moment," a misty white organdy *mousseline de soie* with hundreds of handmade loops on the hemline of the floor-length full skirt, accented with small pearl earrings.

Needless to say, with all the Metro star power packed into *Ziegfeld Girl*, the film did very well when it was released on April 17, 1941, cleaning up at the box office. The picture could have been spectacular had it been shot in Technicolor. Directed by Robert Z. Leonard, who had won the 1936 Best Director Oscar for *The Great Ziegfeld*, with cinematography handled by three-time Oscar-nominated Ray June (and uncredited, Joseph Ruttenberg), *Ziegfeld Girl* was Hedy's one foray into the musical genre. While she did not have to sing or dance, she fulfilled the requirements for her role, with great assistance by MGM makeup expert, the legendary Jack Dawn.

Adrian would be with Metro-Goldwyn-Mayer for but one more year, leaving in 1942 after a bitter dispute with Greta Garbo. The beautiful and gifted Swedish actress was devoted and loyal to only one individual—herself. Her career waning because of the war in Europe, where Metro made most of the profits from her work, her pictures were now infrequent and continuously lost money (with the exception of *Ninotchka*, which took an exorbitant amount of time to earn back its investment). Garbo, whose costumes—indeed, her very image—were in part created by Adrian throughout her heyday with the studio, beginning in the late 1920s, was unhappy with the sketches Adrian had designed for her

for *Two-Faced Woman* (1941). As it turned out, that would be Adrian's last motion picture for MGM, as Garbo had taken her complaints directly to Louis B. Mayer.

This was the ultimate insult for Adrian, who had created contemporary, fashionable, and feminine garments for Garbo's somewhat unfeminine body, helping to create "the illusion" of her beauty. Happily married since 1939 to Janet Gaynor, and recently the father of their son, Robin, born July 6, 1940, Adrian was secure enough with his talent and ability to freelance. With the world at war in Europe and obviously changing, Adrian's designs and flights of fancy were becoming obsolete. And perhaps it was not as enjoyable for him to be creative during this period. His disputes with Mayer and his disappointment with Garbo were major reasons for his leaving the studio. "But he did [say] that the reason he left was because he could see what was in the pipeline of pictures coming up," said his son Robin in 2000. "[N]one of them looked like they would be much fun to design for." [5]

For Metro there would be but one designer who would succeed and rival Adrian with unforgettable fashions during the Golden Age of Hollywood, and that artist was Robert Kalloch. Although Kalloch's tenure at Metro would last just two short years, he would design for almost forty films at the studio.

As for Adrian, he would only design gowns for a couple more motion pictures. After contributing costume designs for Lerner & Loewe's hit Broadway musical *Camelot* in 1959, Adrian suffered a heart seizure and died on September 13, 1959, one of many blows to the stage musical during its pre-Broadway opening. Adrian's glamorous costumes were eventually completed before *Camelot* opened and became a huge hit on Broadway in 1960. They were but another lasting tribute to his name. During his Hollywood career Adrian designed for some 260 films. "Hollywood mourned Adrian's death," wrote one author. "[H]is work was symbolic of the best it could produce." [6]

Beginning with her next motion picture, *H. M. Pulham, Esq.*, in what some say is Hedy Lamarr's best screen performance, her true fashion style would be defined by her new fashion designer, the brilliant Robert Kalloch.

Opposite page: Hedy Lamarr. Metro-Goldwyn-Mayer, 1941.

chapter 9

THE KALLOCH STYLE

To round out her film work in 1940, Hedy embarked on, for her, a most unusual role as an American career woman in the early part of the twentieth century. The picture was *H. M. Pulham, Esq.*, based on the book by John P. Marquand. A very personal project for him, it was directed by six-time Oscar nominee King Vidor, who had helmed *Comrade X*. The story, beginning in 1940, examines the memories told in flashback of successful middle-aged Bostonian advertiser Harry Pulham (Robert Young), happily married for twenty years to his wife Kay (Ruth Hussey) and now retired.

While preparing his biography for an upcoming twenty-fifth high school reunion, Harry Pulham fondly remembers his first love, copy writer Marvin Myles (Hedy Lamarr). (Ironically, most of Hedy's characters in her American pictures up to this

Opposite page: Hedy Lamarr. Metro-Goldwyn-Mayer, 1942.

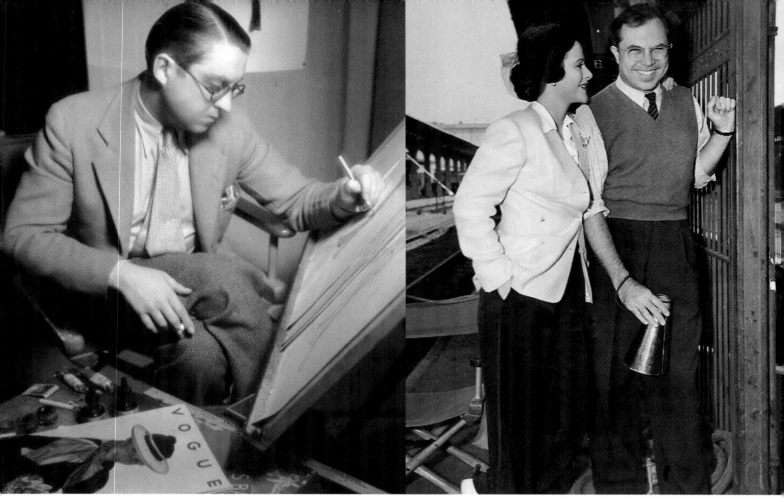

Above left: Robert Kalloch, Metro-Goldwyn-Mayer costume designer for H. M. Pulham, Esq., Tortilla Flat, Crossroads, *and* White Cargo. *(Metro-Goldwyn-Mayer)*
Above right: Hedy Lamarr and director King Vidor off the set of H. M. Pulham, Esq. *(MGM, 1941).*

Hedy Lamarr and cinematographer Ray June on the outdoor set of H. M. Pulham, Esq. *(MGM, 1941).*

point have men's names, possibly to soften her exquisite, almost overpowering beauty: Gaby in *Algiers*, Georgi in *I Take This Woman*, Johnny in *Come Live with Me*, Theodore in *Comrade X*, and Marvin in *H. M. Pulham, Esq.*) Harry's memories of his lost love are bittersweet. As he completes his biography, he is coincidentally contacted by Myles, who is visiting Boston. They meet socially and realize that though their love is as strong as ever, they cannot change who and where they are in life now.

Filming of *H. M. Pulham, Esq.* was conducted on Stage 22 on the Metro lot. Other MGM films in production at that time were *Two-Faced Woman* with Garbo on Stage 18; the first scenes of *Johnny Eager* with Lana Turner and Robert Taylor on Stage 4; *Woman of the Year*, with Katharine Hepburn and Spencer Tracy on Stage 3; and *Tarzan's Secret Treasure* on Stage 12. In Rehearsal Hall A, the blocking (physical direction) of *We Were Dancing* with Norma Shearer was taking place; and at Rehearsal Hall B, Eleanor Powell was developing her tap-dancing routines for what would become *Ship Ahoy*, sharing the space with the cast of Busby Berkeley's *Babes on Broadway*, starring Mickey Rooney and Judy Garland. The factory was at work. All told, Metro-Goldwyn-Mayer would release fifty-two feature motion pictures in 1941.

Hedy was deep into her scientific exploration at that time, having privately worked long and hard with George Antheil on developing a radio-controlled device for the government's Inventors Council in Washington, DC. They had submitted their invention to the government, which didn't know what to do with it. Always fascinated by the way things functioned, and most certainly because of her sincere concern for her homeland and her mother's security, Hedy continued dabbling with inventions. Her creative and active mind was stimulated by work, and this was her most productive period. She worked continuously during the day at MGM and brainstormed with her friend George Antheil during the evenings. It would be years before her scientific work would be acknowledged.

Through a generous endowment from Howard Hughes, Hedy was given two assistants and, through the generosity of MGM, was allowed her own science laboratory area just off the set of *H. M. Pulham, Esq.* (Hughes and Hedy had been lovers briefly, attracted to

Above left: Hedy Lamarr, H. M. Pulham, Esq. (MGM, 1941). Costumes by Robert Kalloch. (Photograph by Clarence Sinclair Bull)
Above right: Hedy Lamarr, H. M. Pulham, Esq. (MGM, 1941). Costumes by Robert Kalloch. (Photograph by Clarence Sinclair Bull)

each other more because of shared intellect than sexual compatibility. Hedy always said Hughes was the worst lover she ever had.)

As noted in his 1972 autobiography, King Vidor wrote lovingly of Hedy at this time. "Her interest seemed to be divided between the part she was playing and another career as an inventor or discoverer of some fascinating new soft drink or useful invention." [1] Hedy's fascination and desire to do something for America was an overwhelming drive in the days just prior to the country's entry into the war.

Most of the storyline of *H. M. Pulham, Esq.* is told in flashback, so period outfits were required for the actors. Hedy's dozen or so costumes were designed by Robert Kalloch, who, more so than any other film fashion designer, created for her "The Lamarr Look," her defining style in films.

Robert Young and Hedy Lamarr in H. M. Pulham, Esq. *(MGM, 1941). Costumes by Robert Kalloch.*

Born Robert Mero Kalloch in New York on January 3, 1893, Kalloch studied at Dwight's Preparatory School on the Upper West Side of Manhattan as well as the New York School of Fine and Applied Art. He eventually worked as a sketch artist prior to World War I in both the London and Paris houses of Lucile Ltd., the couture house of wealthy titled British couture designer (and survivor of the *Titanic* disaster) Lady Duff Gordon, designing for Irene Castle and Anna Pavlova.

Above left: Hedy Lamarr, Tortilla Flat (MGM, 1942). Costumes by Robert Kalloch.
Above right: Hedy Lamarr off the set of Tortilla Flat (MGM, 1942). Costumes by Robert Kalloch.)

Moving to New York, Kalloch worked for five years with Madame Frances & Company Dressmakers before moving over to Hattie Carnegie in 1931 for a year. In 1932 he was contracted by Harry Cohn at Columbia Pictures to be the first important designer at the studio. His creation of more than three dozen "sophisticated, contemporary wardrobes"[2] for Irene Dunne, Nancy Carroll, and Grace Moore established his reputation in Hollywood. His most memorable designs of that period were for Claudette Colbert in the multi-Oscar-winning film *It Happened One Night* in 1934. Before moving over to MGM, his later Columbia films included *The Awful Truth* (1937), *Mr. Smith Goes to Washington* (1939), and *His Girl Friday* (1940). Coming to Metro-Goldwyn-Mayer, Kalloch had already designed costumes and gowns ("Gowns by Kalloch") for several minor Metro films, moving up to the big leagues with *Honky Tonk* (1941) shortly before taking on the demands of *H. M. Pulham, Esq.* He, along with designer Irene (Lentz), would handle the supervision of costumes at MGM when Adrian departed in 1941.

For Hedy's role of Marvin Myles in *H. M. Pulham, Esq.*, Kalloch's challenge was to make the film's period outfits attractive on the actress. Although Hedy Lamarr's beauty could carry that load, his designs still had to be excellent. He was fortunate to have Hedy Lamarr to showcase his work and confirm his credibility. With makeup by Jack Dawn and Jack Young, Hedy's hair was styled by hairdresser Edith Keon. The final fashion look of the era was achieved with the beautiful creations Kalloch presented.

One particularly exquisite design was a simple, light-colored, floor-length, V-necked, light-collared sheer chiffon gown with full sheer sleeves, accentuated with a single-strand pearl necklace and pearl earrings. Other fashions included a mandatory long-sleeved dark day dress with white lace bib; a dark day outfit with a side brooch on the collar, c. 1940, with sequined square hat and veil and gloves; and a smart dark day outfit with a dark coat trimmed in fur, with a dark side beret. Although contemporary to the period, Kalloch's fashionable ensembles for Hedy and the other actors stand the test of time.

Despite a magnificent script with excellent production values, a beautifully dramatic musical score by Bronislau Kaper, and competent directing and performances, the film's box-office future would be hampered by its timing. It premiered December 3, 1941, at New York's Radio City Music Hall, and the following Sunday, December 7, the Japanese would attack the American naval fleet at Pearl Harbor in Honolulu, Hawaii. Within days the United States was effectively at war, in no mood for nostalgic romance.

H. M. Pulham, Esq. was meant to catapult actor Robert Young into leading-man stardom at MGM. Young had begun his movie career in the late 1920s, gaining momentum at Metro in 1931 when he played the male ingenue in Helen Hayes's Oscar-winning melodrama, *The Sin of Madelon Claudet*. Sadly Robert Young lost his bid at stardom in Hollywood, though years later he would achieve immortality on the television screen as the star of *Father Knows Best* (1954–1960) and *Marcus Welby, M.D.* (1969–1976).

"Halfway through 1939 the outbreak of war [in Europe] slammed the door on the Thirties and, with them, on the richest era of American cinema," exclaimed film historian John Kobal. "The Depression, it now appeared, had only been the lull before the storm." [3] With the attack on Pearl Harbor, and the long-awaited entry of the United States into

Hedy Lamarr, Tortilla Flat (MGM, 1942). Costumes by Robert Kalloch.

the fray, motion picture production took a new turn. With the eventual development of more-relevant and timely storylines, there came a more-conservative, resourceful approach to costume design as well. It marked the era where elemental garment design, especially on the home front, gained a noticeable excitement and utilitarian practicality, which has lasted to this very day.

"In the 1940s, especially after our entry into the war, there was a more tailored, more professional look, and that soft, fluffy look started to fade," commented designer Tracy Christensen. "Women's fashion became somewhat 'militaresque' in style as wartime started to transfer over into high fashion, where you suddenly get really broad shoulders, nipped-in waistlines; even though skirts were an A-line, they were pretty trim. It was conserving fabric, keeping things tailored . . . simple but stylish. It stalled a bit through the war. But you see this amazing shift in perspective." [4]

Through necessity, nylon replaced silk, and rayon, a product of the 1920s, made a huge comeback. In Hollywood, Technicolor was making inroads in the industry and many major films of that era appeared with a richness of colors and a farewell to pastels, the palette of the 1930s. Everyday dress design reflected the use of more gabardines and wool and metallics. Large, enormous corsages replaced elaborate embroidered bibs and heavily jeweled accessories. There was a "balance of structure, a proportionate shift . . . [and a] strength in the line which remained still feminine," stated Christensen. "Designers were figuring out through these lines [of their fashions] how to apply a strong harsh silhouette that was very forgiving. That's why the '40s were so dazzling. And it worked for everyone." [5]

"Although the war touched everything, it was not always with the same disastrous results," continued John Kobal in his overview of the 1940s. "The moguls whose business it was to produce movies and fabricate dreams never had it so easy. Anything went . . . The great war created an environment for one long fool's summer for the monolithic film companies, which, as surely as the munitions factories, thrived on man's inhumanity to man."

What followed throughout the war, until about 1946, was a boom in profits at the box office. Except for craftsmen such as directors, actors, studio fashion designers, and cinematographers, little concern for art was given to the output of the studio machine, as long as it provided escape. "The war years were a time of plenty, of rich profits embarrassingly easy to gather," noted Kobal, "of films needing little thought and even less talent to produce. Therein lay the seed of the studios' eventual destruction." [6]

Hedy Lamarr, Crossroads (MGM, 1942). Costumes by Robert Kalloch.

At this time, Hedy Lamarr was still considered a Hollywood glamour queen. Her photographs were in high demand, and her movies were successful. Popular graphic artists clamored to turn her image into high art. One of the most successful of these craftsmen was James Montgomery Flagg (1877–1960). During the filming of *H. M. Pulham, Esq.*, Flagg had the opportunity to sketch her one afternoon after filming had completed that morning. "If you think she is lovely on the screen—well, you'd fall in love with her at sight," he wrote. "[S]he's gay, clear-eyed and healthy and has a delightful speaking voice. And charm enough for twenty."

As Flagg sketched her with charcoal, the conversation landed on marriage. Hedy had just divorced Gene Markey. He asked her if she would marry again. "The trouble with marriages," she tellingly replied, "is that after marriage people relax and become themselves and fight about the littlest of things." [7]

Robert Kalloch designed gowns and costumes for Hedy in four films. *H. M. Pulham, Esq.* was a period piece. His next project with her would require that he design basic, typical Northern California Portuguese *paisano* attire, as well as fish cannery work outfits, which would be contemporary yet thematic in style. The picture was *Tortilla Flat*, based on the 1935 novel by John Steinbeck. It told the story of Pilon (Spencer Tracy), the leader of a handful of colorful inhabitants of Tortilla Flat, a poor fishing village just north of Monterey. The group included Pablo (Akim Tamiroff), Portegee Joe (Allen Jenkins), Jose Maria Corcoran (John Qualen), Pirate (Frank Morgan), Danny Alvarez (John Garfield), and the local beauty, Sweets Ramirez (Hedy Lamarr). Pablo is smitten with Sweets, who in turn is smitten with Danny, and from there the plot develops. Told with humor, pathos, drama, and romance, the film was truly a highlight of Hedy's career, offering her challenging, bordering on brilliant, scenes with the gifted John Garfield.

Hedy's some half-dozen costumes for the picture were basic, simple as per her character's lifestyle. There were no elaborate gowns nor startling hats, veils, and furs. In fact, some of the clothes Hedy wore in the picture were picked right off the rack in the Metro costume department. Nonetheless, the particular costumes Kalloch *did* design for Hedy were lovely. Many consisted of peasant blouses and skirts indigenous to her character's

Hedy Lamarr, Crossroads *(MGM, 1942). Costumes by Robert Kalloch.*

background and position in life. They were working-girl clothes, and quite similar to what Hedy herself wore at home, less the trademark Lamarr flashy gemstones and pearls. Co-star Spencer Tracy called Hedy's costumes her "dime-store wardrobe," and in fact, one outfit cost just $3.95. When required to become sweaty and dirty at a fishing cannery, she relished the opportunity to throw herself into the role. Hedy gained immense respect from the director, Tracy, Garfield, and the entire crew.

Directed by veteran Victor Fleming, Oscar winner for 1939's *Gone with the Wind*, filming on *Tortilla Flat* commenced on November 23, 1941, and ended on February 24, 1942, on a huge soundstage in which the whole village had been erected. Makeup by Jack Dawn helped create the illusion that the actors in the film were of Portuguese descent. Hedy's skin was darkened somewhat with grease, and she wore ten-cent lipstick. Spencer Tracy was of English-Irish heritage, and Hedy, of course, was Viennese; John Garfield was Jewish and from New York, as was Staten Island–born Allen Jenkins; Akim Tamiroff was Armenian-American; and John Qualen was Canadian, born of Norwegian parents. All portrayed Portuguese *paisanos*. Cinema audiences were oftentimes challenged to accept illusion.

Tortilla Flat's cinematography was lensed largely by legendary European film pioneer Karl Freund [8], who had filmed the night sequences in Hedy's *Comrade X*, with additional credit also given to Harold Rosson and Sidney Wagner. Freund had captured in *Tortilla Flat* two key scenes that are breathtaking and emotionally stunning in their mood, their lighting, and their beauty. The first was with Hedy poignantly cradling a baby. The other, the "Francis of Assisi" scene, in the forest with Pilon and his dogs, might possibly have been the singular reason why Frank Morgan, who had portrayed the Wizard in Metro's *The Wizard of Oz* (1939), won a Best Supporting Actor Oscar nomination for his role in *Tortilla Flat* when it was released in May 1942. *Tortilla Flat* turned a tidy profit, and reviews were excellent.

Most motion picture studios, like many factories, were often in operation seven days a week. And so it was that on Sunday, December 7, the cast was in rehearsal on the set of *Tortilla Flat* when news came through of the early-morning surprise attack on Pearl

175

Harbor. Hedy secluded herself in a corner of the soundstage and privately wept. She knew her mother Trude was now safe in Canada, but she was afraid for her friends and remaining family in Europe. Having just received full custody of Jamesie on November 3, Hedy's tears were for her child's future as well. Living with Jamesie, her Great Dane, Donner, and some twenty chickens at her comfortable Hedgerow atop the hill on Benedict Canyon, it seemed Hedy hadn't much to worry about.

Hedy's next motion picture was *Crossroads*, which would define both "The Kalloch Style" and "The Lamarr Look." "No expense was spared in gowning the ladies or on the elaborate sets constructed for the picture," wrote film biographer Christopher Young. [9] A very stylized film, the first of two co-starring vehicles for Hedy and William Powell, *Crossroads* was directed with great care by Jack Conway. The moody cinematography was handled by Joseph Ruttenberg, and an exceptional musical score was composed by Bronislau Kaper.

The story, set in 1935 Paris, tells of a mysterious demand for repayment of a million-franc loan sent to David Talbot (Powell), who works for the French government and is up for a position as ambassador to Brazil. His younger, beautiful wife is Lucienne (Lamarr). The mystery develops as to who sent the note, and why. When the facts come out there are twists and turns, which include murder, blackmail, lies, and deception. Into the mix is thrown the competent talent of Claire Trevor, menacing Basil Rathbone, and a supporting cast of some of the best character actors in Hollywood.

The gowns and costumes Kalloch carefully designed for Hedy and the rest of the cast are some of the most elegant, iconic screen fashions of the era, ranging, at least in Hedy's case, from elegant fashionable daywear and business attire to exquisite evening gowns and feminine negligees. Hedy's hairstyles were primarily upswept in line with the 1930s high-society European fashion. Hedy's wardrobe of nearly a dozen chic and lush costumes included a long-sleeved, shimmering royal black floor-length dinner gown with a bib collar of jet, pearls, and beads, accentuated with pearl drop earrings; another, a two-toned dress with a light raspberry long-sleeved top, loose-fitting upper arms with snug-fitted pleated folds to the wrist, and a deeper-toned skirt; still another, a fluffy, full,

Opposite page: Hedy Lamarr, Crossroads (MGM, 1942). Costumes by Robert Kalloch.

177

long-sleeved, flesh-colored negligee, all puffy, as the publicity called it, "in souffle," with floor-length full skirt; and a breathtaking periwinkle-blue velvet, floor-length hostess gown with trailing hemline, featuring long sleeves, a stiff wide girdle dividing the bodice and skirt, and a V-neck with gold-leaf embroidery its only trimming.

Kalloch's designs for Hedy continued with a simple dark daywear suit ensemble, worn in a courtroom sequence; it had long sleeves and matching gloves, and a most intriguing V-design hat on the side of her hairdo, with delicate, dark, trailing laced veil. Another beautiful dark, long-sleeved, tulle-covered, floor-length evening gown with plunging bodice is as contemporarily couture now as it was then. Kalloch outdid himself with the loving care he applied to Hedy's character's wardrobe in *Crossroads*, successfully imbuing each and every one with a flair of glamour and rightness.

When the picture was released in July 1942, it received decent reviews and made a nice profit. Hedy's performance is controlled and quite respectable. It's possible that Hedy Lamarr achieved the pinnacle of her film career glamour through Robert Kalloch's stunning costumes in this film, for curiously, after *Crossroads* there was a marked decline in the perception of Hedy as an alluring glamour goddess. While her style still endured, society as a whole was evolving.

Quite strangely, it was at this precise juncture in Hedy's career, after she had garnered such strong, positive acting reviews in a series of moderately successful films (at least, they made back their negative costs), that Louis B. Mayer found the most unsubtle property to sabotage her career. He cast her as a wanton jungle siren in *White Cargo*, with the tagline, "I am Tondelayo." *White Cargo* would prove to be one of Metro's biggest moneymakers of 1942, although it remains to this day nothing more than a tawdry, tropical sex fantasy. It is almost blasphemous to see the breathtakingly beautiful Hedy Lamarr playing a half-caste, sex-starved jungle wanton in dark body makeup, in what was most likely Mayer's form of lewd punishment. "Stars who a year earlier were thought supreme now were peremptorily tossed from the illuminating shadows of their glamour to sink or swim in the garish spotlight of the pinup," wrote film historian John Kobal, quite accurately. "Dietrich's legs now made way for Betty Grable's pins; the image of Hedy Lamarr

Above left: Hedy Lamarr,
Crossroads (MGM, 1942).
Costumes by Robert Kalloch.
Above right: Hedy Lamarr. Metro-
Goldwyn-Mayer, c. 1941.
Bottom right: Hedy Lamarr at her
home, Hedgerow. Metro-Goldwyn-
Mayer, 1941.

was transformed into a more prosaic, albeit delightful, popcorn-fed siren like Yvonne De Carlo." [10]

Based on the 1923 Leon Gordon play of the same name, which he had based on a 1912 novel called *Hell's Playground* by Ida Vera Simonton, the story told the lurid tale of African plantation overseer Harry Witzel (Walter Pidgeon), who must deal with the mental and physical loss of his assistant, Wilbur Ashley (Bramwell Fletcher), and now must break in a new worker, Mr. Langford (Richard Carlson). Witzel blames his problems with his colleagues' deterioration on the native "Congo Queen," Tondelayo. The carnal desires of the "Chocolate Cleopatra," as she is also called, are dangerous.

Of course, to appease the censors of the era, Tondelayo is not a true African; her parents, it seems, were of Egyptian and Portuguese heritage. So when Tondelayo eventually seduces Langford on screen, it is made acceptable for the puritanical film audiences of the era. In the end, the film remains seamy and vulgar. Stretching the limits of moral decency at the time, naturally the picture cleaned up at the box office. Those in the armed forces, especially, lined up by the droves to buy tickets to *White Cargo*.

Directed by Richard Thorpe, with a score by Bronislau Kaper, the whole affair was photographed by Harry Stradling. Hedy's entire body was painted to photograph darker, and her lines, not well written, were spoken in broken English. Tondelayo always shows up at night, with darkening ominous shadows prevailing throughout her every scene. Cinematically, however, there is one astonishing moment in the film when Tondelayo moves her beautiful face into the camera lens in a deep, extreme close-up. That one sequence almost redeems the picture. In this, the last film for which Robert Kalloch designed costumes for Hedy, he is credited with just "additional" and "native costumes."

In 1942 alone Robert Kalloch supervised the gowns and costumes for over two dozen Metro films. But for this picture he had little to work with for Hedy's character Tondelayo other than his take on the traditional sarong, in different one- and two-piece designs and colors, with jungle jewelry. Hedy is the only female in the cast, and her outfits vary little in her half-dozen lengthy scenes. Kalloch designed three "body bandannas" for Hedy, which could be re-draped or reversed for variation. Metro publicity ballyhooed the

Hedy Lamarr. Metro-Goldwyn-Mayer, c. 1942.

Above left: Hedy Lamarr. Metro-Goldwyn-Mayer, 1942. (Photograph by Clarence Sinclair Bull)
Above right: Hedy Lamarr. Metro-Goldwyn-Mayer, 1941. (Photograph by Eric Carpenter)

designs, calling them either the "Larong" or the "Chiffong." As explained in the press, "Hedy LaMarre's [*sic*] sarong is called a chiffon . . . because it sounds more high-class," wrote columnist Sidney Skolsky. "The . . . chiffong amuses Miss LaMarr [*sic*] almost as much as the actors in the picture. Every so often Hedy . . . would go over to her full-length mirror and study her costume. 'I suppose,' she mused, 'it just stays up by itself.' " [11]

When *White Cargo* was released in September 1942, with national taglines such as "90% allure, 10% sarong—adds up to LURONG!" and "She rings the GONG in her LURONG," one knew immediately that MGM was not offering up art. *White Cargo* made the list as one of the 10 Worst Films of 1942—and the only one to show a profit. Like it or not, Hedy was now a sex siren. Although the picture was a huge hit, it did nothing to further her credibility as an actress. Louis B. Mayer, ever in supreme control, would not lend Lamarr out to other studios, which proved unfortunate, as she was wanted for some

182

Greer Garson, Ronald Colman, Lynn Bari and Irene Dunne (on train), and Hedy Lamarr. First war bond tour, 1942.

major motion picture roles. Warner Brothers had approached Mayer right before production took off on *White Cargo*, asking the studio to lend them Hedy for the role of Ilsa, their original choice for *Casablanca*, which became the Best Picture of 1943. Old friend Otto Preminger from their Reinhardt days wanted Hedy for *Laura* (20th Century-Fox, 1944). To them both, and others, Mayer said, "No!"

Unfortunately *White Cargo* was an undistinguished picture for Robert Kalloch after his brilliant designs for Hedy in *Crossroads*. His innovative fashions for MGM during

his brief tenure were many. When World War II began, the studios came under pressure by the government to express more confidence in design, more energy, movement, and spontaneity. For his fashion sensibility Robert Kalloch largely abandoned elaborate, studied designs, eliminating belts, pleats, and elaborate openings. With a renewed focus on trimming, shoulder lines were made broader, and skirts made shorter, usually to the knee, and fuller in design, though not swirling with an abundance of material because of limitations on certain fabrics. Kalloch introduced crocheted hats and knitted scarves, and piping for belt substitution. Silk prints, because of war rationing, were simply not available. So Kalloch produced appliqués on silk in many of his designs, and for many of his clientele, Hedy included, for home use.

After his last film for the studio, *Journey for Margaret* (1942), Robert Kalloch went independent. That summer of 1942, per his wife's suggestion, Louis B. Mayer brought in Irene (Lentz) as the studio's chief fashion designer, demoting Kalloch to just fashion designer. When Kalloch had been named successor to Adrian in 1941, he created fashions and wardrobes for such MGM films as *Babes on Broadway* (1941), the Oscar-winning Best Picture *Mrs. Miniver* (1942), along with *Random Harvest* and *Her Cardboard Lover*, also in 1942. Because of his lack of experience creating costumes for period films, Mayer was unhappy with Kalloch. When Howard Shoup came on board at Metro later that same year, Kalloch's authority was broken, and he left MGM.

Other more-serious reasons may have come into play, as the designer was experiencing personal problems at this time as well. His longtime life partner since the early 1930s, Joseph Demaris, was an alcoholic, and suffering from failing health. The two bought a home at 4329 Agnes Avenue in Studio City in 1939. As a freelance designer, Kalloch's last two films were *Suspense* for Warner Brothers in 1946, and *Mr. Blandings Builds His Dream House* for RKO, in 1948. On October 19, 1947, suffering from arteriosclerosis and varying phobias that affected his health, Robert Kalloch died of cardiac arrest at his home at six o'clock that morning. Later that same day, around three in the afternoon, his partner Joseph Demaris succumbed to alcoholic fatty liver disease. Former Paramount fashion designer Travis Banton paid for Kalloch's burial and funeral expenses.

Hedy Lamarr selling war bonds, 1942.

Robert Kalloch's unique, contemporary couture fashions, such as those he executed in *Crossroads*, remain timeless. He is largely forgotten today in the industry, Adrian and Edith Head far surpassing his memory. Yet he most assuredly deserves a place in the legendary pantheon of great film fashion designers. He was never nominated for an Oscar for his remarkable and unforgettable achievements in chic cinema fashion design. Too late the hero, the category of Best Fashion Design would only be established by the Academy of Motion Picture Arts & Sciences the year after his death, 1948.

chapter 10

THE LAMARR LOOK AND 1940S STYLE

Hedy's mother Trude arrived in the United States in January 1942 after spending months in Canada awaiting her papers. Throughout 1942 Hedy was dating again, seen in the company of actors Orson Welles, Howard Hughes, Jean-Pierre Aumont, Charles Chaplin, Craig Stevens, and, most frequently, with George Montgomery, with whom she would become engaged. That is until she found out his studio, 20th Century-Fox, was backing his courtship with her. Brokenhearted, Hedy licked her wounds and continued working.

When she was between pictures, Hedy dedicated herself to selling war bonds with other film stars around the country. In one day, September 11, 1942, in Essex County, New Jersey, Hedy Lamarr raised $991,377 ($15,830,405.25 today), the largest war bond sales in one day by *any* star in all three war bond campaigns.

Opposite page: Hedy Lamarr. United Artists, 1946. (Photograph by Laszlo Willinger)

Above left: Hedy Lamarr, White Cargo (MGM, 1942). Costumes by Robert Kalloch.
Above right: Hedy Lamarr and Walter Pidgeon, White Cargo (MGM, 1942). Costumes by Robert Kalloch.

On December 24, 1942, Hedy, like so many other patriotic Hollywood stars of the era, volunteered to work at the Hollywood Canteen. Allegedly the brainchild of actress Bette Davis and actor John Garfield in response to New York's Stage Door Canteen, it was a venue where servicemen and women could come for respite, dining and dancing, and a chance to meet the stars. Hedy was there every Friday evening, either serving as a hostess, signing autographs, handing out sandwiches and coffee, or working in the kitchen washing and drying dishes. That Christmas Eve Hedy met tall, good-looking British actor John Loder, currently under contract with Warner Brothers, who helped her dry dishes in the kitchen.

Born in York, England, in 1898, and educated at Eton, Loder (whose real name was John Muir Lowe) and his father, Major General Sir William Lowe, both enlisted in World War I, and were present at the surrender of Patrick Pearse, leader of the 1916 Irish Rebellion. Because of that historical event Loder was knighted. He was later captured

and imprisoned by the Germans. After his release he remained in Germany and entered silent cinema, appearing with young actress Marlene Dietrich before her 1929 breakthrough film *The Blue Angel*. Coming to America upon the advent of talkies, John Loder failed to establish himself in Hollywood, appearing in such films as *The Racketeer* (Pathe, 1929) with Carole Lombard, *Lilies of the Field* (First National, 1930) with Corinne Griffith, and even a Hal Roach comedy short, *On the Loose*, starring Thelma Todd and Zasu Pitts and featuring Laurel and Hardy.

Loder's career gained momentum when he returned to England, with roles in *The Private Life of Henry VIII* (London Films, 1933); *My Song Goes Round the World* (BIP, 1934), which starred the tragic Joseph Schmidt; Alfred Hitchcock's *Sabotage* (Gaumont, 1936); and *King Solomon's Mines* (1937). Now back in Hollywood in 1943, he'd been featured in *How Green Was My Valley* (20th

Above: Director Richard Thorpe, hairdresser Eadie Hubner, and Hedy Lamarr on the set of White Cargo *(MGM, 1942).*
Bottom: Hedy Lamarr with her hairdresser Eadie Hubner on the set of White Cargo *(MGM, 1942).*

Richard Carlson and Hedy Lamarr, White Cargo *(MGM, 1942). Costumes by Robert Kalloch.*

Century-Fox, 1941), which won the Best Picture Oscar, and *Eagle Squadron* (Universal, 1942) with Diana Barrymore. Under contract with Warner Brothers, in 1942 he had just completed supporting roles in *Now, Voyager* with Bette Davis and *Gentleman Jim* with Errol Flynn. Married once before and the father of a young daughter, Loder was quite mannered, charming, and attractive. He and Hedy soon became an item.

Hedy's career, especially after the moderate success of *Crossroads* and the huge box-office hit, *White Cargo*, was truly at a crossroads. Though she still maintained star status at the studio, she had sued Metro over the years for better contracts. Somehow agreements were hammered out. She had just lost a major contemporary wartime role in *Cry Havoc* (it went to Margaret Sullavan). Her film persona was difficult to peg at this juncture, the studio only offering her comedies at this time.

After a long break between pictures, production began in May 1943 on Hedy's second film with the durable William Powell, a comedy called *The Heavenly Body* with

Above left: Hedy Lamarr. Paramount Pictures, c. 1951.
Above right: Hedy Lamarr, Let's Live a Little (Eagle-Lion, 1948). Costumes by Elois Jenssen.
Bottom right: Costume by Elois Jenssen for Hedy Lamarr in Let's Live a Little (Eagle-Lion, 1948), on display today. (Photo courtesy of Roy Windham)

a lighthearted screenplay by Michael Arlen and Walter Reisch. Produced by Arthur Hornblow Jr., the script was originally offered to Joan Crawford. She rejected the role outright, stating that she didn't want to play a woman who stood around doing nothing. She imperiously suggested they give it to the younger and much more glamorous Hedy Lamarr. It's possible that playing this role could have done Crawford a lot of good and revived her

Official MGM 20th Anniversary photograph, with stars seated showing their relative importance to the studio. Hedy Lamarr is in the first row, fourth from left. Lucille Ball and Katharine Hepburn are on either side of her. Louis B. Mayer is front and center. (Such MGM stars as Clark Gable and Lana Turner are not shown.) (Photofest)

severely waning career at Metro. Her snub led Metro to terminate her pricey contract on June 29, and Crawford left the studio within the month.

Directed by Alexander Hall and (uncredited) Vincente Minnelli, with cinematography by Robert H. Planck and (uncredited) William H. Daniels, and a musical score composed by Bronislau Kaper, the lightweight *The Heavenly Body* dealt with marriage, astrology, wartime hoarding, and a marital mix-up.

For Hedy's wardrobe, Metro assigned their new head of fashion, Irene, with whom Hedy had worked well on *Algiers* in 1938. Since signing with MGM Irene had set trends with the use of nude souffle creations, the tailored masculine wide-shouldered suit, and the reintroduction of a more-functional cap sleeve. The contemporary costumes Irene designed for Hedy in *The Heavenly Body* set standards for the next few years. Hoping that lightning would strike twice after *Algiers*, Irene would create over a dozen new outfits for *The Heavenly Body*. Unfortunately, although attractive, the results were pedestrian at best.

Above left: Dishonored Lady *(United Artists, 1947). Costumes by Elois Jenssen.*
Above right: Hedy Lamarr. Metro-Goldwyn-Mayer, c. 1943.

Irene was brought to MGM by her brother-in-law, the legendary Cedric Gibbons, head of MGM's art design, to replace Adrian upon his departure, and at the same time to maneuver and usurp the position of then head of the studio's costume department, Robert Kalloch. Irene was assigned to devote "her attention exclusively to costuming motion picture stars—Lana Turner, Greer Garson, Hedy Lamarr, Irene Dunne, Marlene Dietrich, Laraine Day and other 'big names' on the M-G-M lot." [1] That month, along with preparing costumes for *Three Men in White*, Irene created mandatory modern daywear outfits for Hedy's character in *The Heavenly Body*, with the help of sketch artists Katy Bill and Virginia Fischer. In a wartime movie magazine, Irene stated, "Today, women who made a career of clothes now make a career of war activities, and motion pictures depicting modern times have [be]come as down-to-earth as they were once exaggerated." [2]

To create the illusion through costumes of the glamorous Hedy Lamarr as a fashionably attired middle-class housewife would have challenged any designer. Once again, because

Hedy Lamarr, Metro-Goldwyn-Mayer, c. 1943.

Above left: Hedy Lamarr, The Heavenly Body (MGM, 1943). Costumes by Irene. (Photograph by George Hurrell)
Above right: Hedy Lamarr, Crossroads (MGM, 1942). Costumes by Robert Kalloch.
Bottom right: Hedy Lamarr. Metro-Goldwyn-Mayer, c. 1943.

Lamarr's beauty was so overpowering, the costumes she wore in the film by necessity were fairly standard. For outerwear, Irene fashioned a versatile short, belted swagger coat of black-and-white-checked wool with a black velveteen collar for multiple uses (sports, business, or afternoon activities). For exclusively afternoon or dinner wear, Irene designed a sheer, tight-fitting, plain black woolen jacket trimmed with

Hedy Lamarr, The Heavenly Body (MGM, 1943). Costumes by Irene.

Hedy Lamarr, The Heavenly Body *(MGM, 1943). Costumes by Irene.*

Opposite page: Hedy Lamarr, The Heavenly Body *(MGM, 1943). Costumes by Irene. (Photograph by George Hurrell)*

heavy silk braiding, with matching bag and stiffened black lace hat. Another creation was a flowing baby-blue silk full-sleeved nightgown with a matching chiffon negligee and girdle belt, which again emphasized Irene's use of the nude souffle.

"Hedy is so beautiful she doesn't have to worry about clothes, so she doesn't worry," Irene wrote. "If I were as beautiful as she I wouldn't worry about clothes either. You could stand her in a gunny sack and she'd still be gorgeous." [3] Of the numerous outfits Hedy wore in the film, another was a startling throwback to the late 1930s, a black long-sleeved day suit with a

Above left: John Loder and Hedy Lamarr on their wedding day, May 27, 1943. (Metro-Goldwyn-Mayer)
Bottom: Postcard of Hedy Lamarr's home, 919 North Roxbury Drive, Beverly Hills, 1943.

821 HOME OF HEDY LAMARR

John Hughes Photo

Above left: Hedy Lamarr. Metro-Goldwyn-Mayer, 1942. (Photograph by Clarence Sinclair Bull)
Above right: Leah Rhodes, costume designer for The Conspirators *and* Experiment Perilous, *Warner Brothers Pictures.*

flashy white lace bib and matching white lace-cuffed gloves; another, a floor-length, flow-ing long-sleeved chiffon evening gown with sequined belt and appliqués; and yet another, a clever pleated light-colored woolen skirt and matching loose-fitting jacket worn over a polka-dot dark blouse, accessorized with a simple beret, pearl earrings, and three-strand pearl necklace.

One negligee Irene designed for Hedy for *The Heavenly Body* was a pale silk floor-length nightgown with a gathered peasant bodice, over which Hedy wore an ivory vel-veteen long-sleeved robe with bell sleeves, accented with a row of faux pearls down the front and lined in ivory. Hedy's character was dressed in the most fashionable outfits throughout this film. It's no wonder that with her numerous attractive costume changes, more than one cinemagoer pondered whether the true heart of the film was the plot, or the number of costume changes Hedy made. "I wonder how any person could wear so many clothes in one picture," wrote California stylist Richard M. Wilkes. [4]

Above left: Hedy Lamarr, Experiment Perilous *(RKO, 1944). Costumes by Leah Rhodes.*
Above right: Hedy Lamarr and the script woman on the set of Experiment Perilous *(RKO, 1944). Costumes by Leah Rhodes. (Photograph by Alex Kahle)*

Filming wrapped on *The Heavenly Body* in August 1943, but it would not be released until the following March, when it did brisk business. By then Hedy had married John Loder in a private ceremony at the home of actor Conrad Veidt on May 27, 1943. After moving in with Hedy at Hedgerow, he formally adopted four-year-old Jamesie, changing his last name to Loder. John Loder was a good father to the boy. Years later James Loder would recall the many good times his father spent with him when he was a young boy, taking him to events and playing ball with him.

More roles were offered to Hedy at this time, including a significant co-starring role opposite Charles Boyer in Metro's *Gaslight* (1944), which she rejected, as she did not want to co-star with the French actor again. Ingrid Bergman stepped in and won an Oscar. From Warner Brothers came an offer for Hedy to star in *Mr. Skeffington* (1944). Mayer declined, and Bette Davis took it and chewed up the scenery. Still another appropriate Warner

201

Above left: Leah Rhodes costume sketch for Hedy Lamarr, Experiment Perilous *(RKO, 1944).*
Above right: Hedy Lamarr, Experiment Perilous *(RKO, 1944). Costumes by Leah Rhodes.*

Brothers part was opposite Gary Cooper in *Saratoga Trunk* (1945). Mayer declined again, and Ingrid Bergman happily stepped in again. Not having another project for Hedy per her recently revised contract, or possibly just to dismiss her, Mayer finally did lend Hedy to Warner Brothers for *The Conspirators.* Mayer's negotiation guaranteed him $2,000 a week for eight weeks, and $2,500 a week thereafter (a minimal weekly profit).

A precursor to the popular James Bond 007 films of the 1960s and 1970s, *The Conspirators*, co-starring Paul Henreid and Peter Lorre, was based on a novel by Frederic

Hedy Lamarr, Experiment Perilous (RKO, 1944). Costumes by Leah Rhodes.

Prokosch, and tastefully directed by Jean Negulesco. A story of wartime espionage and intrigue, it was exactly the type of thriller in which Hedy was perfectly cast. In *The Conspirators*, unlike most of her other films, Hedy's at times distracting, lilting Viennese accent actually complements those of the other stars in the film, providing a sense of realism. The script was written by Vladimir Pozner and Leo Rosten, and the cinematography was handled by Arthur Edeson. Lavishly produced to create the feeling of European locations, as was typical of Warner Brothers at that time, no expense was spared.

The talented Leah Rhodes was assigned to create Hedy's many memorable costumes in the film. Born Leah Montgomery in Port Arthur, Texas, on July 21, 1902, the designer

Hedy Lamarr, The Conspirators *(Warner Bros., 1944). Costumes by Leah Rhodes.*

married Russell Spurgeon Rhodes in 1921 and moved to Los Angeles, California, in 1926, securing a position as a buyer in the wardrobe department at Warner Brothers. Rhodes became assistant "Girl Friday" to Orry-Kelly for several years before divorcing Rhodes in 1937. In 1939 she began creating costume designs for film shorts, eventually graduating to feature films. She became head of the studio's costume design department in 1943 when Orry-Kelly left to enroll in the army after completing his work for *Old Acquaintance.* Rhodes's own personal style and taste became her trademark. "Some designers, like Edith Head, preferred to dress modestly. Not Rhodes," noted two Hollywood costume historians. "She was known for her personal sense of fashion. 'She always looked so nice,' remembered designer Adele Balkan. 'She was a spic-n-span kind of lady. She always looked like she came out of the bandbox.' " [5]

Hedy began filming her scenes for *The Conspirators* on the Warner Brothers lot on March 10, 1944. As the lusciously beautiful femme fatale Irene Von Mohr, Hedy radiated a sense of mystery and desire. With Austrian-born Paul Henreid as the equally mysterious Vincent Van Der Lyn, the two made a near-perfect screen couple. (One can only wonder how their scenes would have played out had Hedy been allowed the role of Ilsa in *Casablanca.*) A long shoot, filming of *The Conspirators* wrapped on June 12, thirty-four days behind schedule.

Above left: "Orchid Moon" sheet music, The Conspirators *(Warner Bros., 1944).*
Above right: Hedy Lamarr costume test for The Conspirators *(Warner Bros., 1944). Costumes by Leah Rhodes.*

In Hedy's first appearance with Henreid, she is introduced in the magnificent, lush setting of a Lisbon casino stunningly garbed in a floor-length dark gown with flowing sequined veil. Throughout the picture Hedy appears in daywear ranging from a simple colored jumper with embroidered blouse (very modern in style), to stylized light pleated skirt affairs, to more lavish dark ensembles with light-colored, red bolero jackets with a definite European flair. Hedy accentuates her garments with light lace scarves, accented with simple to elaborate jewelry, adding clever berets with matching shoulder-wrapping cloth veils. One feminine and very exquisite garment Rhodes created for Lamarr was a

Hedy Lamarr and Paul Henreid, The Conspirators *(Warner Bros., 1944). Costumes by Leah Rhodes.*

Above left: Hedy Lamarr, The Conspirators *(Warner Bros., 1944). Costumes by Leah Rhodes.*
Above right: Hedy Lamarr costume test, The Conspirators *(Warner Bros., 1944). Costumes by Leah Rhodes.*
Bottom left: One of Leah Rhodes's costumes for Hedy Lamarr in The Conspirators *(Warner Bros., 1944), on display today.*
Bottom right: Hedy Lamarr costume test, The Conspirators *(Warner Bros., 1944). Costumes by Leah Rhodes.*

Makeup man Ben Nye and Hedy Lamarr on the outdoor set of The Conspirators *(Warner Bros., 1944). Costumes by Leah Rhodes.*

simple long-sleeved pale-green chiffon evening garment, floor-length, with laurel design shoulder embroidery and lace floret hemline, with gathered wrists and lace accents. Stunningly beautiful.

These fashions caught the eye of female filmgoers, yet it was the tastefully elaborate evening gowns that attracted the most attention. Rhodes designed one striped V-neck long-sleeved gown that was exquisite in its execution. Worn with a sequined appliqué cloth belt, with tight sleeves, capped wrists, and form-fitting skirt, Hedy was back, at her glamour-defining best. In her final scenes in the picture her gown features a metallic square-shouldered, long-sleeved blouse worn with a severe, form-fitting black floor-length skirt.

Makeup direction for *The Conspirators* was by Perc Westmore, with assistance by Johnny Wallace, Bill Cooley, and Albert Greenway. The six Westmore Brothers of Hollywood, sons

Above left: Hedy Lamarr, The Conspirators *(Warner Bros., 1944). Costumes by Leah Rhodes.*
Above right: Hedy Lamarr, The Conspirators *(Warner Bros., 1944). Costumes by Leah Rhodes. (Photograph by Bert Six)*

of pioneer film makeup artist and wigmaker George Westmore, were Percival ("Perc"), Ernest ("Ern"), Walter ("Wally"), Monte, Bud, and Frank, and they all secured work at the major film studios. Collectively they are credited with creating and designing most of the great makeup creations in Hollywood during its Golden Age. In reference to working with Hedy Lamarr, brother Frank in his family biography stated, "Ern adopted . . . techniques he had learned from Dietrich, and so did the rest of us Westmore brothers. We used the line-down-the-nose, sometimes white instead of silver, on Colbert, Ginger Rogers, Hedy Lamarr, Barbara Stanwyck, and many others." [6]

Under the musical direction of Hugo Friedhofer, with a mesmerizing score by Max Steiner and hairstyles by Jean Burt Reilly, *The Conspirators* represents the type of film—and possibly the very studio—Hedy Lamarr should have been under contract with all along. Warner Brothers *knew* how to cast her. They *knew* how to photograph her. And,

THE BEAUTY OF HEDY LAMARR

Above left: Hedy Lamarr and cinematographer Arthur Edeson on the set of The Conspirators *(Warner Bros., 1944).*
Above right: Hedy Lamarr, The Conspirators *(Warner Bros., 1944). Costumes by Leah Rhodes.*

aside from Robert Kalloch at MGM, they *knew* how to dress her. For these, and various other more-personal reasons, *The Conspirators* is the author's favorite of all of Hedy Lamarr's motion pictures. It exemplifies the glamour and romance of 1940s Hollywood.

The Conspirators was released on October 21, 1944, to mixed reviews. Over the years it has earned a more-commendable reputation. The stars give solid performances, and the sheer glamour of the film sets it apart from most of the other Warner Brothers output of the era. The war was winding down at the time of its release. Had the picture been made a couple of years earlier, it quite possibly would have gained the reputation it truly deserves. Hedy Lamarr was still a top draw. Her 1943 annual salary totaled $88,250 ($1,327,728.90 today), still ahead of Lana Turner, but not anywhere near the Metro salaries of Greer Garson or Judy Garland. It should also be noted that Louis B. Mayer was still king of the heap in the United States, earning a reported annual salary that year of $1,138,992 ($17,136,233.40 today).

Hedy Lamarr, Her Highness and the Bellboy (MGM, 1945). Costumes by Irene and Marion Herwood Keyes.

Before *The Conspirators* was released, Hedy was loaned out a second time to RKO for *Experiment Perilous*, a delicate period thriller, astutely directed by Jacques Tourneur, with cinematography by Tony Gaudio and film score by Roy Webb, under the musical direction of C. Bakaleinikoff. Once again, this was one of the best roles of her career. Hedy's costumes for this film were designed again by Leah Rhodes, with Edward Stevenson credited for gowns and costumes for the rest of the cast. The dozen or so creations fashioned by Rhodes for Lamarr exemplify some of the designer's most exquisite work.

Robert Walker and Hedy Lamarr, Her Highness and the Bellboy *(MGM, 1945). Costumes by Irene and Marion Herwood Keyes.*

Set in 1903 New York, the storyline of *Experiment Perilous*, based on a novel by Margaret Carpenter, deals with the suspicious death of the sister of prominent Nick Bedereaux (Paul Lukas, fresh on the heels of *Watch On the Rhine* for Warner Brothers, for which he had won the 1943 Best Actor Oscar). Dr. Huntington Bailey (George Brent, lending a very bored and lethargic performance) suspects foul play. He is most empathetic with the plight of Bedereaux's wife Allida and her small son. Will Allida be her husband's next victim?

When the picture was released in December 1944, critics made comparisons to the more-popular Warner Brothers' *Gaslight* that same year. But in fact, except for the time period and the relationship between the lead characters, the two films are not very similar at all.

Above: Hedy Lamarr, Her Highness and the Bellboy (MGM, 1945). Costumes by Irene and Marion Herwood Keyes.
Bottom right: Robert Walker and Hedy Lamarr, Her Highness and the Bellboy (MGM, 1945). Costumes by Irene and Marion Herwood Keyes.

For most of the picture Hedy's upswept hairstyles complement an array of gorgeous gowns, such as the off-the-shoulder glittering ball gown, with sleek form-fitting bodice and full billowing skirt with appliquéd flowers and ribbon. A traveling outfit is in itself memorable, featuring a dark woolen, fur lapel–lined overcoat with matching cuffs, accompanied with light-colored gloves, a large jeweled bracelet, and a large period hat with light-colored stiff

THE BEAUTY OF HEDY LAMARR

Hedy Lamarr, Her Highness and the Bellboy (MGM, 1945). Costumes by Irene and Marion Herwood Keyes.

tulle veil. "Possessed . . . by a Love that Destroys!" read the tantalizing trade ads for the picture upon its release. Though it was not a huge hit, Hedy Lamarr's reviews were quite respectable, and she looked lovely in her intricate period costumes and gowns.

It must be said that Hedy Lamarr never looked more feminine and vulnerable than she did in *Experiment Perilous,* with no small credit going to Leah Rhodes. From scenes of Hedy's character in youthful dirndls, her hair allowed to flow to her shoulders, to scenes of dramatic tension with Lamarr dressed all in black, Rhodes carefully constructed Hedy's character's wardrobe to fall in line with the dramatic storyline. Rhodes's understanding of the demands of period dress rank her as one of the leading costumers of the time. She would later win the 1949 Oscar for Best Costume Design for a Color Film for the adventure period film, Warner Brothers' *The Adventures of Don Juan.*

Allowed by Louis B. Mayer and Metro to consider loan-outs, Hedy was approached by David O. Selznick to appear as Pearl Chavez in his upcoming sex-and-sand Western

Above left: Natalie Visart, costume designer for The Strange Woman *(United Artists, 1946).*
Above right: George Sanders and Hedy Lamarr, The Strange Woman *(United Artists, 1946). Costumes by Natalie Visart.*

epic, *Duel in the Sun* at RKO, opposite John Wayne. She had to decline. Toward the end of the filming of *Experiment Perilous*, Hedy had discovered she was pregnant. *Duel in the Sun* would eventually be filmed for Selznick International and released in 1946 starring Gregory Peck and Selznick's *inamorata* and later wife, Jennifer Jones.

Hedy was rushed into her last film of her original Metro-Goldwyn-Mayer contract, a romantic modern-day fantasy, *Her Highness and the Bellboy*, directed by Richard Thorpe with a clever screenplay by Richard Connell and Gladys Lehman. Produced by two-time Oscar-nominated producer Joe Pasternak, and starring opposite the talented and yet

Hedy Lamarr, The Strange Woman *(United Artists, 1946). Costumes by Natalie Visart.*

tragic Robert Walker and rising newcomer June Allyson, the lightweight plot of the film revolves around a European princess who comes to America to learn the customs and reclaim her jilted reporter lover. She is encouraged by a hotel busboy (Walker), who is loved by a disabled girl (Allyson), to experience many adventures in Manhattan firsthand.

Hedy was perfectly cast as the princess in *Her Highness and the Bellboy*, except for the fact that during filming her girth started to expand at an alarming rate. Faced with the task of disguising Hedy's pregnancy while often filming scenes out of sequence, photography was handled ingeniously by Harry Stradling.

Costuming Hedy's character would also be a challenge. Meeting in Irene's office on Monday, August 14, 1944, sketch artist Virginia Fischer began the initial designs for the picture. Though credited to Irene, Hedy's wardrobe of over a dozen outfits and gowns were also created by Irene's assistant, Marion Herwood Keyes. Listed on the credits is also studio designer Valles, who was assigned to handle the men's costumes exclusively.

Hedy Lamarr on the set of The Strange Woman *(United Artists, 1946).*

Between the director, the cinematographer, and even the script, there were several clever ways to camouflage Hedy's pregnancy, including having her hold objects like flowers, outer garments, fans, and large hats, and by blocking her behind chairs and tables. Hedy's full-figure sequences were by necessity filmed first. "Irene was an elegant, sophisticated woman who liked to design for women like herself," said fellow Metro designer Helen Rose, [7] and Irene did exactly that for Hedy's character in *Her Highness and the Bellboy*, extending her love of elegant fashion as best she could, even when confronted with the pressing circumstances at hand.

Attempting to Americanize the princess's wardrobe, Irene included a charming dark daywear outfit with a dark cotton-weave jacket with large white pointed collar and white cuffs, and several evening gowns. Hedy's princess gown, an iconic pale-pink, off-the-shoulder silk affair with heavy lace V-neck trimming, is accentuated with opera-length

217

THE BEAUTY OF HEDY LAMARR

Hedy Lamarr, The Strange Woman *(United Artists, 1946). Costumes by Natalie Visart.*

gloves and stunning jewelry, and of course, the requisite tiara. One evening dress, a light-colored, straight, floor-length skirt with flair hip-length jacket embroidered in a sequin design, is an elegant showstopper. For the scenes in which Hedy is actually show-ing her impending motherhood, she is costumed wearing heavy woolen outerwear and unfortunately outdated headwear (with flowing cloth veils around the shoulders, very much 1930s European-influenced).

When released in September 1945 at the very close of World War II, *Her Highness and the Bellboy* ran 112 minutes. With a charming musical score by Georgie Stoll and the inclusion of the perennial favorite song "Honey" by Seymour Simons, Haven Gillespie,

Hedy Lamarr on the set of Dishonored Lady *(United Artists, 1947).*

and Richard Whiting as a main theme, the picture received only mixed reviews. The *New York Times* ranked it one of the ten worst pictures of the year. Still, *Her Highness and the Bellboy* did turn a minor profit. Sadly, there are very few clever or funny moments in the picture. It is heavily outdated today with wartime humor, and not only are some scenes appalling in their banality, but even perky June Allyson comes across as a saccharine-sweet bore. Robert Walker was a seriously brilliant actor, and his comic performance is laced with moments of delight. But throughout the filming, his personal problems—depression and alcoholism brought on by separation from his wife, actress Jennifer Jones, now deeply involved with David O. Selznick—were overwhelmingly disruptive.

With the help of makeup man Jack Dawn, thirty-year-old Hedy Lamarr was ethereally beautiful, her pregnancy only enhancing her inner contentment. Unfortunately, in private the Loder marriage was rocky. John's own career was on the wane, with prospects in film for a man his age somewhat limited. Free of her Metro contract, Hedy was allowed to prepare for producing her own pictures. As Loder's personal and professional unhappiness grew, Hedy in turn was ready for a new career and a new life with her two children. On May 29, 1945, she gave birth to a baby girl, naming her Denise Hedwig Loder. Denise's godmother was Bette Davis.

James Lamarr Loder's ninth birthday, March 12, 1948. From left to right: Anthony Loder, Hedy Lamarr, James Loder, Denise Loder. (Denise Loder DeLuca Collection)

Now freelancing, Hedy became an independent producer of her own films, creating Mars Productions, Inc., in the late summer of 1945, along with Jack Chertok, who had produced *The Conspirators*. They purchased the steamy Ben Ames Williams novel, *The Strange Woman*, as their first production, to be produced by Hunt Stromberg, also fresh from MGM. They assigned Hedy's Marx Reinhardt–days colleague Edgar Ullmer to direct. He had had success with the low-budget independent films *Detour* (now a noir classic) and *Wife of Monte Carlo*, which had starred John Loder. Releasing arrangements were made through United Artists. Hedy's co-stars for *The Strange Woman* would be George Sanders, Louis Hayward, and *Algiers* actor Gene Lockhart.

Filming began shortly before Christmas 1945, with a rambling potboiler screenplay by Herb Meadows. The plot of the film is long and convoluted, but highly melodramatic, as Jenny Hager (Hedy) marries and destroys the lives of her husband (Lockhart) and lovers (one, his son Hayward), sending them into madness—or to their graves—all the

while in lusty pursuit of the one man she cannot have, John Evered (George Sanders). Over-the-top cinema melodrama, for sure.

Photography was assigned to Lucien N. Andriot. With a rather long and laborious musical score by Carmen Dragon, makeup was handled by Joseph Stinton, and hairstyles were created by Blanche Smith. For this, her first production, Hedy chose former Paramount costume designer Natalie Visart to create over two dozen 1820s–1830s New England period gowns and costumes for her character.

Natalie Visart was born Natalie Visart Schenkelberger in Chicago on April 14, 1910. Raised in California, she met Katharine DeMille, adopted daughter of film director Cecil B. DeMille, at the Hollywood School for Girls, and eventually began designing for DeMille films. Visart started with the 1919 Gloria Swanson picture, *Male and Female*, at Paramount. There she met and fell in love with fellow art director and fashion creator Mitchell Leisen, who later became an elegantly accomplished director for the studio in his own right. When talkies arrived, uncredited and under the direction of Adrian, Visart assisted Leisen with fashion creations for Metro's disastrous 1930 musical/comedy/drama film, *Madam Satan*. Leisen and Visart never wed, as the future director Leisen was gay. Visart did become pregnant by him, but tragically miscarried.

Elois (Eloise) Jenssen, costume designer for Dishonored Lady, Let's Live a Little, *and* Picture Mommy Dead. *Desilu Productions, c. 1954.*

Above left: Hedy Lamarr, Dishonored Lady (United Artists, 1947). Costumes by Elois Jenssen.
Above right: Elois Jenssen costume sketch for Hedy Lamarr, Dishonored Lady (United Artists, 1947).
Bottom right: Hedy Lamarr, Dishonored Lady (United Artists, 1947). Costumes by Elois Jenssen.

When Mitchell Leisen decided to leave with DeMille for Paramount in 1933, Visart became the director's designer, her first job *The Plainsman* (1936). After Leisen suffered a heart attack, he took up with dancer Billy Daniels. Natalie fled to Paris to design for Lily Dache in 1938. When the war broke out, she returned to DeMille and designed costumes for the Technicolor *Northwest Mounted Police*

(1940). She finally left DeMille in 1942 and signed with producer Hunt Stromberg before he went independent. In 1945 she began creating costumes for *The Strange Woman*, using many one-hundred-year-old issues of *Godey's Lady's Book* as a source of inspiration and ideas.

The costumes Visart created for Hedy, with her sketch artist Elois (Eloise) Jenssen, were accurate for their period—fussy, cluttered, opulent—with many of the evening gowns showing a propensity for off-the-shoulder design and fur trim, made to show off Lamarr's allure. While Hedy looks gorgeous, ultimately the gowns become repetitious and nondescript.

In 1946 Natalie Visart married Dwight Bixby Taylor, son of actress Laurette Taylor. Visart died on September 11, 1986.

What is most often talked about in reference to *The Strange Woman* is Hedy's make-it-or-break-it, over-the-top dramatics. While in some ways a delight to watch, at times they border on camp. Her costuming in this film is the element of the production least remembered today, along with the meandering, overly zealous musical score by Carmen Dragon. When it was released in October 1946, *The Strange Woman* received mixed reviews, though Hedy's personal notices were positive, and the film turned a bit of a profit.

The Lamarr and Loder marriage was still volatile, and divorce proceedings were begun during the filming of *The Strange Woman*. But by March 1946, when filming wrapped on the picture, Hedy and John had reconciled shortly before ten-month-old Denise's christening. Their son Jamesie, now in second grade, was enrolled at the Chadwick Military School throughout the week, with weekends, when possible, at home with his parents and new sister. Hedy in the meantime moved on to her next Mars Company production, *Dishonored Lady*. For this film Hedy's leading men would be Dennis O'Keefe, William Lundigan, and, in his only film with his wife, John Loder.

Originally a play, *Dishonored Lady* had been successfully produced on Broadway in 1930 by Guthrie McClintic, starring his wife, actress Katharine Cornell. Written by Margaret Ayer Barnes and Edward Sheldon, and based on an actual trial case, the story tells of a woman who is accused of the murder of her lover yet refuses to take the witness

Hedy Lamarr, Dishonored Lady *(United Artists, 1947). Costumes by Elois Jenssen.*

stand in her own defense. A psychological drama, censors at that time were appalled that the plot touched upon nymphomania. Louis B. Mayer found that intriguing, of course, and used the production as the basis for his Joan Crawford vehicle, *Letty Lynton* (MGM, 1933). Lawsuits ensued from the playwrights and continue to this day. (Thus, the film *Letty Lynton* is the only known existing Joan Crawford picture never to have been televised and still not available on DVD.) By the time Edmund R. North did his screen rewrite for this version of *Dishonored Lady*, a shift had been made away from the sexual implications of the trial to focus more on the psychological aspects.

Directed by Robert Stevenson, with cinematography again by Lucien N. Andriot and another ineffectual musical score by Carmen Dragon, Hedy's hair designs were fashioned by Ruth Pursley, and makeup again applied by Joe Stinton. Refreshingly, though, Hedy's costumes were created by newcomer Elois (Eloise) Jenssen.

Born on November 5, 1922, Jenssen had studied at the New York School of Fine and Applied Arts (now Parsons School of Design) and its Paris atelier. Coming to California at the outbreak of World War II, Jenssen enrolled in a four-year course at the Chouinard Art Institute (now the California Institute of the Arts). In 1943, Jenssen was hired by Natalie Visart, who had just been employed by producer Hunt Stromberg upon his leaving MGM, as a sketch artist. Hedy liked the sketches Jenssen had done for *The Strange Woman* and requested her for *Dishonored Lady*.

"An argument between Miss Lamarr and Stromberg almost caused the project to abort before it started," wrote Elizabeth Leese in *Costume Design in the Movies*, "but peace was restored, and a very young Miss Jenssen created a stunningly sophisticated series of outfits for Hedy Lamarr. She also received her first screen costume credit for the picture." [8] The gowns and outfits Jenssen created for Hedy Lamarr in *Dishonored Lady* were the ultimate in couture, this just before the attack of the lower-hemline, full-skirted "New Look," which when first introduced jarred the sensibilities of late-1940s couture. Plush and elegantly romantic, the garments and gowns that Lamarr wore in *Dishonored Lady* firmly established Elois Jenssen's reputation.

Above left: Hedy Lamarr. United Artists, 1946. (Photographed by Laszlo Willinger)
Above right: Hedy Lamarr. Metro-Goldwyn-Mayer, c. 1949.

Of the more than two dozen costumes Jenssen designed, perhaps the most photographed and sensuously beautiful of them all was a long, snug-sleeved, emerald-green, soft woolen evening gown with a sequin-and-bead-encrusted and embroidered off-the-shoulder neckline, which exquisitely set off Hedy's trademark classic face and long hair, parted in the middle. Hedy's daywear in *Dishonored Lady* was very typical of her own style. One was a dark dirndl design, worn over a long, loose-sleeved, buttoned-to-the-neck, light-colored blouse; another was a very simple elbow-length, loose, light-colored blouse with a dark-patterned skirt. Another costume was a tried-and-true flashback ensemble featuring a fur beret with a flowing, sheer shoulder-length veil and matching fur-cuffed dress, which worked for Hedy. And there was yet another light-colored off-the-shoulder gown with dark crocheted embroidery. With each costume, Hedy was accessorized with amazing yet simple jewels. In *Dishonored Lady* Hedy Lamarr was truly stunning.

Filming of the picture began in May 1946, and was completed by late July, $1.2 million over budget. When it opened in March 1947, *Dishonored Lady* was not a hit, though once again Hedy received respectable reviews. The whole enterprise of acting in and producing her own films had been a nightmare for Hedy, as her marriage to Loder was now over as well. Her tenure as an independent producer of two not very profitable pictures had left her career right where it had been when she'd left Metro.

After she and Loder separated, she put Hedgerow on the market (it was purchased by newlyweds Humphrey Bogart and Lauren Bacall), and in June she and her two children moved to 919 North Roxbury Drive in Beverly Hills. The following month she advised Loder yet again that she wanted a divorce. According to Loder, in the next breath she informed him he was going to be a father for a second time. In early March 1947, Hedy gave birth to a boy, whom she named Anthony John Loder. In May, a bit slow for her, Hedda Hopper broke the announcement that Hedy Lamarr and John Loder were divorcing.

Hedy's life started to unravel somewhat at this time. Her divorce from Loder was anything but amicable, but mercifully, it was settled quite quickly. She kept custody of the three children. He left with the clothes on his back. Hedy wasted little time and started dating the married actor Mark Stevens almost immediately, but they broke up when he met her at an airport with liquor on his breath. He returned to his wife and new baby. Hedy also started pursuing Orson Welles in hopes he would cast her opposite him in a production of Shakespeare's *Macbeth*. He, to his credit, distanced himself very quickly from her.

Faced with several lawsuits for broken and ill-advised contracts, and concluding her business arrangements with the Mars Company, Hedy accepted a role in a picture called *Let's Live a Little*. The film was a product of independent film company United California Productions, owned by producer Eugene Frenke and actor Bob Cummings, and would be released by Eagle-Lion Films, Inc.

Now represented by the William Morris Agency, Hedy starred in this change-of-pace comedy opposite Cummings and the producer's wife, Anna Sten. With photography by the competent Ernest Laszlo, music by Werner R. Heymann, makeup by Ern Westmore

Above left: Hedy Lamarr and John Hodiak, A Lady Without Passport *(MGM, 1950). Costumes by Irene and Helen Rose.*
Above right: Hedy Lamarr, Let's Live a Little *(Eagle-Lion, 1948). Costumes by Elois Jenssen.*

and Joe Stinton, for her wardrobe in the film, Hedy secured Elois Jenssen. Now independent after producer Hunt Stromberg closed his offices, Jenssen was much in demand. Hedy's hairstyles were created by Joan St. Oegger and Helen Turpin, and stills for the picture were made by George Hommel.

At eighty-five minutes long, *Let's Live a Little* was a quickly shot lightweight comedy about a somewhat neurotic ad agent, Duke Crawford (Cummings), who is being black-mailed by his former sweetheart, Michele Bennett (Sten). He nervously seeks counseling from Dr. J. O. "Jo" Loring (Lamarr), who is promoting her book, *Let's Live a Little*. Jo eventually falls in love with Duke after several comedic situations. Not at all to be taken seriously, this film fluff is typical of the post–World War II moral climate. It ages badly when viewed today. Filming commenced in February 28, and Hedy was paid $200,000 for her participation, with 10 percent of the profits.

Elois Jenssen's gowns and outfits for Hedy are superb. Of the dozen garments she created for Hedy, one features a stunning light-colored, knee-length, full-sleeved woolen coat with sharp arrow collar, accentuated with auburn-colored shoulder highlights and matching stripes. With this Hedy wore a matching side beret. In one restaurant sequence in the picture, Hedy is sporting a somewhat "New Look"–influenced, off-the-shoulder, ankle-length ivory print evening gown with a defined lower waist, its full skirt made of satin brocade and embroidered with a floral print, accented with silver sequins and bugle beads. Hedy kept this garment after filming, and auctioned it off in 1951 when she left Hollywood. It was bought at another auction some years later by a private collector for a paltry $150. Still, Jenssen was flattered that Hedy had owned it.

In another scene Jenssen has incorporated the side-cap with long mesh-net shoulder-wrapped veil to good effect, though in the canon of Hedy's films, it seems almost mandatory, and a bit repetitious.

During the filming of *Let's Live a Little* Hedy befriended her manicurist, a young Holocaust survivor named Manya Breuer, who was born on September 14, 1922. Surviving the 1938 *Anschluss*, Manya had made it to America during the war, crossing treacherous waters on board a ship, deathly afraid of being torpedoed after her breathless escape from the Nazis. Breuer's life would later be dramatized in the 2001 CBS miniseries, *Haven*. She would appear in the 2017 documentary *Bombshell: The Hedy Lamarr Story*, talking about her friendship with Hedy Lamarr. Manya Breuer died on March 27, 2018.

The once-great Russian film actress Anna Sten was known as "Goldwyn's Folly" when film producer Samuel Goldwyn brought her to Hollywood in the early 1930s, in a futile attempt to make her the next Garbo or Dietrich. After a couple of disastrous flops, her career fizzled. Sadly, in *Let's Live a Little*, she comes across as ridiculous in this, her only American film comedy. For some reason the Jenssen gowns and costumes created for Sten are made to seem almost Euro-chic, circa 1935. This may have been done on purpose, to further highlight Lamarr's spectacular look. "Although her costumes for Hedy

229

Hedy Lamarr and Ray Milland, Copper Canyon *(Paramount, 1950). Costumes by Edith Head.*

Lamarr were as elegant as any Dior or Chanel creation," wrote two film fashion historians, "Jenssen believed an actress should dress as she pleased off-screen, no matter how tasteless or over-the-top." [9] One wonders if the vain Anna Sten may have worn her own clothes in the picture.

Elois Jenssen firmly established her career with the costumes she designed for Hedy Lamarr's two films. Eventually signing with 20th Century-Fox, Jenssen (as Elois W.

Hedy Lamarr, The Strange Woman *(United Artists, 1946). Costumes by Natalie Visart.*

Jenssen) created stunning wardrobes for actress Patricia Neal in two Fox films in 1952, *Diplomatic Courier* and *Something for the Birds*. During the latter 1950s Jenssen supervised the wardrobe for Lucille Ball in several episodes of the TV sitcom *I Love Lucy*. Elois Jenssen died on Valentine's Day in 2004.

Elois Jenssen would win an Academy Award for Hedy's next film, working in tandem with Edith Head and others, though it is questionable whether she herself actually designed any of Lamarr's costumes. The picture was Cecil B. DeMille's *Samson and Delilah*.

231

chapter 11

SAMSON AND DELILAH AND THE DEMISE OF THE STUDIO SYSTEM

hortly before her work on *Samson and Delilah* began, Hedy journeyed to Paris, arriving on July 7, 1948, for a press junket for a circus, *La grande nuit de Paris*, in benefit of the United Nations Overseas Aid for Children. Hedy later spoke about the affair she had with a young US naval officer, John F. Kennedy, long before he was elected president of the United States. According to Hedy the liaison took place in Paris. In a tabloid article she said, "That was about a year after the *PT-109* incident," which happened in 1943. [1] (That would be incorrect, because of the war.)

On this trip—Hedy's first to Europe since her departure in 1937, and now, after the war—Hedy stayed at the Lancaster Hotel in Paris, where Kennedy would pick

Opposite page: Hedy Lamarr. Paramount Pictures, 1950.

Above left: Edith Head, Paramount costume designer for Samson and Delilah, Copper Canyon, *and* My Favorite Spy. *(Paramount Pictures)*
Above right: Hedy Lamarr and Victor Mature, Samson and Delilah *(Paramount, 1949). Costumes by Edith Head (Lamarr) and Gile Steele (Mature).*

her up to go nightclubbing. When he asked what she would like him to bring her on their first date, she told him oranges. In the article Hedy did not mention that he was married, so their affair most like occurred in 1948. She did say he was jealous of the attention given her by other men, and went on to speak of an unpleasant incident at the Casa Nova nightclub with writer Henri Bernstein, who died in 1953. Kennedy and Hedy went out a great deal, but she did not love him, as she found him very tense and nervous.

Back in Hollywood by the end of July, Hedy reported for work at Paramount. Perhaps the one motion picture for which Hedy Lamarr is best remembered is Cecil B. DeMille's sex-and-sand blockbuster, *Samson and Delilah* (Paramount, 1949), which starred the alluring Hedy opposite the masculine and appealing Victor Mature. A lush, lavish, Technicolor production as only DeMille could mastermind, *Samson and Delilah* became the first in a series of epic 1950s biblical sagas.

Hedy Lamarr, Samson and Delilah (Paramount, 1949). Costumes by Edith Head.

Conceived and directed by the master film showman Cecil B. DeMille (1891–1959), what the screenplay lacked in fact and logical screen dialogue was made up for in flashy pageantry and mesmerizing spectacle. DeMille had been a somewhat unsuccessful actor and vaudevillian for years before partnering with film producers Jesse L. Lasky and Samuel Goldwyn. Together they created the Jesse L. Lasky Famous Players, with film production beginning in California in 1913. DeMille is credited with directing the first full-length moving picture ever made in Hollywood, *The Squaw Man*, released in 1914.

Over the course of the next thirty years DeMille created historical romances, a few contemporary potboilers, and a couple biblical sagas with plenty of sex and retribution, such as *The Ten Commandments* (1923) and *The King of Kings* (1927). The talkies were a bit challenging for the director, as he continued to use the same scenarists he had employed during the silent era. Unfortunately for DeMille, none of his eventual sound films were ever heralded for their intelligent screenplays. After three early talkie box-office failures for MGM—*Dynamite* (1929), *Madam Satan* (1930), and his dull

235

Above left: Hedy Lamarr wearing the peacock costume (colorized) from Samson and Delilah *(Paramount, 1949). Costumes by Edith Head.*
Above right: Edith Head's peacock costume for Hedy Lamarr in Samson and Delilah *(Paramount, 1949), on display today.*

third remake of *The Squaw Man* (1931)—DeMille was back at Paramount, where he produced and directed two fairly successful religious dramas, *The Sign of the Cross* (1932) and *The Crusades* (1935). *Samson and Delilah* would be his only return to that genre during the 1940s.

Based on the three books of Judges in the Bible, and on *Antiquities of the Jews* by Flavius Josephus, for good measure DeMille purchased the film rights to the 1877 French opera *Samson et Dalila*, by Camille Saint-Saëns. (He also purchased the 1930 novel *The Judge and the Fool* by Vladimir Jabotinsky, so as to cover all bases.) Assigning Jesse

Hedy Lamarr, Samson and Delilah *(Paramount, 1949). Costumes by Edith Head.*

Lasky Jr. and Frederick M. Frank to develop a screenplay, he began his casting. For his leading lady in *Samson and Delilah*, DeMille needed a beautiful, alluring, tempestuous Delilah who would be able to tempt and seduce the strongest man in the land, shepherd Samson (Victor Mature) from the land of Dan.

In the film, after Samson has betrayed Delilah, she, in revenge and with the aid of the powerful Philistine, the Saran of Gaza (George Sanders), drugs the mighty Samson and cuts off his hair, which he believed gave him his power and strength. Blinded and tortured, his faith in the end empowers him to physically topple and destroy the Temple of Dagon.

DeMille had created an eclectic list of potential beauties to consider for the role of Delilah, including Rhonda Fleming, Lana Turner, Patricia Neal, Rita Hayworth, and Jean Simmons. On May 25, 1948, DeMille screened *The Strange Woman* and found his

Delilah. Circling the name of Hedy Lamarr, his choice was made. DeMille assigned Edith Head, head costume designer at Paramount, to design his fantasy vision of sensual and alluring costumes for the picture. She would be assisted by a staff of other leading fashion experts, including Dorothy Jeakins, Gwen Wakeling, Elois Jenssen (credited as Eloise W. Jenssen), and Gile Steele, who along with Jenssen was specifically assigned to create costumes for the male leads and extras. Hairstyles for Hedy were created by Lenore Weaver, with Nellie Manley, Elaine Ramsey, and Doris Clifford assigned to the rest of the cast. Makeup was handled by Wally Westmore, Hal Lierley, and William Woods. Cinematography was helmed by the great George Barnes, and the impressive musical score was composed by Victor Young.

Fashions for Delilah, as well as her sister Semadar (Angela Lansbury), were designed by Edith Head, who was born in California on October 28, 1897. After enrolling in night classes at Otis College of Arts and Design in Los Angeles, Head later transferred to the Chouinard Art Institute. She was eventually hired as a sketch artist by costume designer Howard Greer for a DeMille film, and continued working at Paramount with Greer and Travis Banton in the mid-1920s. Greer left the studio in 1927. When Paramount did not renew Banton's contract in 1937, Head became head designer, a position that would last until 1967. "In her new position," succinctly reported the authors of *Creating the Illusion: A Fashionable History of Hollywood Costume Design*, "Head influenced fashion." [2]

Much to Head's credit, when she first encountered Hedy Lamarr in 1949, she recognized the challenge, saying later, "The greatest beauties that I have worked with were Carole Lombard, Marlene Dietrich, and Hedy Lamarr." [3] While her evaluation of Hedy's beauty might have been sound, Head's working relationship with Hedy was not. "There were easier stars to work with than Hedy Lamarr," Head once said. "Beautiful, yes. A great actress? I had my doubts. But DeMille wanted her, so she was Delilah. Dressing her wasn't easy. . . . She did, however, have very specific demands about how things should fit. DeMille wanted her to look voluptuous, but she was small-busted and she wouldn't wear padding. She told me she couldn't act if she felt she had unnatural proportions. So I draped her

Edith Head costume sketch for Hedy Lamarr,
Samson and Delilah *(Paramount, 1949).*

and shaped her until I finally achieved DeMille's required sensuousness and Hedy's requested natural look." [4]

Filming commenced on *Samson and Delilah* on October 4, 1948. Hedy was paid $10,000 a week for her work beginning on October 9. Cameraman George Barnes relished talking to the press about Lamarr, saying, "You can shoot her from any angle. She has no bad angles." But Edith Head did not

care at all for Hedy Lamarr, recalling DeMille's behavior during the actual filming of the picture: "I can still see that old goat riding his camera crane, booming out over the stage, 'Miss Lamarr! Please! God DAMN it! Come out of that MASK!' " [5]

In an interview Jesse Lasky said of Lamarr, "The spectacular face and figure were enhanced by a miraculous grace . . . DeMille said she was like a gazelle, incapable of a clumsy or wrong move. She filled the beholder with such breathless beauty that her acting hardly mattered." [6] Complimenting her director in the same conversation, Hedy gushed to the press, "Mr. DeMille has knowledge and charm such as few people have. . . . When he gets mad, I do not listen." [7]

"Lamarr's cleavage and navel were never exposed in the film," read one captioned photo in *Edith Head's Hollywood*. " 'The censors had a thing about women's belly buttons,' Edith explained." For the collapse of the temple scene, DeMille wanted something special created for Delilah as she sat on the throne. "Her costume was to be nothing like the scant things she had worn in the more erotic scenes. Here she was to demonstrate the power of her position; she was to be beautiful, but not a seductress. . . . He wanted a costume with feathers—for what reason, I don't know. He never gave reasons. Beyond that, he was leaving the rest up to me." [8]

For the role of Delilah, Head was supplied with the following measurements to follow for the even dozen costumes she created for Hedy Lamarr: "bust: 34½, un. 31, ab. 32½; waist: 25; shoe size: 7½; head size: 21½; dress size: 12; hip: upper 33, lower 35; etc." [9] Seeing that none of Delilah's costumes were contemporary in design, Head had to "wing it," as there are no true Minoa fashion guidelines for that biblical era. Most of the individual costumes for Hedy were constructed with fabrics and accessories in varying colors of gold, red, purple, iridescent emeralds and greens, blacks, and silver. Fashions made of satin, lamé, gauze, and wool ranging from $200 to $1,810 each were created for Hedy at a total cost of $12,230 ($134,307.35 today).

The most opulent of all of these outfits by far was the famous peacock costume Hedy wears at the end of the film, ordered by DeMille, in which Delilah appears at the Temple of Dagon to witness Samson's final torture. The amazing creation consisted of a

Hedy Lamarr, A Lady Without Passport *(MGM, 1950). Costumes by Irene and Helen Rose.*

short-sleeved, V-neck bodice top embroidered with peacock-feather designs, an open midriff, a long flowing matching blue skirt with waistband, with beaded and feathered embroidery, worn with the famous gold satin–lined, long trailing peacock-feather cape. With this outfit Hedy wears high-heeled sandals as she guides Samson up the steps to position him for his destruction of the temple.

" 'There wasn't any place in America where we could buy peacock tails,' " Head recalled in Cecilia De Mille Presley and Mark Vieira's defining book on DeMille. [10] Eventually Head and her crew would spend endless hours gathering peacock feathers from a pride of molting birds on DeMille's Paradise ranch in Tujunga, then stitching and gluing them onto a blue light wool cape and train. "Of course, he didn't go out and gather dirty bird feathers," declared Head. "My own staff helped collect them [from Paradise] and bring them in. We sorted them by size, color and brilliance. It took days." [11] Recalled Paramount's then-publicist Herb Steinberg, "I watched wardrobe people carrying bushels

THE BEAUTY OF HEDY LAMARR

Edith Head costume design for Hedy Lamarr, Copper Canyon *(Paramount, 1950).*

of feathers onto the lot." [12] This extraordinary outfit is one of only two fashions DeMille kept in his personal collection until his death on January 21, 1959.

Edith Head was to write, "I have always had the feeling that it was entirely wrong. I doubt very much that there were any peacocks around or nearby in the days of Samson and Delilah. Nor would anyone, even Delilah, have worn the kind of cape that I designed— or any of the other costumes, for that matter. I suppose only scholars would know that the costumes were not historically correct, but it bothered me terribly. I was never able to find anything authentic to indicate what Samson and Delilah looked like, so I improvised." [13]

The feathered cape may have been inspired by another peacock-plumed ensemble worn by Theda Bara in Fox's 1917 now-lost silent-film version of *Cleopatra*. At any rate, Head later remarked, "Lamarr's garb, shimmering and revealing as it was, was all too reminiscent of costumes shown in films of the past." [14]

Needless to say, in glorious Technicolor and worn in the much-anticipated finale of *Samson and Delilah*, the costume is incredibly impressive, even though Delilah discards the cape quickly after her entrance as she steps off her throne beside the Saran of Gaza (George Sanders), to enter the arena.

Hedy Lamarr and Bob Hope, My Favorite Spy *(Paramount, 1951). Costumes by Edith Head.*

For this massive endeavor of costuming, Edith Head and her staff, Gile Steele, Elois Jenssen, Dorothy Jeakins, and Gwen Wakeling, were each awarded Oscars at the 1950 Academy Awards, for Best Costume Design for a Color Film in 1949. *Samson and Delilah* was also nominated for four other Oscars: Best Score, Best Special Effects, Best Cinematography Color, and Best Art and Set Direction Color. *Samson and Delilah* cost $3 million and became the third-highest-grossing film of the 1940s, and the largest-grossing picture for Paramount up to that point. Once again, Hedy was an important star, as designated on her Paramount contract, and once more a highly sought-after commodity.

Lamarr's next motion picture under her Paramount contract was the Technicolor Western *Copper Canyon*, directed by John Farrow, and co-starring Ray Milland and Mac-Donald Carey. For this film Hedy was paid $100,000 for five weeks of work. The story takes place in post–Civil War Coppertown, with feuding between the Northerners and

Hedy Lamarr, My Favorite Spy *(Paramount, 1951). Costumes by Edith Head.*

the Southerners over the ore mined at the Balfour Smelter. Milland is the good guy, Johnny Clark; Carey, the bad man, Lane Travis; and incongruously, Hedy Lamarr as Lisa Roselle is the "French" proprietor of the local saloon. Hedy's character has little to do other than be gorgeous and alluring. Battles and deception are prevalent in the plot, as well as a mandatory love story. And somewhere in the mix of this colorful shoot-'em-up is the Jay Livingston / Ray Evans song "Copper Canyon," which became a hit pop song upon the film's release in October of 1950.

The film's score was composed by Daniele Amfitheatrof, and Edith Head was assigned to create the eight costumes and sumptuous gowns Hedy wore in the picture, the most memorable being an off-the-shoulder, ice-blue striped satin dress trimmed with pearled embroidery, accentuated with a multi-strand, looped pearl necklace. Hedy's hair designs were by Lenore Weaver, and her makeup by Harold Lierley and Carl Silvera, supervised by Wally Westmore. *Copper Canyon* was filmed between mid-April and early June of 1949 at a cost of some $1.7 million. Upon its completion the Western's release was held up until Hedy's next film for her home studio, MGM, was filmed and released in August 1950.

Critics were respectful, though not exactly overwhelmed by *Copper Canyon*, finding its magnificent photography by Charles B. Lang Jr. and the overall acting memorable. But

Hedy Lamarr and Bob Hope, My Favorite Spy *(Paramount, 1951). Costumes by Edith Head.*

still, audiences were somewhat taken back by the casting of the still radiantly beautiful, alluring Hedy Lamarr as a saloon keeper alongside Welsh-born Ray Milland as a Confederate soldier. Sophisticated and urbane, Milland had won the Best Actor Oscar of 1945 for *The Lost Weekend.* Paramount's ads for the film had reached sublime ridiculousness, and possibly even ruined the picture's chances at the box office. They featured Lamarr looking more like a young Linda Darnell, her legs wide apart, her knee-length *sheer* cowgirl outfit caressing her body, feet in boots, holding a rifle, her long hair flowing in the wind. "Hot Lead, Blue Steel and Red Lips were her Brands! With Them She Ruled the Valley of Violence!" blared the ads. Sadly, *Copper Canyon*, despite its visual beauty and classic musical score, eventually ended up on the bottom half of double bills.

After the immense box-office success of *Samson and Delilah* for Paramount, Louis B. Mayer wanted Hedy back on the Metro lot for his picture *Visa*, which became *A Lady*

Without Passport. While Hedy knew Mayer's claim that this film would be even bigger than *Samson and Delilah* wasn't true—it was really just a potboiler about illegal immigration, not a very popular theme of that time—by signing a most generous contract for the film, Hedy allowed her name to be exploited in what was actually for MGM a B-picture. Mayer was clever enough to know that by signing a major star in a cheap film, he could be guaranteed block bookings of other minor pictures. As produced by Samuel Marx, directed by Joseph H. Lewis, and starring Hedy opposite newcomer John Hodiak, *A Lady Without Passport* was released on August 18, 1950, with little fanfare. Most unusual for MGM, over the decades this film has become a minor film noir classic.

With cinematography by Paul C. Vogel and a gripping musical score by David Raksin, the seventy-two minutes of the film explore the social issue of illegal immigration from Cuba into Florida combined with a simple love story thrown in for the two stars. Studio hairdresser Sydney Guilaroff once again supervised Hedy's hairstyles, along with June Roberts. Jack Dawn as head of the department supervised the makeup for the film, with Metro makeup artist Gene Hibbs assigned to handle Hedy. Along with such stars as Judy Garland, Rosalind Russell, and later Elizabeth Taylor, Hedy would insist on Hibbs for the remainder of her films.

As early as Tuesday, May 24, 1949, MGM head of fashion Irene met with her staff, Kay Dean, Marion Herwood Keyes, J. Arlington Valles, and Gile Steele, to discuss three upcoming projects that were to be filmed almost simultaneously—*Shadow on the Wall*, *A Lady Without Passport*, and *Crisis*. Wrote Irene's sketch artist Virginia Fisher, "Among those films Irene received credit for only one [*Shadow on the Wall*]. However, looking at the wardrobe worn by Ann Sothern, Signe Hasso, and Hedy Lamarr, it is obvious that they are wearing Irene's designs." [15] Irene, who won an Oscar nomination for her designs for Barbara Stanwyck in *B.F.'s Daughter* in 1946, had remarked to Travis Banton that staying at MGM had been a terrible mistake. She abruptly left Metro after a major falling-out with Katharine Hepburn and her arrogant demands on the film *Adam's Rib*, and with Mayer himself, leading the mogul to sigh heavily and snidely remark, "So quiet she was—and expensive, Miss Don't-Melt-Ice-Cube." [16]

Hedy Lamarr, Copper Canyon (Paramount, 1950). Costumes by Edith Head. (Photograph by A. L. Whitey Schafer, Photofest)

Tragically for Irene, her drinking had become a major issue at the studio. She would behave irrationally, sometimes not appearing at all for meetings. Leaving the industry, Irene opened her own fashion house, but returned to film to design for a couple of Doris Day pictures in 1960; she would be nominated for a second Oscar for Universal's 1960 thriller *Midnight Lace*. Confiding to Day that the only man she ever loved was actor Gary Cooper, who died of cancer in 1961, Irene grew ever more despondent. She took her life by leaping out of an eleventh-story window of the Knickerbocker Hotel in Hollywood on November 15, 1962.

The credits for *A Lady Without Passport* list no designer. Irene had met with her sketch artist Virginia Fisher as late as June of 1949 to work on Hedy's wardrobe. Although similar in style to Irene's costumes of 1949, Hedy's costumes for this film were nonetheless accredited in the press to Helen Rose.

Rose was born in Chicago on February 4, 1904. After studying at the Chicago Academy of Fine Arts, she moved to Hollywood in 1929, eventually designing ice-skating costumes for films at 20th Century-Fox in the 1930s. She eventually moved over to MGM in 1942 and would remain with them until 1966.

Rose found designing for beautiful women could be difficult. "If you have a magnificent jewel—you put it in a simple setting," Rose once said. "[Y]ou don't distract from it with a lot of detail." [17] A favorite designer of other Metro actresses at MGM in the 1950s, Rose would privately create wedding gowns for Elizabeth Taylor, Jane Powell, Debbie Reynolds, and Grace Kelly.

Los Angeles Times drama and film critic Edwin Schallert wrote at the time: "Helen Rose is designing seventeen evening dresses for Hedy Lamarr in *Visa* [*A Lady Without Passport*], at Metro, which will afford this star her most modernly sartorial role in a long while." [18] But there is conjecture that Irene had actually finished the costumes for Hedy, and that Helen Rose had merely been assigned as supervisor of costuming for the film.

In *A Lady Without Passport*, Hedy wore a two-piece sequined outfit with a single-strap halter top and wrap-around open ruffled skirt for her character's "cigarette girl" garb. It is distinctly out of place in the film and appears to be an old Adrian flashback moment. The

Hedy Lamarr, Copper Canyon (Paramount, 1950). Costumes by Edith Head. (Photograph by A. L. Whitey Schafer)

other costumes Hedy wears in the film are contemporary in design, and include a lovely off-the-shoulder white V-neck with lattice lining, flared open elbow-length sleeves, and matching lattice lining. One sees both Irene's distinct influence and Helen Rose's flair in the designs.

Rose would later earn eight Oscar nods, winning for her costume creations in *The Bad and the Beautiful* (1952) and *I'll Cry Tomorrow* (1955). On a commercial level,

thousands of copies of her iconic chiffon V-neck white dress, designed for Elizabeth Taylor for *Cat on a Hot Tin Roof* (1958), sold for $250 apiece at Joseph Magnin in San Francisco and Bonwit Teller in New York. In her memoir, *Just Make Them Beautiful*, Helen Rose does not mention *A Lady Without Passport* as one of her credits. She died on November 9, 1985.

At Paramount Hedy appeared in her last film for the studio starring opposite comedian Bob Hope in *My Favorite Spy*, which began filming in April 1951. A silly spy spoof comedy about some missing microfilm, it was photographed by Victor Milner. Bob Hope played a double role: comic Peanuts White and master spy Eric Augustine. Hedy's part was that of a nightclub singer named Lily Dalbrey. Ineffectively directed by Norman Z. McLeod, Hope once again plays the same smart-mouthed wisecracker he had portrayed for nearly twenty years. His tiring character, Peanuts, becomes a bore all too quickly. Hope is now older, his punches are a bit too slow, and his pratfalls and humorous physical efforts are clearly provided in the film by stuntmen.

Hedy's character is only required to look glamorous. (This is especially true given that Hope had many of Hedy's more-comedic scenes cut, probably due to his massive ego.) For Hedy's costumes Edith Head designed contemporary outfits that were stylish and chic, thankfully a bit more mature in design for a bit-more-mature-looking Hedy Lamarr. Her six costumes, except for a firefighter's outfit, are feminine and detailed in design and fabric, featuring flowing chiffons, with jewelry prominent, the evening apparel in the nightclub sequences the most appealing. Hedy's makeup was created by Wally Westmore. When it was released in December 1951, *My Favorite Spy* did respectable business primarily because of Bob Hope's popularity.

During her lengthy career in film, Edith Head would receive eight Oscars for Best Costume Design, for *The Heiress* (1949); *Samson and Delilah* and *All About Eve* (both 1950); *A Place in the Sun* (1951), *Roman Holiday* (1953), and *Sabrina* (1954), all at Paramount; *The Facts of Life* (United Artists, 1960); and *The Sting* (Universal, 1973). In total Head was nominated for thirty-five Oscars for her film fashions. She would eventually depart Paramount in the 1960s and design for Universal and other studios until her death

on October 24, 1981. During Head's lifetime, writes one historian, "Her even-tempered, dependable approach to seemingly insurmountable problems earned her the unqualified respect of her associates." [19]

By the early 1950s Hedy Lamarr's once-influential impact on film glamour and style had become minimal. Without a studio contract, her film career floundered just as the Golden Age of Hollywood was coming to a close. Temperamental and aging, Hedy had refused to cooperate with Paramount when asked to appear in a cameo sequence along with DeMille and other cast members from *Samson and Delilah* for Billy Wilder's *Sunset Boulevard*, demanding enormous financial compensation. And for both *My Favorite Spy* and *Copper Canyon*, Hedy had vehemently refused to do any promotion.

Paramount dropped her. Faced with no forthcoming film offers, and being a single mother, for the next several decades Hedy Lamarr's life spiraled out of control.

chapter 12

THE END OF
AN ERA

As Hedy's film career waned after 1951, her private life took many unfortunate and uncomfortable turns. She had divorced John Loder in 1947 shortly after the birth of their son Anthony. Hedy then married Austrian musician and Acapulco restaurateur Ernest Heinrich "Teddy" Stauffer in 1951, leaving Hollywood and taking her two younger children with her. For reasons quite personal to both mother and son, Hedy abandoned her eleven-year-old elder son James at this time, although she did finance his education. The reason given was that he was going to be reared by the proprietors of his school.

Hedy Lamarr would not make another motion picture for two more years.

Ernest Stauffer, born on May 2, 1909, in Switzerland, had been a popular European jazz band leader. He eventually became a leading figure in Acapulco hospitality, opening restaurants and hotels and bringing the glittering international set to

Opposite page: Hedy Lamarr. Metro-Goldwyn-Mayer, c. 1942. (Photograph by George Hurrell)

Hedy Lamarr, Denise Loder, Anthony Loder, and Howard Lee, 1953. (Photofest)

popularize Mexico. Selling everything she owned at auction in Hollywood, Hedy and the two younger children followed Stauffer to Acapulco to begin life anew. It proved to be a disaster, with their marriage over by January 1952.

Back in Hollywood, Hedy's career was sporadic, as the times and the culture were in flux. Hedy worked periodically on television variety and game shows, and on radio dramas and popular comedy shows. She became a US citizen on April 10, 1953.

Resuming the role of producer, Hedy traveled to Italy to finance two films in Rome. The first project, eventually completed and released in English as *The Love of Three Queens* (*L'amante di Paride*), was originally conceived as a series of one-hour television dramas dealing with famous historical beauties throughout history. Produced by Hedy Lamarr Productions, the projected monumental series was directed by Marc Allegret, with Hedy's longtime friend Edgar G. Ullmer, whom she had worked with in *The Strange Woman*, listed as associate director. Filming in Technicolor commenced in Europe, with

Vittorio Nino Novarese, costume designer for The Love of Three Queens *(L'amante di Paride) and* Eternal Woman *(L'eterna femmina)*.

cinematography by Desmond Dickinson and Fernando Risi, and script by Nino Novarese (who also created the costumes), Marc Allegret, and Salka Viertel. The musical score was composed by the prolific Nino Rota.

With all of this international talent, including Hedy's leading men, Gerard Oury, Massimo Serato, Cesare Danova, Terence Morgan, and the late John Fraser, one would think it would have been a masterpiece in the making. From the outset, however, filming of the series was a nightmare, with continual disputes erupting behind the scenes and on the set, beginning with Edgar Ullmer and the project's unstable financing, troubled casting, and changing screenplay.

Most of the difficulties were compounded by Hedy herself. Pressured from the start with the responsibility of bringing to life the epic tales of tragic beauties Helen of Troy,

Massimo Serato and Hedy Lamarr in The Love of Three Queens *(L'amante di Paride) (Cino del Duca-P.C.E. Productions, 1953). Costumes by Vittorio Nino Novarese.*

Genevieve de Brabent, and Empress Josephine (and at one time or another, Queen Esther and Mary of Scotland), it's possible the whole project was simply too ambitious. Eventually just the stories of Helen, Genevieve, and Josephine were assembled into a rambling trilogy held together by a fourth storyline that dealt with a traveling Tuscan theatrical troupe. The introduction of each episode, called *I cavalieri dell'illusione*, involved the Gods on Mount Olympus choosing their games with earthbound humans.

Complicated and rambling, poorly edited and savagely reviewed, *The Love of Three Queens*, long available in black-and-white, was never released in the United States. Today it is somewhat restored in beautiful Technicolor, an interesting timepiece. Sadly, Hedy Lamarr, once known as the "most beautiful girl in the world," had matured, and showed her age on the screen. Had the project starred the young Audrey Hepburn, or even Sophia Loren, it might have drawn more interest and made money.

Above left: Hedy Lamarr, Eternal Woman (L'eterna femmina) *(Cino del Duca–P.C.E. Productions, 1955). Costumes by Vittorio Nino Novarese. Unreleased.*
Above right: Hedy Lamarr in "Proud Woman" for Dick Powell's Zane Grey Theatre *(CBS, 1957). Costumes by Robert B. Harris.*

One redeeming aspect of *The Love of Three Queens* was Hedy's wardrobe, created for all three of her completed episodes by Nino Novarese. Born in Rome on May 15, 1907, Vittorio Nino Novarese designed costumes for Italian films before coming to Hollywood in 1949, the year he won an Oscar nomination for his designs in color for *Prince of Foxes* (20th Century-Fox). His creations for *The Love of Three Queens* are of period design, with the expected flowing gowns for Helen, plain and somewhat ordinary costuming for Genevieve, and elaborate yet appropriate designs for Josephine. In his autobiography, actor John Fraser wrote of a freakish situation during the filming of this project when Hedy ruined "a priceless lilac velvet gown embroidered with seed pearls and semiprecious stones," a design she had insisted upon for Genevieve, according to Fraser. Supposedly, in anger after repeated heated takes, Hedy impulsively and maliciously tore this costume to

THE BEAUTY OF HEDY LAMARR

Above left: Hedy Lamarr and director Irwin Allen on the set of The Story of Mankind *(Warner Bros., 1957). Costumes by Marjorie Best.*
Above right: Hedy Lamarr, The Story of Mankind *(Warner Bros., 1957). Costumes by Marjorie Best.*

shreds, holding up production until another costume could be substituted. [1] In the film, however, the costume Genevieve wears bears no resemblance to what Fraser describes.

The costumes were nonetheless brilliantly crafted. In later years Nino Novarese would win the Best Costume Design Oscar for Color for his startling creations for *Cleopatra* (20th Century-Fox, 1963), and be nominated twice more, in 1965, for both *The Greatest Story Ever Told* (UA) and *The Agony and the Ecstasy* (20th Century-Fox). He would win yet another Oscar in 1971 for *Cromwell* (Columbia, 1970). An expert craftsman, his costume designs unmatched for a particular era and time, Vittorio Nino Novarese died on October 17, 1983.

For Hedy's next Italian film, *Eternal Woman* (*L'eterna femmina*), a contemporary costumer was required. Originally titled *White Ermine* because of an ermine wrap that

features prominently in the story of romance in modern Rome, *Eternal Woman*, with musical score again by Nino Rota, was a troubled venture from the start. Filming had commenced in mid-October of 1954, but the weather in Rome did not cooperate, nor did the financing hold out. The picture was shut down indefinitely for months. It co-starred Hedy once again with Massimo Serato and used most of the same cast and crew of *The Love of Three Queens*. After the shutdown in mid-production, Hedy returned to the United States, eventually returning to Italy to complete the film in 1955. Unfortunately *Eternal Woman* was never released, due to legal entanglements.

"It was tough for a woman to last [in the industry]," wrote film historian Jeanine Basinger. "Those who ran the studios and operated the star machine knew only too well that the beautiful female stars they were manufacturing were going to lose in popularity sooner than the males. Glamorous women were a fragile product. . . . But longevity for women was tricky. The camera was a cruel observer, and it saw age: wrinkles, thickness, the loss of that glistening shine of the first blush of ripe sexuality. The standards of beauty were stricter for women, and society's attitude toward romantic pairings of older women and younger men was less accepting. If a female star could last for a decade, she really paid off. If she could last for two decades, she was a phenomenal success." [2]

Hedy Lamarr had had a good run, but her dark, mysterious, sensual allure became irrelevant as the decade of 1950s produced a new crop of glamour queens like Marilyn Monroe, who was curvaceous and sexy, and Debbie Reynolds, who was the opposite— homespun, healthy, and cute. These images became the trend. As moviegoers' tastes changed, Hedy no longer quite fit the mold.

Hedy chose to exchange the limelight for domesticity in Texas. On December 21, 1953, she married oilman W. Howard Lee, left Hollywood, and settled comfortably in Houston for the next five years. Lee's money enabled her to finance the completion of the ill-fated *Eternal Woman* in Rome. As her life focused more and more on domesticity and family, Hedy's unavoidable aging weighed heavily on her mind. Her beauty had always been her ticket to acknowledgment and recognition, and she longed to be in films again.

Above left: Bill Thomas, costume designer for Slaughter on Tenth Avenue *and* The Female Animal. *Universal-International Pictures.*
Above right: Denise Loder, Hedy Lamarr, and Anthony Loder on the beach set of The Female Animal *(Universal-International, 1958). Lamarr costumes by Bill Thomas.*

Eventually she was offered a brief role at Warner Brothers in Irwin Allen's preposterous "epic," *The Story of Mankind*, based on the best-selling nonfiction book by Hendrik van Loon. Advertised as "THE BIGGEST STAR CAST EVER ON ONE SCREEN," with the exception of Ronald Colman (in his last film appearance) and Hedy Lamarr, the other fifteen names on that list were primarily character actors and minor players, including Agnes Moorehead, Peter Lorre, Cesar Romero, Franklin Pangborn, and the Marx Brothers—Groucho, Harpo, and Chico.

On purpose or accidentally, and rather tongue-in-cheek, the ludicrous screenplay written by Allen and Charles Bennett revolves around The Spirit of Man (Ronald Colman), who comes before the High Tribunal to debate with the Devil (Vincent Price) over the worth of humanity and its possible redemption from hell. For his defense the history

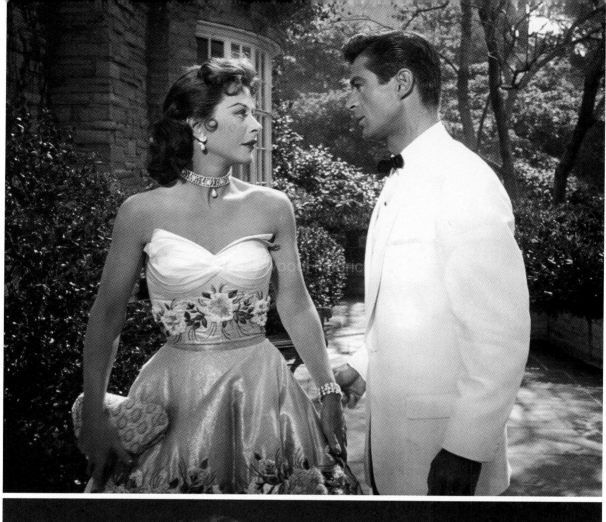

Hedy Lamarr and George Nader, The Female Animal *(Universal-International, 1958). Costumes by Bill Thomas.*

Hedy Lamarr and George Nader, The Female Animal *(Universal-International, 1958). Costumes by Bill Thomas.*

of mankind is ponderously told to prove its redemption. As one critic put it when *The Story of Mankind* was unleashed on the public, "It is my personal observation that if the High Tribunal ever catches this picture, we're goners." [3] The film's minimal musical score was composed by Paul Sawtell. In the Technicolor film Hedy portrays a somewhat mature Joan of Arc in five brief scenes, all told within a matter of minutes. Her contract, signed in November of 1956, gave her $2,500 for one week's work.

The film's costume designer was Marjorie Best. Born in Illinois on April 10, 1903, Best came to Los Angeles and studied at the Chouinard Art Institute, becoming a designer at the Western Costume Company in 1926. She came to the costume department at Warner Brothers in 1936, her forte in designing men's costumes and wardrobe for period

pictures. In 1949, along with Leah Rhodes and Travilla, Marjorie was awarded the Best Costume Design Oscar for *The Adventures of Don Juan*.

For Hedy's character of Joan of Arc in *The Story of Mankind*, Best designed costumes ranging from a scarfed tunic and long skirt to a long white tunic and long-sleeved chain-mail shirt and tights, which Joan wears while astride a horse. Another costume consisted of blue tights and a long-sleeved turtleneck sweater, which Hedy wears during Joan's trial. Joan's final costume is a long white robe that she wears as she is tied to the stake. In the film Hedy sported a short hairstyle created by Margaret Donovan, and her makeup was supervised by Gordon Blau and handled by Ray Romero and Emile Lavigne.

The final result of the picture is painful. It is excruciating to watch, with unintentional bad acting, and even worse dialogue. *The Story of Mankind* opened on October 23, 1957, and quickly tanked at the box office. *Newsweek*'s review summed it up succinctly: "Unearthly . . . a poor excuse to use a bunch of available actors in some of the weirdest casting ever committed." [4] It quite properly ranks as one of the worst films of all time. Yet, the costumes stand out. Surprisingly, that same year Marjorie Best was nominated for an Oscar for Best Costume Design again, along with Moss Mabry, for the Warner Brothers epic *Giant*. Best would be nominated twice more for Best Costume Design—for *Sunrise at Campobello* (Warner Brothers, 1960), and, along with Vittorio Nino Novarese, for *The Greatest Story Ever Told* (MGM, 1965), which was her last film. Marjorie Best died on June 14, 1997.

Approached by Universal-International producer Albert Zugsmith to accept the lead in *Hideaway House*, Hedy agreed, accepting the role for $50,000 for six weeks' work. But first she appeared in a cameo scene with leading lady Julie Adams in the studio's *Slaughter on Tenth Avenue*, directed by Arnold Laven, and starring Richard Egan, Dan Duryea, and Walter Matthau. The gratuitous sequence with Julie Adams was intended to add a bit of femininity to an already male-dominated, gritty crime drama. The role of Mona, the proprietress of a fashion house, was originally begun—and aborted—by Zsa Zsa Gabor, when producers realized Gabor could not act.

Above left: Hedy Lamarr, Picture Mommy Dead *(Embassy, 1966). Costumes by Leah Rhodes.*
Above right: Hedy Lamarr, c. 1953. (Denise Loder DeLuca Collection)

On May 11, 1957, Hedy underwent camera tests, followed by a day of filming, with pickup shots completed later, on a third day. Her makeup was created by both Monte and Bud Westmore, and her hairstyle (a wig, actually) was managed by Edith House and Virginia Jones. But it was all for naught. When the picture was released on November 5, 1957, the boutique sequence featuring Hedy was deleted.

Hedy's costume in *Slaughter on Tenth Avenue* consisted of a simple, dark, form-fitting, three-quarter-length-sleeve business attire ensemble with white button-front, accessorized by a loose-fitting white scarf. The costume was created by nine-time Oscar-nominated designer Bill Thomas, born in Chicago on October 13, 1921. He too attended Chouinard Art Institute in Los Angeles, later working briefly at MGM with Walter Plunkett. In existing stills from the aborted scene, Thomas's design was stylish and very flattering to Hedy.

Above left: Hedy Lamarr, c. 1960.
Above right: Robert Osborne and Hedy Lamarr, 1965. (Photofest)

Hedy was offered an acting role in a thirty-minute television drama, "Proud Woman," for *Dick Powell's Zane Grey Theatre*, hosted by Powell. In it Hedy portrayed a South American ranch owner (possibly to explain her accent) who tangles with a couple of unscrupulous wranglers over a stallion. Filmed in August 1957 for CBS, the show aired on October 25. Directed by Louis King, with cinematography by Guy Rose and original music by Harry Lubin, Hedy's makeup was applied by television makeup artist Karl Herlinger. Hedy's costumes for the teleplay were designed by Robert B. Harris, who specialized in supplying period wardrobe for the television anthology *You Are There* (CBS, 1953–1972).

It should be mentioned here that in the mid-1950s it became popular for young actresses to apply eyeliner below their lower lids and then dramatically sweep upward at the outer point, creating an almost exotic look. This was done either because of new

Above left: Hedy Lamarr on an episode of Shindig! *(ABC, 1965), which aired on October 21, 1965.*
Above right: Hedy Lamarr and Lewis Boies Jr., c. 1964.

cinematic techniques, because of the European influx of new nubile starlets, or merely for vanity's sake. This effect was used most creatively by such cinema stars as Shirley MacLaine, Audrey Hepburn, and Sophia Loren, as well as innumerable other pixie-ish starlets up until the mid-1960s.

However, this heavy technique did *not* work for Hedy Lamarr and her classic beauty. With the freshness and glow of youth fast disappearing from her face, this technique came across as hard, and too harsh. Though she kept remarkably physically fit—at one point in the 1950s Hedy was featured in ads for a popular dietetic candy called AYDS— the fact was, Hedy was aging.

Back at Universal, the title of Hedy Lamarr's film was changed from *Hideaway House* to *The Female Animal*. Filmed in Cinemascope and black-and-white, it would also become Hedy Lamarr's last completed motion picture. Directed by Harry Keller, with musical score by Hans J. Salter and photography by Russell Metty, *The Female Animal* told the story of a love triangle featuring, ironically enough, an aging film beauty who falls

Above left: Anthony Loder and Hedy Lamarr, after her divorce from Lewis Boies Jr., 1965.
Above right: Hedy Lamarr on holiday, 1969. (Denise Loder DeLuca Collection)

obsessively in love with a hunky film extra (John Gavin / George Nader), who by mere chance falls in love with the woman's almost adult daughter (Jane Powell). Perhaps Hedy could relate to her character. Certainly young actor John Gavin could not, as he was later replaced by George Nader. This was an unusual casting choice, because real-life gay actor George Nader portrayed a sexy hapless Romeo garbed in 1950s (gay-appropriate) tight, rolled-up beach jeans, with open shirts and rolled-up sleeves, which at significant moments he would discard. Simultaneously, twenty-eight-year-old former Metro musical-comedy star, the cuddly Jane Powell, portrayed the wild-child teenager daughter, to much embarrassment, and was totally out of her depth in a dramatic role.

Lillian Burkhart and Virginia Jones were assigned the hairstyles for the leading actresses, repeating a most unflattering, youngish 1950s flip style for Hedy's character. Hedy was now forty-three years old, and makeup by Bud Westmore, Vincent Romain, and Nick Marcelino was again heavily applied, stressing the "pixie" look. Costumes, listed

Hedy Lamarr and Merv Griffin on an episode of The Merv Griffin Show *(CBS, 1969), which aired on August 18, 1969.*

in the credits as "Gowns by," were by Bill Thomas, with the assistance of Rose Brandi and Truman Eli.

For Hedy, Thomas created a dozen contemporary and period fashions, plus a two-piece bathing outfit, which unfortunately could not match the male beauty of Nader's torso and body in swim trunks. Thomas's gowns—light-colored pieces with prints and lace—were exquisitely designed and modern, sleeveless, full-skirted, and feminine. Though they were quite fashionable, on younger women they would have been sensational. They just did not represent the iconic Hedy Lamarr style. Bill Thomas would remain with Universal until 1960, winning a Best Costume Design Oscar, along with Valles, for *Spartacus* (1960). Thomas would later join the Disney organization in 1961, freelancing as well, and earn more Oscar nominations. Bill Thomas died on May 30, 2000.

Bored with Houston, Hedy's marriage to Howard Lee, an alcoholic, ended. Taking the children to Hollywood in June 1958 and settling at 614 North Beverly Drive, Hedy

filed for divorce on August 8. Haggling back and forth led to Lee filing suit against Hedy in February 1959. Her capriciousness led to many acrimonious disputes, and the courts continually ruled against her. Her stubbornness lost her a large amount of community property, including the beautiful and profitable Villa Lamarr, which she had built in Aspen, Colorado, as a ski resort, effectively placing Aspen on the map. By 1960 it was over, and later Howard Lee married actress Gene Tierney. He died on February 17, 1981.

Hedy's personal life and equilibrium started to come under question during this time. Years later it was discovered she had

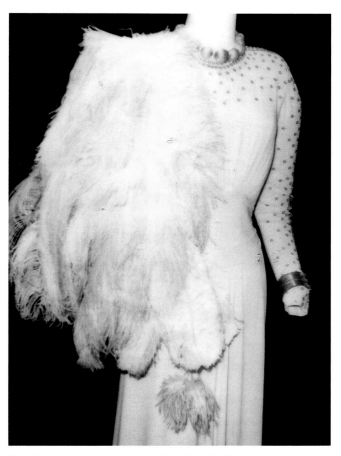

The Hedy Lamarr gown worn on The Merv Griffin Show *(CBS, 1969), on display today. (Arlene Roxbury Collection)*

begun taking "vitamin B" shots from Dr. Max Jacobson in the 1950s, and would continue this practice until 1974. She was not the only celebrity to receive these injections under the guise of vitamin boosters. President John F. Kennedy, both before and after his election in 1960, director Cecil B. DeMille, Eddie Fisher, Alan Jay Lerner, and Charlton Heston were also familiar with "Dr. Feelgood" Jacobson. Each shot was actually a 40mg injection of methamphetamine, a highly addictive stimulant affecting the central nervous system, which many well-heeled clients were absolutely convinced was beneficial to them. As a result, Hedy's behavior became quite erratic throughout the next two decades, and she would experience a nervous breakdown following her divorce from Howard Lee.

269

Above left: Hedy Lamarr, 1967.
Above right: Hedy Lamarr, c. 1960s.

As her career wound down, Hedy continued appearing on various television interview, game, and variety shows. By selling off her valuable art collection Hedy was able to keep her children in private schools, as well as support older son James's higher education. Hedy once owned priceless paintings by Renoir, Guillaumin, and Dufy, as well as sculptures by Rodin and Daumier. By selling them she was able to keep the wolf at bay.

But sadly, her life was falling apart. After moving into an apartment at 1802 Angelo Drive in Beverly Hills, on March 4, 1963, Hedy got married for the sixth and final time, to lawyer Lewis Boies Jr. The couple took a two-year lease on a house at 9550 Hidden Valley Road, across the street from Jack L. and Ann Warner. However, the marriage was short-lived, and the two separated and divorced in 1965.

Both Denise and Anthony had attended the prestigious Stockbridge School in Interlaken, Massachusetts, until their respective graduations. Denise then attended

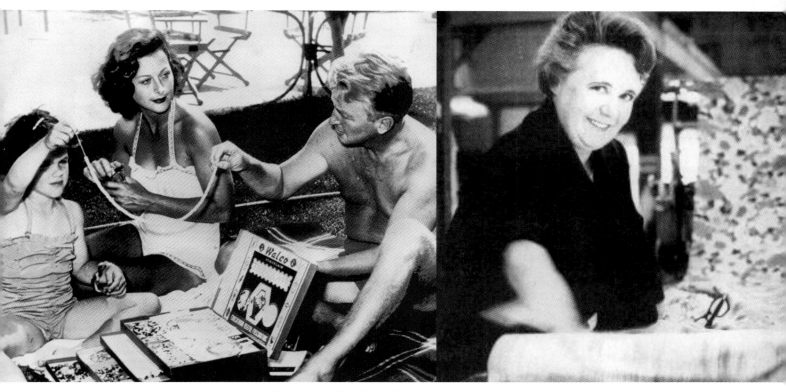

Above left: Denise Loder, Hedy Lamarr, and Teddy Stauffer in Carmel, California, June 1951 (Photofest)
Above right: Marjorie Best, Warner Brothers costume designer for The Story of Mankind *(Warner Brothers)*

the University of California–Berkeley, and eventually wed then–Philadelphia Phillies baseball player Lawrence "Larry" Colton in July 1965. Upon his graduation, Anthony attended the University of California–Los Angeles. That October, Hedy, appearing much younger that her fifty years, appeared on the popular ABC evening television teen show, *Shindig!* Still ravishingly attractive, dressed in tight slacks and a sleeveless blouse, her hair short and streaked with highlights, she did not appear at all like the Hedy Lamarr of her film stardom heyday.

In January 1966 Hedy was elated to be asked to star along with Don Ameche and Martha Hyer in independent film producer/director Bert I. Gordon's thriller film, *Picture Mommy Dead* for Embassy Pictures. This would be her first film in some eight years and, needless to say, Hedy was quite excited about her return to the screen. Her role was a brief one, that of a murdered wife and mother of a young daughter, clumsily performed by

THE BEAUTY OF HEDY LAMARR

Hedy Lamarr and her painting, c. 1967.

Gordon's real-life daughter Susan. Still gorgeously beautiful, and looking younger than her fifty-one years, Hedy's makeup was handled by Wally Westmore, Hal Lierley, and Daniel C. Striepeke, and her hair was styled by Nellie Manley and Sherry Wilson.

Hedy was particularly delighted to be gowned in her only costume for the film by Leah Rhodes once again. Rhodes designed for Hedy's character a stunning floor-length, strapless chiffon-over-silk creation with a fur-trimmed bodice and bow, accessorized with matching opera-length gloves and heavy woven gold necklace integral to the plot of the picture. It was said that the costume only cost $165. Jewelry was supervised by Dorothy Hughes. For Hedy, though, this was a true pleasure, to be gowned by one of her favorite film fashion designers. As for Leah Rhodes, *Picture Mommy Dead* would be one of her last films. She retired the following year and died on October 17, 1986.

One evening in January at the home of actor George Hamilton, shortly before the start of filming, photographs were taken of Hedy made up and wearing the gown and jewels, so they could be used to create a portrait, important for the finale of the film. Hairstylist Joel Israel had created a short chic hairstyle for Hedy, and Bill Tuttle had taken care of her makeup. Afterwards everyone went out for a celebratory dinner.

But something happened to Hedy soon after this photo session, on Thursday, January 27. Accompanied by her business manager, Earl Mills, Hedy was unceremoniously arrested for shoplifting at the May Company department store in Los Angeles.

Filming for *Picture Mommy Dead* was scheduled to begin immediately. Hedy's notoriety killed her participation in the project. Because the role demanded little dramatically from its character other than beauty, the part was given to Zsa Zsa Gabor, who squeezed herself into the Leah Rhodes gown at the last minute and smirked her way through the film. The picture ended up a mess and a financial fiasco when it was released later in the year.

Hedy's film career was effectively over. Throughout the subsequent court proceeding, which eventually acquitted her, Hedy was supported by old Hollywood friends like Lucille Ball, and new friends like young actor/writer Robert Osborne. A day-by-day accounting of the trial is chronicled in *Beautiful: The Life of Hedy Lamarr*. It was a tragedy that such a huge and important star would be dragged through the tabloids as she was.

But worse events were still to come.

The following year Hedy's memoir *Ecstasy and Me* was published by Bartholomew House, with Fawcett Publications given the paperback rights. On October 3, 1966, the book hit the stands, effectively killing Hedy Lamarr's reputation in Hollywood.

Ghostwritten by Leo Guild, from Hedy's tape-recorded interviews conducted by Cy Rice, *Ecstasy and Me* is filled with passages of actual Hollywood history, clearly recognizable in Hedy's voice, combined with fictionalized sexual exploits, fabricated to sell the book. Hedy, paid an advance, never read the manuscript before it went to press.

273

According to Robert Osborne, who was with Hedy when she read it for the first time, "she was shocked by it. But that was the foolish side of her. She wanted money." Osborne sighed, adding, "They simply made up passages in that book and she allowed them to. It was her own fault she let them do that. . . . It was part of her capriciousness." [5]

Hedy sued to halt the distribution of the book, but failed. She was in court over the next several years, trying to make it go away.

In 1967, her life and film career in Hollywood over, Hedy moved to New York. Years later, perhaps to justify the move, she said that she had relocated because she did not feel safe in

Hedy Lamarr, c. 1970.

California after the Manson murders (which didn't happen until August of 1969). In reality Hedy was fleeing from her Hollywood life in the spotlight.

As she aged her eyesight began to fade. It was somewhat restored by surgeries in the 1970s. Still attractive, she dated Dr. Herbert Ross, former husband of actress Glenda Farrell, in 1971. In New York she had many affairs, including a lengthy romance with another Manhattan doctor, and a significant relationship with her romantic and financial benefactor, former US Navy commodore Thomas McGlaughlan. Hedy attended more social events as her confidence and financial situation improved, because of her lover's support. In the mid-1970s Hedy also started undergoing a series of plastic surgeries, which for the most part were unsuccessful.

In 1981, as her romantic affairs in New York were ending, one after the other, Hedy met New Yorkers Larry and Arlene Roxbury in Miami, on the beach. They became friends, and she would visit them regularly at their Long Island home, sometimes staying with them for weeks at a time. Hedy eventually moved to Florida in 1987, where she preferred the weather. New York had ultimately proven to be a vast disappointment for her, both romantically and financially. (She could no longer afford to remain in Manhattan once her affair with "The Commodore" had ended.)

Living on a modest income, Hedy soon retired from public view. Her surgeries had transformed her appearance drastically. In Florida she enjoyed a quiet retirement out of the limelight.

Hedy's son James had wed Ona Minor in 1967, and fathered four children. For many years he was a policeman in Milwaukee. Sometime in the

Hedy Lamarr's final resting place in Wiener Zentralfriedhof Cemetery, Vienna, Austria.

mid-1980s James and Hedy would reconnect, maintaining a respectful bittersweet relationship via telephone.

Hedy's beautiful daughter Denise gave birth to a baby girl she named Wendy in 1966. She would divorce first husband Larry Colton in 1970. After a brief second marriage, Denise wed Vincent DeLuca, a commercial real estate investor in Seattle, in 1987. Son

THE BEAUTY OF HEDY LAMARR

Anthony, or Tony, as he was called, had studied to be an actor, and even appeared in a play on Broadway. Tall and handsome like his absentee father, he gave up acting to become an artist and filmmaker. Tony married briefly in 1966 only to divorce in 1968. Then in 1970 he wed Dominique Rongier, and the couple had three children, daughter Lodi, and sons Andrew and Thomas. They divorced in 1982, the year he founded PhonesUSA in Los Angeles, a business specializing in information technology. His third marriage to Lise Marie Verzotti in 1987 produced their son, Max.

Hedy's life in Florida was quiet. She had settled originally in Miami Beach's North Bay Village. As her health declined she moved to a second-floor, two-bedroom condo in the Sandy Cove Condominium in Altamonte Springs, north of Orlando. There was yet another unsavory shoplifting event on August 1, 1991, when Hedy was arrested at a drugstore in Casselberry, Florida. Charged for taking without paying some $21.48 in personal health-care items, Hedy once again made embarrassing news. The charges were mercifully dismissed.

But she became more reclusive, to such an extent that she did not go out in public anymore. Hedy befriended select people but unfortunately denied even her family visits. Fritz Mandl, with whom she had kept in touch throughout the years, died in 1977, in South America. Gene Markey died in 1980. John Loder passed away in 1988, and Teddy Stauffer died in 1991. Howard Lee died in 1981. Hedy's last husband, Lewis Boies Jr., passed away in 2012. Hedy's mother Trude died quietly on February 27, 1977, while living her last years with Anthony and his family.

The last decade of Hedy Lamarr's life, the 1990s, would prove to be a revelation for her and the world upon the recognition of a long-forgotten patent of such importance and magnitude that its significance quite literally changed the world.

Hedy Lamarr's true legacy would finally be recognized.

Opposite page: Hedy Lamarr. Metro-Goldwyn-Mayer, c. 1942.

Aug. 11, 1942.   H. K. MARKEY ET AL   2,292,387

SECRET COMMUNICATION SYSTEM

Filed June 10, 1941   2 Sheets–Sheet 1

Aug. 11, 1942.   H. K. MARKEY ET AL   2,292,387

SECRET COMMUNICATION SYSTEM

Filed June 10, 1941   2 Sheets–Sheet 2

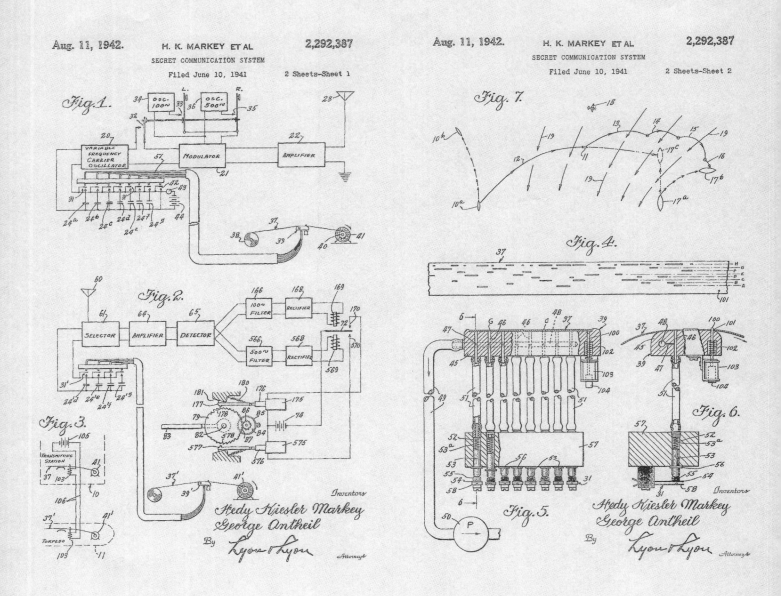

Hedy Kiesler Markey–George Antheil "Secret Communications" Patent. (Courtesy of the United States Patent and Trademark Office)

chapter 13

LEGACY: THE DICHOTOMY OF BEAUTY AND BRAINS

hen in June 1940 Hedy Lamarr was one of two guests at a small dinner at the home of Metro-Goldwyn-Mayer fashion designer Gilbert Adrian and his wife Janet Gaynor, it was with the distinct purpose of meeting avant-garde musical composer George Antheil. Hedy was eager to meet and talk with the man for various reasons, one of which was because of her quest for intelligent minds to complement her own. Hedy had just completed her work with Clark Gable in *Boom Town*, and was set to begin work in *Comrade X*, again with Gable, at the end of the month.

Born on July 9, 1900, in New Jersey, George Antheil was famously remembered for his amazing cacophonous musical work *Ballet Mécanique*, a 1924 musical piece he composed to accompany a silent sixteen-minute, 35mm, avant-garde film produced by Dudley Murphy, Fernand Leger, and Man Ray. For this presentation

Antheil had devised a fascinating musical score originally intended for a player piano (also known as a pianola), synchronized with the film. Antheil expanded on the piece over the years, extending it to thirty minutes in length, with the inclusion of doorbells, automobile horns, and airplane propellers, and later jet engines. *Ballet Mécanique* debuted in Vienna in 1924 by arrangement of Frederick John Kiesler, who ironically was Hedy's father's second cousin.

As far as Adrian and Janet Gaynor were concerned, the original purpose of that fateful meeting in June of 1940 was for Hedy to engage in conversation with Antheil regarding her bosom. Long before the era of breast augmentation, Hedy had been pressured by Louis B. Mayer, her boss at Metro, to consider ways to increase her bustline. To that end, she casually read three articles in *Esquire* magazine about just that. All of the articles were written by George Antheil, who as an avocation had studied the then-popular idea of human glands affecting human psychology. His 1936 *Esquire* articles, "Glands on a Hobby Horse," "Glandbook for the Questing Male," and "The Glandbook in Practical Use," delved into the issue of glandular alteration by hormonal injection. In 1937 he penned a book, *Every Man His Own Detective: A Study of Glandular Criminology*, to advocate his theories.

Hedy had another reason to speak to Antheil; she wanted to know what he thought about the war in Europe, and in particular, whether he had concerns about America's inevitable entry into it. In November 1939 Antheil wrote a most prophetic *Esquire* article titled "Germany Never Had a Chance," which he expanded into a novel the following year and published anonymously. *The Shape of the War to Come* was set in 1950, and as I wrote in *Beautiful: The Life of Hedy Lamarr*, "Anticipating the coming conflict with Germany, Antheil predicted with uncanny accuracy the events of World War II and its outcome, including Hitler's defeat." [1]

Antheil's younger brother Henry, born on September 23, 1912, was a clerk with the US legation in Helsinki. Serving as a diplomatic courier and carrying several pouches designated for US legations in Tallinn and Riga, he boarded a Finnish passenger plane

on June 14, 1940, the week before George and Hedy met. It was shot down ten minutes later by two Soviet bombers over the Gulf of Finland, near Tallinn, Estonia.

That night at the dinner, Antheil was mourning the loss of his brother. Because of his work in Hollywood, Antheil's wife Boski had flown out east to be with his grieving parents. Antheil was set to score *Angels Over Broadway* with Rita Hayworth and Douglas Fairbanks Jr. for Columbia, gearing up to commence shooting on June 20. That evening of the dinner at Adrian's, Hedy was prompt and on time for cocktails. Antheil, however, arrived late; they'd finished the appetizers and dinner had already begun.

Excusing himself to his hosts and Hedy, eventually conversation got around to Hedy's breasts. As told in both Antheil's own autobiography, *Bad Boy of Music*, and my biography of Lamarr, the discussion on the size of her breasts was more or less just a ploy for Hedy to meet the eccentric composer. They enjoyed their time together, and when Hedy left early, she scrawled her name and phone number in lipstick on Antheil's car windshield.

Antheil did contact Hedy, and they met for dinner the following evening at Hedy's home atop Benedict Canyon. It must be said that their subsequent meetings were not of a romantic or sexual nature at all. Antheil was grieving the loss of his brother, and he was very much a married man and the father of two boys. Hedy, a single mother with a young boy as well, was not attracted to short men, nor did she deliberately seek out lovers who were already married. Their relationship was strictly intellectual.

Before that evening at Hedy's home was over they had latched on to a serious discussion of the coming war. Both were keenly patriotic, even though Hedy would not become a naturalized US citizen until the 1950s. George was extremely distraught and angered over the loss of his brother because of the conflict in Europe, and Hedy for her part was anxious to see her mother brought to the United States.

Military weaponry in the early part of the war was less than efficient for both the fascists and the Allies. After a Nazi torpedo was embedded in the side of the Holland America liner *Volendam* in the North Atlantic in September 1939, it was found to be a

dud. Refugee children were on board that ship, and had it exploded, many lives would have been lost.

Throughout her marriage to Fritz Mandl, Hedy had listened carefully at the dinner table as Fritz and his colleagues discussed the fascist leaders and their desire to develop wireless communication to advance and control the destruction of their weaponry. Though the Nazis never developed a way to implement such wireless communication, engineers at Mandl's munitions factory did play with the possibilities. Hedy may not have had any tangible information regarding the practical application of wireless communication to share with the US government when war broke out in Europe, but she *knew* that the fascists were searching for just that breakthrough.

Hedy believed she had insight as to how war machinery might be improved through what she called "spread spectrum"—wireless communication. Her relationship with Howard Hughes had allowed her to explore her ideas for airplane design, combining the physical structures of the fastest birds and fastest fish, developing a curved wingspan instead of a straight design, which Hughes *did* develop for aircraft. Hughes called Hedy a genius for her ideas. He had also supplied her with a studio laboratory and two assistants to experiment with her other varied ideas, one of which was for a soda cube that could dissolve in water for the armed forces. (It proved to be a dud because of the varying quality of water available.)

For the war effort it was Hedy's idea to invent a system of radio transmission that would constantly change frequencies for wireless weaponry, making it difficult for the Axis powers to decode. Hedy had figured out a way to jam interference of a radio-controlled torpedo through the idea of a mechanism similar to that of the Philco Magic Box of 1939, a top-of-the-line remote-control device then on the market for home radios. She had sketched the box in her spiral notebook, detailing it for the patent she sought with Antheil. By changing the frequency of the radio transmission, whether from air, land, or sea, to the torpedo—frequency hopping, in other words—she believed one could secure the radio transmission.

To this end, she suggested to Antheil that combining her ideas with his musical and mechanical understanding of the eighty-eight-key piano roll, together they might be able to invent a device that would enable a torpedo to deliver its destruction without interception, avoiding the enemy. Using the idea of two piano player rolls, they could possibly activate radio transmission from the ship simultaneously with that of the torpedo and coordinate the frequencies. (Many of the technical aspects of this design are detailed in Rob Walters's masterful book *Spread Spectrum: Hedy Lamarr and the Mobile Phone.*)

Hedy and Antheil worked on three inventions together that were meant to fight the Axis powers. Interestingly, during this period of development of the Lamarr Antheil device, Hedy was at her most prolific as an actress, working on four major motion pictures back to back. She truly became a pest to Antheil, calling him in the middle of the night with ideas, and prodding him continuously to expedite the process of getting the plan into operation.

Thus, these two unlikely people—Hedy Lamarr, glamorous leading lady of Hollywood films, and George Antheil, eccentric music composer and writer—designed and developed what became known as the Hedy Kiesler Markey–George Antheil "Secret Communications" patent, #2,292,387, which they eventually filed with the National Inventors Council in Washington, DC, on June 10, 1941, after recommendation from Charles Kettering and Samuel Stuart Mackowen at Cal-Tech.

The patent was granted for their Secret Communications System on August 11, 1942. Hedy and Antheil gave it to the US Navy. Considered top secret and referred to by Colonel L. B. Bent as a "red hot" idea, it was not used during the war because the government had no idea how to further develop it. Because of its importance it was filed away and seized in 1942 as being the concept of an "enemy alien," meaning it had come from a citizen outside the United States. (Again, Hedy would not become a US citizen until 1953.)

Stunned by the government's decision to forego further development of their idea, Hedy volunteered her services to the Inventors Council, going so far as to tell Louis B. Mayer that she would prefer to leave films and move to Washington, DC, and work for the government herself. He instead advised her that her place was still at Metro, and

that participation in war bond tours would prove more beneficial. As Hedy attended war bond rallies to fulfill her patriotism, the Hedy Kiesler Markey–George Antheil patent remained locked away.

In 1959, the same year George Antheil died, the patent expired. It had not been renewed, and thus no money was made by either Hedy or Antheil. However, in later years it was discovered that in 1955 an early application to use the patent came from contractor Sir Romuald Ireneus Scibor-Marchocki (1926–2010). He utilized the patent in the design of one of the first devices to deploy the technology, the Sonobuoy, which relayed messages through frequency hopping to passing naval vessels. It was further used in the creation of surveillance drones. "The Secret Communications System saw use in the 1950s during the development of CDMA network technology in the private sector, while the Navy officially adopted the technology in the 1960s," confirmed Jesse Kratz. [2]

With the advent of transistor radios and other methods of wireless transmission around the world, by October 1962, during the Cuban Missile Crisis, Hedy and Antheil's invention was already in practical use, allowing communications between US Navy vessels without the threat of Soviet interception. Later in the 1960s the patent was further utilized in the advancement in design of military armaments in Vietnam. Eventually the patent became the nucleus of every wireless communication device, from GPS to secure Wi-Fi and Bluetooth, from the billion-dollar expansion of military satellites and the US Milstar military communications system to current-day mobile phone systems.

Recognition for Hedy Lamarr for her contributions to science was slow in coming. For the May 1990 issue of *Forbes* magazine, writer Fleming Meeks, who had interviewed Hedy extensively, published a definitive article that for the first time fully acknowledged Hedy's and George Antheil's scientific contribution to modern technology. In 1997 Hedy and Antheil were awarded the prestigious Pioneer Award at the Electronics Frontier Foundation (the Computers, Freedom, and Privacy Conference). That same year TRW, Lockheed Martin, and the US Air Force awarded Hedy the Milstar Award. According to electrical engineer and spread spectrum historian Robert Price in 1998, the Hedy Kiesler Markey–George Antheil patent was "the generic invention—the first

in the field" of such technology. [3] Hedy was also awarded the Viktor Kaplan medal of invention in 1998.

Hedy's recognition came just three years before her death. Around the world her birth date, November 9, is recognized as International Science Day. In India November 9 is actually called Hedy Lamarr Day. Scientists have acknowledged Hedy Lamarr as having possessed "one of the most brilliant minds of the twentieth century," recognizing the true legacy of her lifetime accomplishment. No other film star has left behind not only a canon of impressive film work, but also the gift of a scientific invention that impacts the entire world with its pioneering technology. "It was the one thing she did for others that she wanted to be remembered for a long, long time," stated her friend Robert Osborne in the definitive 2017 PBS *American Masters* feature documentary *Bombshell: The Hedy Lamarr Story*.

The only financial compensation Hedy Lamarr ever received for their invention was a multimillion-dollar out-of-court settlement in 1999 from the Canadian technology company Corel, which used her image on their labeling without her permission. Hedy died quietly, and comfortably well off, in her home in Casselberry, Florida, on January 19, 2000.

Hedy Lamarr once stated in 1970, "I am always Austrian." In her later years she reminisced frequently about her Austria, and especially, her cherished Vienna. Her children Anthony and Denise laid her to rest there, spreading part of her ashes in her beloved Vienna Woods. Hedy was home again, having given us her remarkable beauty on celluloid as well as a significant, world-changing technology.

Because of the glory of cinema, the exquisite vision of actress Hedy Lamarr still radiates glamour and style in movie after movie from the 1930s to the 1950s. Yet there was so much more to Hedy Lamarr than just her celluloid image. As author Annette Tapert wrote in her book *The Power of Glamour*, "[The] concept of glamour is not, in the end, reducible to fashion and cosmetics—it's about the woman herself." [4]

ACTING APPEARANCES

For a more-comprehensive list of Hedy Lamarr's acting appearances, please see my book, *Beautiful: The Life of Hedy Lamarr* (Thomas Dunne / St. Martin's Press-Macmillan, 2010).

Stage

Das schwache Geschlecht (The Weaker Sex), Deutsches Theater, Berlin, December 1930. Staged by Max Reinhardt; assistant director, Otto Preminger; written by Édouard Bourdet. *Cast*: Hedy Kiesler (2nd American Girl).

Das schwache Geschlecht (The Weaker Sex), Theater in der Josefstadt, Vienna, 1931. Staged by Max Reinhardt; assistant director, Otto Preminger; written by Édouard Bourdet. *Cast*: Joseph Schildkraut (?), George Weller (An American Man), Hedy Kiesler (2nd American Girl).

Private Lives, Theater in der Josefstadt, Vienna, 1931. Staged by Max Reinhardt; assistant director, Otto Preminger; written by Noël Coward. *Cast*: George Weller (Victor Prynne), Hedy Kiesler (Sibyl Chase).

Intimitäten (Intimacies), Vienna, 1931 or 1932. *Cast*: Hedy Kiesler.

Sissy, Theater an der Wien, Vienna, December 1932. Staged by Otto Langer; produced by Hubert Marischka; written by Ernst and Hubert Marischka, based on the comedy by Ernst Decsey and Gustav Holm; music by Fritz Kreisler; musical director, Anton Panlik; women's costumes by Lillian; shoes loaned by Leopold Jellinek; jewelry loaned by R. Fleischer; men's and Vienna opera ballet costumes by Alfred Kunz; ballet under the direction of Hedy Pfundmayr from the state opera; set decorator, Ferdinand Moser, carried out in the workshops of the Theater an der Wien; Davison managers Marie Skreischofsky and Alois Strommer; choreography, Camillo Feleky; dance master, Budapest; film sequence between acts painted and animated by Lotte Reiniger; tapestries by Wr. Gobeline-Manufaktur, Hofburg; stage manager, Hubert Marischka-Karezag.

Cast: Hans Jaray (Franz Joseph, Emperor of Austria), Paula Fiedler (Archduchess Sophie, Empress of Austria), Hubert Marischka (Duke Max of Bavaria), Traute Carlson (Ludovika "Luise," his wife), Maria Tauber (Helene "Rene"), Hedy Kysler [Kiesler] (Elisabeth "Sissy"), Kl. Bartelmus (Karl Theodore "Gackl"), Kl. Leitner (Sophie "Spats"), Kl.

287

Wytek (Rupprecht), Kl. Wrede (Annemarie), Kl. Wilhemede (Maxmilian), Ernst Arndt (Field Marshal Count Radezky), Otto Maran (Prince Thurn-Taxis), Rudolf Carl (Master of Ceremony), Hermann Lenau (Count Creneville, aide de camp von Kempten), Vinzenz Kaiser (Prince Menschilow, envoy of the Czar), Irene V. Zilahy (Jlona Barady, ballet dancer), Edi Holm (Ballet Master, Vienna Opera), Felix Dombrowsky (Petzelberger, *Zum goldenen Ochsen* innkeeper), Ada Klement (Zenzi, waitress), Leopold Wallinger (Peter, manservant), Erich Kaufmann (Watchman), Ludwig Herold (Policeman), Paul von Hernreid (Paul Henreid).

(*Sissy* opened in Vienna in December 1932 starring Paula Wessely in the title role. Hedy Kiesler took over the title role in March 1933. When she left the production at the end of the summer 1933, the role was assumed by Rose Stradner.)

Feature Films

Geld auf der Strasse (Money on the Street), Sascha-Felsom Films, 85 minutes, released December 29, 1930. Producer, Nicolas Deutsch; director, Georg Jacoby; screenplay, Rudolf Osterreicher, Friedrich Raff, Julius Urgiss; based on a play by Rudolph Bernauer and Rudolf Oesterreicher; musical score, Stefan Weiss; cinematography, Nicolas Farkas.

Songs: "*Lach mich nicht, weil ich Dir so true bin!*" and "*Mir ist alles einerlei ganz einerlen,*" by Peter Herz and Stefan Weiss.

Cast: Lydia Pollman (Dodo), Georg Alexander (Peter Paul Lutz), Rosa Albach-Retty (Lona Reimnacher), Hans Moser (Albin Jensch), Hugo "Hans" Thimig (Max Kesselberg), Harry Payer (singer in the Carlton Bar), Hedwig Kiesler (young girl at nightclub table).

Sturm im Wasserglas (Storm in a Water Glass), Sascha-Felsom Films, 70 minutes, released April 21, 1931. Producer, director, Georg Jacoby; screenplay, Walter Wassermann, W. Schlee, Felix Salten; cinematography, Guido Seeber, Bruno Timm.

Cast: Hansi Niese (Frau Vogel), Renate Müller (Viktoria), Paul Otto (Dr. Thoss), Harald Paulsen (Burdach), Hedy Kiesler (Burdach's secretary).

(Note: This film is also known as *Die Blumenfrau von Lindenau* in Germany, and *The Flower Woman of Lindenau* in English-speaking countries.)

Die Koffer des Herrn O.F. (The Trunks of Mr. O.F.), Tobis-Klangfilm Production, 80 minutes, released December 2, 1931. Producers, Hans Conradi, Mark Asarow; director, Alexis Granowsky; screenplay, Leo Lania, Alexis Granowsky; costumes, Edward Suhr; cinematography, Reimar Kuntz, Heinrich Balasch.

Songs: "Hausse-Song," "Cabaret Song," "Barcarole," *"Die Kleine Ansprache,"* and "Schluss-song"; music by Dr. Karl Rathaus, lyrics by Erich Kastner.

Cast: Alfred Abel (The Mayor), Peter Lorre (Stix), Harald Paulsen (Stark), Hedy Kiesler (Helene, the Mayor's daughter), Ludwig Stössel (Brunn), Margo Lion (Viola Volant), Alfred Döderlein (Alexander), Aribert Mog (Stark's assistant), The Wild Harmonists, and Jack's Laughing Girls.

Wir Brauchen kein Geld (We Need No Money), Allianz-Tonfilm Productions, 92 minutes, February 2, 1932. Producers, Arnold Pressburger, Dr. Wilhelm Szekely; director, Karl Boese; screenplay, Karl Noti, Hans Wilhelm; cinematography, Willy Goldberger; costumes, Margarete Scholz and still photographer, Rudi Brix.

Cast: Heinz Rühmann (Heinz Schmidt), Hedy Kiesler (Kathe Brandt), Hans Moser (Thomas Hoffmann), Ida Wüst (Frau Brandt), Hans Junkermann (Herr Brandt), Kurt Gerron (Bank President), and Lilia Skala.

(Note: This film is also known as *Man Brach kein Geld* in Germany, and *His Majesty, King Ballyhoo* in English-speaking countries.)

Symphonie der Liebe (Symphony of Love), Elekta Film Production, 85 minutes, January 20, 1933. Executive producers, Frantisek Horky, Moritz Grunhut; producer, Gustav Machaty for Elekta Film AG; executive producer, Otto Sonnenfeld; director, Gustav Machaty; screenplay, Gustav Machaty, Frantisek "Franz" Horky, Vitezslav Nezval; musical score, Dr. Josef "Guiseppe" Becce, Walter Kiesow; cinematography, Jan Stallich, Hans Androschin; photography, Josef Staetter, Herr Stal. Filmed at the AB Vinohrady, Prague; Schonbrunn Atelier, Vienna.

Cast: Hedy Kiesler (Eva Hermann), Zvonimir Rogoz (Emil), Aribert Mog (Adam), Leopold Kramer (Eva's father).

(Note: This film is also known as *Ekstase* in Germany, and *Ecstasy* in English-speaking countries.)

Algiers, United Artists release of a Walter Wanger Production, 95 minutes, released May 23, 1938. Producer, Walter Wanger; director, John Cromwell; musical score by Vincent Scotto and Muhammed Ygner Buchen; lyricist, Ann Ronell; costumes, Omar Kiam and Irene (for Ms. Lamarr); hairstylist, Nina Roberts; cinematography, James Wong Howe; still photography, Robert Coburn.

Cast: Charles Boyer (Pépé le Moko), Hedy Lamarr (Gaby), Sigrid Gurie (Ines), Joseph Calleia (Slimane), Gene Lockhart (Regis), Johnny Downs (Pierrot), Alan Hale (Grandpère).

Lady of the Tropics, Metro-Goldwyn-Mayer, 91 minutes, released August 11, 1939. Producer, Sam Zimbalist; director, Jack Conway, Leslie Fenton (uncredited); screenplay, Ben Hecht; costumes and gowns, Adrian; men's costumes, Valles; musical score, Franz Waxman; cinematography, George Folsey, Norbert Brodine (uncredited); still photographer, Clarence Sinclair Bull.

Song: "Each Time You Say Goodbye (I Die a Little)" by Phil Ohlman and Foster Carlin.

Cast: Robert Taylor (Bill Carey), Hedy Lamarr (Manon DeVargnes), Joseph Schildkraut (Pierre Delaroch), Gloria Franklin (Nina).

I Take This Woman, Metro-Goldwyn-Mayer, 96 minutes, released January 26, 1940. Producers, Lawrence Weingarten, Louis B. Mayer, James K. McGuiness, Bernard H. Hyman; director, W. S. (Woodbridge Strong) Van Dyke II, Josef von Sternberg, Frank Borzage; screenplay, James Kevin McGuiness, Charles MacArthur, Ben Hecht; based on a story by Charles MacArthur; musical score, Bronislau Kaper, Arthur Guttmann (Artur Guttmann); costumes and gowns, Adrian; cinematography, Harold Rosson, Bud Lawton Jr.; still photographer, Clarence Sinclair Bull.

Cast: Spencer Tracy (Dr. Karl Decker), Hedy Lamarr (Georgi Gragore), Verrée Teasdale (Madame Maresca), Kent Taylor (Phil Mayberry), Mona Barrie (Sandra Mayberry), Paul Cavanaugh (Bill Rodgers), Jack Carson (Joe), Louis Calhern (Dr. Martin Sumner Duveen), Laraine Day (Linda Rodgers), Reed Hadley (Bob Hampton), Frances Drake (Lola Estermonte), Marjorie Main (Gertie).

Starring cast: for Josef von Sternberg (1938): Fanny Brice (Madame Maresca), Walter Pidgeon (Phil Mayberry),

Starring cast: for Frank Borzage (1938/1939): Ina Claire (Madame Maresca), Walter Pidgeon (Phil Mayberry), Adrienne Ames (Linda Rodgers), Leonard Penn (Bob Hampton) (Note: This film was also known as *A New York Cinderella*.)

Boom Town, Metro-Goldwyn-Mayer, 119 minutes, released August 30, 1940. Producer, Sam Zimbalist; director Jack Conway; screenplay, John Lee Mahin, based on the short story "A Lady Comes to Burkburnett" by James Edward Grant; costumes and gowns, Adrian, Gile Steele; hairstylist, Sydney Guilaroff; makeup artists, Robert J. Schiffer; musical score, Franz Waxman; cinematographer, Harold Rosson, Elwood Bredell.

Cast: Clark Gable (Big John Masters), Spencer Tracy (Square John Sand), Claudette Colbert (Betsy Bartlett), Hedy Lamarr (Karen Vanmeer), Frank Morgan (Luther Aldrich), Lionel Atwill (Harry Compton), Chill Wills (Harmony Jones).

Comrade X, Metro-Goldwyn-Mayer, 87 minutes, released December 3, 1940. Producer, Gottfried Reinhardt; director, King Vidor; screenplay, Ben Hecht, Charles Lederer, Herman J. Mankiewicz (uncredited); women's costumes and gowns, Adrian; men's costumes, Gile Steele; makeup, Jack Dawn; musical score, Bronislau Kaper; cinematographer, Joseph Ruttenberg; special night photography, Karl Freund (uncredited).

Songs: "Funiculi Funicula," lyricists, Peppino Turco and Luigi Denza; "To Vania," arranged by Bronislau Kaper; "Buriel Chant," music by Bronislau Kaper, lyrics by Andrei Tolstoy; "We Are Free," music by Bronislau Kaper, lyrics by Andrei Tolstoy.

Cast: Clark Gable (McKinley B. "Mac" Thompson), Hedy Lamarr (Theodore Yahupitz, "Lizzie"), Oscar Homolka (Commissar Vasiliev), Felix Bressart (Igor Yahupitz, "Vanya"), Eve Arden (Jane Wilson), Sig Rumann (Emil von Hofer), Natasha Lytess (Olga Milanava), Vladimir Sokoloff (Michael Bastakoff).

Come Live with Me, Metro-Goldwyn-Mayer, 86 minutes, released January 29, 1941. Producer-director, Clarence Brown; screenplay, Patterson McNutt; based on a story by Virginia Van Upp; musical score, Herbert Stothart; lyricists, Christopher Marlowe "Come

Live with Me," Ed Rose, "Oh Johnny, Oh Johnny"; gowns and costumes, Adrian; cinematography, George J. Folsey.

Cast: James Stewart (Bill Smith), Hedy Lamarr (Johanna Janns [Johnny Jones]), Ian Hunter (Barton Kendrick), Verree Teasdale (Diana Kendrick), Adeline de Walt Reynolds (Grandma).

Ziegfeld Girl, Metro-Goldwyn-Mayer, 133 minutes, released April 17, 1941. Producer, Pandro S. Berman; director, Robert Z. Leonard; musical numbers staged by Busby Berkeley; specialty dance sequence and ensemble dance direction, Danny Darel; screenplay, Marguerite Roberts, Sonya Levien, Annalee Whitmore, based on a story by William Anthony McGuire; musical score, Herbert Stothart; musical director, costumes and gowns, Adrian; makeup, Jack Dawn; hairstylist, Larry Germain; cinematography, Ray June, Joseph Ruttenberg.

Songs: "You Stepped Out of a Dream," music and lyrics by Gus Kahn and Nacio Herb Brown; "Whispering," music and lyrics by John Schonberger, Richard Coburn, and Vincent Rose; "Mr. Gallagher and Mr. Shean," music and lyrics by Edward Gallagher and Al Shean; "I'm Always Chasing Rainbows," music and lyrics by Joseph McCarthy and Harry Carroll; "Caribbean Love Song," lyrics by Ralph Freed and music by Roger Edens; "The Kids from Seville," music and lyrics by Antonio and Rosario; "You Never Looked So Beautiful Before," music and lyrics by Walter Donaldson (from MGM's *The Great Ziegfeld*, 1936); "Minnie From Trinidad," "Ziegfeld Girls," and "Laugh? I Thought I'd Split My Sides," music and lyrics by Roger Edens; "You Gotta Pull Strings," music and lyrics by Harold Adamson and Walter Donaldson (from MGM's *The Great Ziegfeld*, 1936), "Too Beautiful to Last" and "We Must Have Music," both cut from final film. Filmed in sepia.

Cast: James Stewart (Gilbert "Gil" Young), Judy Garland (Susan Gallagher), Hedy Lamarr (Sandra Kolter), Lana Turner (Sheila "Red" Regan, later Hale), Tony Martin (Frank Merton), Jackie Cooper (Jerry Regan), Ian Hunter (Geoffrey Collis), Charles Winninger (Ed "Pop" Gallagher), Edward Everett Horton (Noble Sage), Philip Dorn (Franz Kolter), Paul Kelly (John Slayton), Eve Arden (Patsy Dixon), Dan Dailey, Jr. (Jimmy

Walters), Al Shean (Himself), Fay Holden (Mrs. Regan), Felix Bressart (Mischa), Rose Hobart (Mrs. Merton).

H. M. Pulham, Esq., Metro-Goldwyn-Mayer, 119 minutes, December 3, 1941. Producer-director, King Vidor; costumes and gowns, Robert Kalloch; men's costumes, Gile Steele; wardrobe men, Bill Beatty; wardrobe women, Myrtle Gallagher; makeup, Jack Dawn; makeup man, Jack Young; hairstylist, Edith Keon; cinematography, Ray June; still photographer, Jimmy Manatt.

Songs: "Three O'Clock in the Morning," music by Julian Robeldo, lyrics by Dorothy Terriss, "The Wedding March" from *A Midsummer's Night Dream*, by Felix Mendelssohn-Bartholdy, "The Bridal Chorus" by Richard Wagner, "The Band Played On" by John E. Palmer.

Cast: Robert Young (Harry Pulham Jr.), Hedy Lamarr (Marvin Myles Ransome), Ruth Hussey (Kay Motford Pulham), Charles Coburn (Mr. Harry Pulham Sr.), Van Heflin (Bill King), Fay Holden (Mrs. Pulham), John Raitt (Soldier), Ava Gardner (Young socialite at the wedding, back row).

Tortilla Flat, Metro-Goldwyn-Mayer, 105 minutes, released April 21, 1942. Producer, Sam Zimbalist; director, Victor Fleming; fill-in director, Sam Zimbalist; screenplay, John Lee Mahin, Benjamin Glazer; based on the novel *Tortilla Flat* by John Steinbeck; musical score, Franz Waxman; gowns and costumes, Robert Kalloch; men's costumes, Gile Steele; makeup, Jack Dawn; cinematography, Karl Freund, Harold Rosson, Sidney Wagner; Monterey exteriors cinematography, Jack Smith.

Song: "Ay, Paisano!" music by Franz Waxman, lyrics by Frank Loesser.

Cast: Spencer Tracy (Pilon); Hedy Lamarr (Dolores "Sweets" Ramirez); John Garfield (Danny Alvarez); Frank Morgan ("The Pirate"), Akim Tamiroff (Pablo); Sheldon Leonard (Tito Ralph).

Crossroads, Metro-Goldwyn-Mayer, 83 minutes, July 23, 1942. Producer, Edwin Knopf; director, Jack Conway; screenplay, Guy Trosper and Frederick Kohner; gowns and costumes, Robert Kalloch; makeup, Jack Dawn; cinematography, Joseph Ruttenberg.

Song: "Till You Return," music by Arthur Schwartz, lyrics by Howard Dietz.

293

Cast: William Powell (David Talbot), Hedy Lamarr (Lucienne Talbot), Claire Trevor (Michelle Allaine), Basil Rathbone (Henri Sarrou), Felix Bressart (Dr. Andre Tessier), Margaret Wycherly (Mme. Pelletier), Reginald Owen (Concierge).

White Cargo, Metro-Goldwyn-Mayer, 89 minutes, September 20, 1942. Producer, Victor Saville; director, Richard Thorpe; screenplay, Leon Gordon, based on his play *White Cargo*, based on the novel *Hell's Playground* by Ida Vera Simonton; musical score, Bronislau Kaper; makeup, Jack Dawn; hairstylist, Eadie Hubner; native costumes, Robert Kalloch; cinematography, Harry Stradling.

Song: "Tondelayo," music by Vernon Duke, lyrics by Howard Dietz.

Cast: Hedy Lamarr (Tondelayo), Walter Pidgeon (Harry Witzel), Frank Morgan (Doctor), Richard Carlson (Langford), Reginald Owen (Skipper), Henry O'Neill (Reverend Roberts), Bramwell Fletcher (Wilbur Ashley).

The Heavenly Body, Metro-Goldwyn-Mayer, 93 minutes, March 23, 1944. Producer, Arthur Hornblow Jr.; director, Alexander Hall; fill-in director, Vincente Minelli; screenplay, Michael Arlen, Walter Reisch; based on a story by Jacques Thery, adapted by Harry Kurnitz; musical score, Bronislau Kaper; costumes, Irene; cinematography, Robert H. Planck, William H. Daniels.

Songs: "Happiness Is Just a Thing Called Joe," music by Harold Arlen, lyrics by E. Y. Harburg; "Hungarian Dance No.1 in G Minor," by Johannes Brahms; "I'm Dying for Someone to Love Me," unknown; "The Volga Boatman," unknown; "The Merry Widow Waltz" by Franz Lehar.

Cast: William Powell (Prof. William Stewart Whitley), Hedy Lamarr (Vicky Whitley), James Craig (Lloyd X. Hunter), Fay Bainter (Margaret Sibyll), Henry O'Neill (Professor Stowe), Spring Byington (Nancy Potter).

The Conspirators, Warner Brothers, 101 minutes, release October 21, 1944. Executive producer, Jack L. Warner; producer, Jack Chertok; director, Jean Negulesco; screenplay, Vladimir Pozner, Leo Rosten; based on a novel by Fredric [Frederic] Prokosch; gowns and costumes, Leah Rhodes; wardrobe, Mildred Duncan, Marie Pickering, Leon Roberts; makeup, Perc Westmore, Bill Cooley, Albert Greenway, Johnny Wallace; hairstylist,

Jean Burt Reilly; musical score, Max Steiner, Hugo Friedhofer; cinematography, Arthur Edeson; still photographer, Milton Gold.

Songs: "The Blue Danube Waltz, Opus 314," by Johann Strauss; "Maringa," music by Joubert de Carvalho; "Orchid Moon," music by Max Steiner, lyrics by Albert Stillman.

Cast: Hedy Lamarr (Irene Von Mohr), Paul Henreid (Vincent Van Der Lyn), Sydney Greenstreet (Ricardo Quintanilla), Peter Lorre (Jan Bernazsky), Victor Francen (Hugo Von Mohr), Joseph Calleia (Captain Pereira), Carol Thurston (Rosa).

Experiment Perilous, RKO Radio, 91 minutes, December 18, 1944. Executive producer, Robert Fellows; producer, Warren Duff; director Jacques Tourneur; screenplay, Warren Duff; based on the novel *Experiment Perilous* by Margaret Carpenter; costumes, gowns for Ms. Lamarr, Leah Rhodes; other gowns, Edward Stevenson; musical score, Roy Webb; cinematography, Tony Gaudio.

Cast: Hedy Lamarr (Allida Bedereaux), George Brent (Dr. Huntington Bailey), Paul Lukas (Nick Bedereaux), Albert Dekker ("Clag" Claghorne), Carl Esmond (John Maitland), Olive Blakeney (Clarissa "Cissie" Bedereaux), George N. Neise (Alec Gregory), Margaret Wycherly (Maggie).

Her Highness and the Bellboy, Metro-Goldwyn-Mayer, 112 minutes, September 11, 1945. Producer, Joe Pasternak; director, Richard Thorpe; screenplay, Richard Connell, Gladys Lehman; musical score, George (Georgie) E. Stoll; costumes, Irene; associate costumes, Marion Herwood Keyes; men's costumes, Valles; makeup, Jack Dawn; cinematography, Harry Stradling.

Songs: "Honey," music and lyrics by Seymour Simons, Haven Gillespie, and Richard A. Whiting; "Wait 'Til the Sun Shines, Nellie" music by Harry Von Tilzer, lyrics by Andrew B. Sterling; "The Fountain in the Park" ("Strolling Through the Park One Day"), music and lyrics by Ed Hailey; "dream" music and lyrics by Georgie Stoll and Calvin Jackson.

Cast: Hedy Lamarr (Princess Veronica), Robert Walker (Jimmy Dobson), June Allyson (Leslie Odell), Rags Ragland (Albert Weaver), Agnes Moorehead (Countess Zoe),

Carl Esmond (Baron Zoltan Faludi), Warner Anderson (Paul MacMillan), Ludwig Stossel (Mr. Pufi).

The Strange Woman, United Artists release of a Hunt Stromberg Production, 101 minutes, released October 25, 1946. Executive producers, Hedy Lamarr, Hunt Stromberg; producers, Jack Chertok, Eugen Schufftan; director, Edgar G. Ullmer; based on the novel *The Strange Woman* by Ben Ames Williams; costumes, Natalie Visart; hairstylist, Blanche Smith; makeup, Joseph Stinton; musical score, Carmen Dragon; cinematography, Lucien N. Andriot.

Cast: Hedy Lamarr (Jenny Hager), George Sanders (John Evered), Louis Hayward (Ephraim Poster), Gene Lockhart (Isaiah Poster), Hillary Brooke (Meg Saladine), Rhys Williams (Deacon Adams), June Storey (Lena Tempest), Moroni Olsen (Reverend Thatcher), Olive Blakeney (Mrs. Hollis).

Dishonored Lady, United Artists release of a Hunt Stromberg Production, 86 minutes, May 16, 1947. President, Hunt Stromberg; producer Jack Chertok; director, Robert Stevenson; screenplay, Edmund H. North; contributing writers, Andre de Toth, Ben Hecht; based on the stage play *Dishonored Lady* by Edward Sheldon and Margaret Ayer Barnes; gowns, Elois [Eloise] Jenssen; makeup, Joseph Stinton; hairstylist, Ruth Pursley; musical score, Carmen Dragon; cinematography, Lucien Andriot. Special thanks for Robert Stevenson to David O. Selznick.

Cast: Hedy Lamarr (Madeleine Damien), Dennis O'Keefe (Dr. David Cousins), John Loder (Felix Courtland), William Lundigan (Jack Garet), Morris Carnovsky (Dr. Caleb), Paul Cavanaugh (Victor Kranish), Natalie Schafer (Ethel Royce), Douglas Dumbrille (District Attorney), Margaret Hamilton (Mrs. Geiger, landlady).

Let's Live a Little, Eagle-Lion, 85 minutes, December 9, 1948. Producers, Eugene Frenke, Robert Cummings; screenplay, Howard Irving Young, Edmund L. Hartmann, Albert J. Cohen, Jack Harvey; based on an original story by Albert J. Cohen, Jack Harvey; costumes, Elois [Eloise] Jenssen; makeup, Ern Westmore, Joe Stinton; hairstylist, Joan St. Oegger, Helen Turpin; musical score, Werner R. Heymann; cinematography, Ernest Laszlo; still photographer, George Hommel.

Cast: Robert Cummings (Duke Crawford), Hedy Lamarr (Dr. J. O. Loring), Anna Sten (Michele Bennett), Robert Shayne (Dr. Richard Fields), Mary Treen (Miss Adams), Harry Antrim (James Montgomery), Hal K. Dawson (M.C.), Billy Bevan (Morton), Curt Bois (Chemist).

Samson and Delilah, Paramount, 121 minutes, December 21, 1949. Producer-director, Cecil B. De Mille; screenplay, Jesse L. Lasky, Jr., Frederic M. Frank; based on the story of Samson and Delilah in the Holy Bible, Judges 13-16, and *Judge and Fool* by Vladimir Jabotinsky; screen treatment by Harold Lamb and Vladimir Jabotinsky; musical score and director, Victor Young; women's costumes, Edith Head, Gus Peters, Gile Steele, Gwen Wakeling; men's costumes, Dorothy Jeakins; Miss Lamarr's costumes, Elois [Eloise] W. Jenssen; wardrobe, Frank Richardson, Pat Williams, Roger Weinberg, Frank Tait, Lloyd Ritchie, George Clark, Julie Cockerill, Hazel Haggerty, Sam Benson; makeup, Wally Westmore, Hal [Harold] Lierley, William Woods; hairstylist, Nellie Manley, Elaine Ramsey, Doris Clifford; hairstylist for Hedy Lamarr, Lenore Weaver; musical score, Victor Young; cinematography, George Barnes; still photographers, G. E. Richardson, Ed Henderson. Filmed in Technicolor.

Song: "Song of Delilah," music by Victor Young, lyrics by Ray Evans and Jay Livingston.

Cast: Hedy Lamarr (Delilah), Victor Mature (Samson), George Sanders (The Saran of Gaza), Angela Lansbury (Semadar), Henry Wilcoxon (Ahtur, military governor of Dan), Olive Deering (Miriam), Fay Holden (Hazel), Julia Faye (Hisham), Rusty [Russ] Tamblyn (Saul).

A Lady Without Passport, Metro-Goldwyn-Mayer, 74 minutes, August 18, 1950. Producer, Samuel Marx; director Joseph H. Lewis; screenplay, Howard Dimsdale; adapted by Cyril Hume; suggested by a story by Lawrence Taylor; musical score, David Raksin; costumes, Helen Rose; makeup creator, Jack Dawn; makeup, Gene Hibbs; hairstyle designs, Sydney Guilaroff; hairstylist, June Roberts; cinematography, Paul C. Vogel; still photographer, Sam C. Manatt.

Cast: Hedy Lamarr (Marianne Lorress), John Hodiak (Pete Karczag, "Joseph Gammush"), James Craig (Frank Westlake), George Macready (Palinov), Stephen Geray (Frenchman), Bruce Cowling (Archer Delby James).

Deleted scenes: James Whitmore and Peter Coe.

Copper Canyon, Paramount, 83 minutes, November 15, 1950. Producer, Mel Epstein; director, John Farrow; screenplay, Jonathan Latimer [Marquis Warren]; based on a story by Richard English; women's costumes, Edith Head; men's costumes, Gile Steele; makeup supervisor, Wally Westmore; makeup, Harold Lierley, Carl Silvera; hairstylist, Lenore Weaver; musical score, Daniele Amfitheatrof; choreography, Josephine Earl; cinematography, Charles B. Lang Jr.; still photography, Jack Koffman. Filmed in Technicolor.

Songs: "Copper Canyon" music by Ray Evans, lyrics by Jay Livingston; "Square Dance Calls," music by Phil Boutelje, lyrics by Les Gotcher.

Cast: Ray Milland (Johnny Carter), Hedy Lamarr (Lisa Roselle), MacDonald Carey (Lane Travis), Mona Freeman (Caroline Desmond), Harry Carey Jr. (Lieutenant Ord), Frank Faylen (Mullins), Hope Emerson (Ma Tarbet).

My Favorite Spy, Paramount, 93 minutes, December 25, 1951. Producer, Paul Jones; director, Norman Z. McLeod; screenplay, Edmund L. Hartmann, Jack Sher; adapted from a story by Edmund Beloin, Lou Breslow; costumes, Edith Head; makeup, Wally Westmore; musical score, Victor Young; cinematography, Victor Milner.

Songs: "I Wind Up Taking a Fall," music by Robert Emmett Dolan, lyrics by Johnny Mercer; and "Just a Moment More," music by Jay Livingston, lyrics by Ray Evans.

Cast: Bob Hope (Peanuts White/Eric Augustine), Hedy Lamarr (Lily Dalbrey), Francis L. Sullivan (Karl Brubaker), Arnold Moss (Tasso), Tonio Selwart (Harry Crock), [Alden] Stephen Chase (Donald Bailey), John Archer (Henderson), Morris Ankrum (General Fraser).

L'Amant de Paride, Cino Del Luca—P.C.E. Productions, 181 minutes, released 1953. Producer, Victor Phalen; associate director Edgar G. Ullmer; director, Marc Allegret; story and screenplay, Salka Viertel, Vadim Plemiennikov [Roger Vadim], Aeneas MacKenzie; costumes, Vittorio Nino Novarese; cinematography, Desmond Dickinson. Filmed in Technicolor. A Hedy Lamarr Production.

Cast of "The Face That Launched a Thousand Ships": Hedy Lamarr (Helen of Troy), Massimo Gerato (Paris), Sunrise Arnova (Venus), Elli Parvo (Juno), Cathy O'Donnell (Enone).

Cast of "Teatro Romani": Hedy Lamarr (Liala), Luigi Pavese (Romani), Girard Oury (Actor).

Cast of "*I cavalieri dell'illusione*": Hedy Lamarr (Genevieve de Brabant), Cesare Donova (Count Seigfride), Terence Morgan (Golo), Richard O'Sullivan (Benoni), John Fraser (Drago).

Cast of "Napoleon and Josephine": Hedy Lamarr (Empress Josephine), Girard Oury (Napoleon), Milly Vitale (Maria Luisa).

Released in Great Britain as *The Loves of Three Queens*. Edited to 97 minutes in 1955.

Narration: Hans Conried.

L'eterna femmina (Eternal Woman), Cino Del Luca—P.C.E. Productions, completed 1955. Producer, Victor Pahlen; director, Marc Allegret; screenplay, Nino Novarese, Marc Allegret; original music, Nino Roti; cinematography, Desmond Dickinson, Ferdinand Risi. Filmed in Technicolor.

Cast: Hedy Lamarr, Massimo Gerato: Franco Coop, Mino Doro, Lia Nitali, Andre Hildebrand, Anna Arena.

Film shut down in December 1954. It was eventually completed, but never released.

The Story of Mankind, Warner Brothers, 100 minutes, released October 23, 1957. Associate producer, George E. Swink; producer, Irwin Allen; director, Irwin Allen; screenplay, Irwin Allen, Charles Bennett; based on the book *The Story of Mankind* by Hendrik van Loon; art director, Art Loel; costumes, Marjorie Best; men's wardrobe, Ted Schultz; women's wardrobe, Florence Hackett; makeup, Ray Romero, Emile Lavigne; hairstylist, Margret Donovan; original music and musical director, Paul Sawtell; cinematography, Nick Musuraca; still photography, Pat Clark. Filmed in Technicolor.

Cast: Ronald Colman (Spirit of Man), Hedy Lamarr (Joan of Arc), Groucho Marx (Peter Minuit), Harpo Marx (Sir Isaac Newton), Chico Marx (Monk), Virginia Mayo

(Cleopatra), Agnes Moorehead (Queen Elizabeth), Vincent Price (Mr. Scratch, the Devil), Peter Lorre (Nero).

Slaughter on Tenth Avenue, Universal-International Pictures, 103 minutes, released November 5, 1957. Producer, Albert Zugsmith; director, Arnold Laven; screenplay, Lawrence Roman; based on the book *The Man Who Rocked the Boat* by William J. Keating and Richard Carter; musical score, Herschel Burke Gilbert, Richard Rodgers, Henry Mancini; costumes, Bill Thomas; cinematography, Fred Jackman Jr.

Musical Theme: "Slaughter on Tenth Avenue" by Richard Rodgers.

Cast: Richard Egan (William "Bill" Keating), Jan Sterling (Madge Pitts), Dan Duryea (John Jacob Masters), Julie Adams (Dee Pauley), Walter Matthau (Al Dahlke), Hedy Lamarr (Mona, scenes deleted).

The Female Animal, Universal-International Pictures, 82 minutes, released January 22, 1958. Producer, Albert Zugsmith; director, Harry Keller; screenplay, Robert Hill; based on a story by Albert Zugsmith; costumes, Bill Thomas; wardrobe, Rose Brandi, Truman Eli; makeup, Bud Westmore, Vince Romain, Nick Marcelino; hairstylists, Lillian Burkhart, Virginia Jones; musical score, Hans J. Salter; cinematography, Russell Metty; still photographer, Sherman Clark. Filmed in Cinemascope.

Cast: Hedy Lamarr (Vanessa Windsor), Jane Powell (Penny Windsor), George Nader (Chris Farley), Jan Sterling (Lily Frayne), Jerry Paris (Hank Galvez), Gregg Palmer (Piggy), Mabel Albertson (Irma Jones), James Gleason (Tom Maloney), Casey Adams [Max Showalter] (Charlie Grant). John Gavin (Chris Farley), scenes cut.

Television Appearances

Dick Powell's Zane Grey Theatre, CBS, "Proud Woman," 30 minutes, October 25, 1957. 8:30–9:00 p.m. Producer, Hal Hudson; director, Louis King; from a story by Harold Shumate; story supervisor, Aaron Spelling; cinematography, Guy Roe; original music, Harry Lubin; wardrobe, Robert B. Harris; makeup, Karl Herlinger; production executive, Bill Bauer; casting, Lynn Stalmaster.

Cast: Dick Powell (Host), Hedy Lamarr (Consuela Bowers), Paul Richards (Frank Frayne), Roy Roberts (Don Miguel Bowers), Donald Buka (Laredo), Edward Colmans (Esteban), Iphigenie Castiglioni (Maria Delgado).

Radio Appearances

LUX RADIO THEATRE (CBS). *"Algiers."* July 7, 1941. 60 minutes. Monday, 9:00–10:00 p.m., from Hollywood. Seventh Season. Presented by Lever Brothers–Lux Toilet Soap (Kathleen Fritz as "Libby Collins" in Lux commercials).

Producer, Cecil B. DeMille; director, Sanford Barnett; music, Louis Silver; writers, George Wells, Sanford Barnett, based on the screenplay by John Howard Lawson from the novel *Pépé le Moko* by Henri La Barthe; set decorator, George Sawley; special effects, Max Uhlig, David Light, Walter Person, Charlie Forsyth; announcer, Melville Ruick.

Cast: Charles Boyer (Pépé le Moko), Hedy Lamarr (Gabrielle "Gaby"), Alan Napier (Inspector Slimane), Bea Benaderet (Ines), Hans Conrad (Regis/Gendarme), Bruce Payne (Grandpère), Frederick Worlock (Janvier/Man), Jeff Corey (L'Arbi), Leo Cleary (Andre), Lou Merrill (Carlos), Virginia Gordon (Marie/Girl), Paul Dubov (Pierrot), Noreen Gammell (Aicha), Howard McNear (Max). Cecil B. DeMille (Host).

Commercials: Frances Litaker (United Artist stewardess), Charles Seel (Man), Jane Morgan (Woman).

Lux broadcast another version of *Algiers* on December 14, 1942, again with Boyer and Loretta Young as Gaby.

THE EDGAR BERGEN/CHARLIE McCARTHY SHOW (NBC). November 30, 1941. 30 minutes. Sunday, 8:00–8:30 p.m., from Hollywood. Presented by Chase and Sanborn Coffee.

Director, Earl Ebi; music, Ray Noble and His Orchestra; writers, Carroll Carroll, Dick Mack, Shirley Ward, Stanley Quinn, Joe Bigelow, Joe Connelly, Bob Mosher, Alan Smith, Zeno Klinker, Royal Foster, Roland MacLane, etc.; sound effects, John Glennon, etc.

Cast: Edgar Bergen, Charlie McCarthy, Bud Abbott, Lou Costello, Hedy Lamarr (Guest Star). Announcer, Buddy Twiss.

Skits: "Charlie's Orchestra"; Abbott & Costello in "Department Store"; Hedy Lamarr leads Charlie on teaching lesson.

LUX RADIO THEATRE (CBS). "The Bride Came C.O.D." December 29, 1941. 60 minutes. Monday, 9:00–10:00 p.m., from Hollywood. Eighth Season. Presented by Lever Brothers–Lux Toilet Soap (Kathleen Fritz as "Libby Collins" in Lux commercials).

Producer, Cecil B. DeMille; director, Sanford Barnett; music, Louis Silver; writers, George Wells, Sanford Barnett, based on the screenplay by Julius J. and Philip G. Epstein, story by M. M. Musselman and Kenneth Earl; set decorator, George Sawley; special effects, Max Uhlig, David Light, Walter Person, Charlie Forsyth; announcer, Melville Ruick.

Cast: Bob Hope (Steve Collins), Hedy Lamarr (Joan Winfield), Gene O'Donnell (Alan Brice), Wally Maher (Tommy Keenan), Ferdinand Munier (Jones's uncle), Eddie Marr (Pee Wee Defoe/Pilot), Warren Ashe (Man/Reporter), Torey Carleton (Gertie), Edwin Max (Hinkle/Announcer), Griff Barnett (Sheriff), Felix Vallee (Judge). Cecil B. DeMille (Host).

Commercials: Frances Litaker (United Artist stewardess), Charles Seel (Man), Jane Morgan (Woman).

Based on the 1941 Warner Bros. film *The Bride Came C.O.D.*, which starred James Cagney and Bette Davis.

THE EDGAR BERGEN/CHARLIE MCCARTHY SHOW (NBC). February 22, 1942. 30 minutes. Sunday, 8:00–8:30 p.m., from Hollywood. Presented by Chase and Sanborn Coffee.

Director, Earl Ebi; music, Ray Noble and His Orchestra; writers, Carroll Carroll, Dick Mack, Shirley Ward, Stanley Quinn, Joe Bigelow, Joe Connelly, Bob Mosher, Alan Smith, Zeno Klinker, Royal Foster, Roland MacLane, etc.; sound effects, John Glennon, etc.

Song: "Rose O'Day," sung by The Mellowaires.

Cast: Edgar Bergen, Charlie McCarthy, Mortimer Snerd, Bud Abbott, Lou Costello, The Mellowaires, Hedy Lamarr (Guest Star). Announcer, Buddy Twiss.

Skits: "Bundles for Bergen"; Abbott & Costello in "The Life of George Washington"; Hedy Lamarr, Charlie and Mortimer in "Red Cross."

THE GULF SCREEN GUILD THEATER (WABC). "Too Many Husbands." March 8, 1942. 30 minutes. Sunday, 7:30–8:00 p.m., from Hollywood. Presented by Gulf Oil.

Producer, Bill Lawrence; director, Bill Lawrence; writers, Bill Hampton, Harry Kronman; based on the comedy *Too Many Husbands* by William Somerset Maugham, and screenplay by Claude Binyon. Music by The Oscar Bradley Orchestra.

Cast: Roger Pryor (Host), Bob Hope (Bill Cardew), Bing Crosby (Henry Lowndes), Hedy Lamarr (Vicky Lowndes).

THREE RING TIME (WJZ). April 14, 1942. 30 minutes. Tuesday, 8:30–9:00 p.m., from Hollywood. Presented by Ballantine Ale.

Cast: Milton Berle (Host), Hedy Lamarr (Guest).

COMMAND PERFORMANCE (AFRS). May 14, 1942. Thursday evening, Armed Forces Radio. Presented by Campbell Soups.

Created by Louis G. Cowen; producers, Maury Holland, Vick Knight, Cal Kuhl; director, Glenn Wheaton; writers, Melvin Frank, Norman Panama; announcers, Ken Carpenter, Paul Douglas.

Cast: Edward G. Robinson (Host), Hedy Lamarr, Parkyakarkus, Milton Berle, Glenn Miller Orchestra, Ginny Simms, Ray Eberle, Cliff Edwards "Ukelele Ike," The Modernaires, Leith Stevens Orchestra, Maxie Rosenbloom, Dick Ryan, Abe Reynolds, Joe Forte (voices).

LUX RADIO THEATRE (CBS). *H. M. Pulham, Esq.* July 13, 1942. 60 minutes. Monday, 9:00–10:00 p.m., from Hollywood. Eighth Season. Presented by Lever Brothers–Lux Toilet Soap (Kathleen Fritz as "Libby Collins" in Lux commercials).

Producer, Cecil B. DeMille; director, Sanford Barnett; music, Louis Silver; writers, George Wells, Sanford Barnett, based on the book by John P. Marquand, screenplay by King Vidor and Elizabeth Hill; set decorator, George Sawley; special effects, Max Uhlig, David Light, Walter Person, Charlie Forsyth; announcer, Melville Ruick.

Cast: Hedy Lamarr (Marvin Myles), Robert Young (H. M. Pulham Jr.), Josephine Hutchinson (Kay Motford), Norman Field (Mr. Pulham Sr.), Verna Feldon (Mrs. Pulham/Nurse), Fred MacKaye (Bill), Thomas Mills (Hugh), Diane Thompson (Miss Rollo/Miss

303

Percival), Jack Mather (Bo-Jo/Driver), Tris Coffin (Ridge/Artist), Leo Cleary (Bullard/Conductor), Charles Seel (Kaufman), Eugene Forsyth (Page Boy). Cecil B. DeMille (Host).

Commercials: Sandra Coles (Sally), Doris Sederholm (Mary), Janet Waldo (Girl).

After the curtain call, a tribute to Captain Melville Ruick, with the show six years, now joining the Army Air Corps.

Based on the 1941 MGM film, *H. M. Pulham, Esq.*

THE VOICE OF BROADWAY (WABC). August 8, 1942. 15 minutes. Tuesday 6:15–6:30 p.m.

Cast: Hedy Lamarr (Guest).

COMMAND PERFORMANCE (AFRS). August 30, 1942. 30 minutes. Thursday evening, Armed Forces Radio. Presented by Campbell Soups.

Created by Louis G. Cowen; producers, Maury Holland, Vick Knight, Cal Kuhl; director, Glenn Wheaton; writers, Melvin Frank, Norman Panama; announcers, Ken Carpenter, Paul Douglas.

Cast: Bing Crosby (Host), Hedy Lamarr, Connee Boswell, Ginny Simms, Abbott and Costello, Dr. Frank Black Orchestra.

Recorded in Washington, DC.

THE EDGAR BERGEN/CHARLIE MCCARTHY SHOW (NBC). September 27, 1942. 30 minutes. Sunday, 8:00–8:30 p.m., from Hollywood. Presented by Chase and Sanborn Coffee.

Director, Earl Ebi; music, Ray Noble and His Orchestra; writers, Carroll Carroll, Dick Mack, Shirley Ward, Stanley Quinn, Joe Bigelow, Joe Connelly, Bob Mosher, Alan Smith, Zeno Klinker, Royal Foster, Roland MacLane, etc.; sound effects, John Glennon, etc.

Song: "Let Freedom Ring," music by Thesarus Nusicus, lyrics by Samuel F. Smith.

Cast: Edgar Bergen, Charlie McCarthy, Bud Abbott, Lou Costello, Don Ameche, Dale Evans, Jane Powell, Hedy Lamarr (Guest Star), Buddy Twiss (Announcer).

Skits: "Charlie and Trust"; Hedy Lamarr in "The Tropics."

LUX RADIO THEATRE (CBS). "Love Crazy," October 5, 1942. 60 minutes. Monday, 9:00–10:00 p.m., from Hollywood. Eighth Season. Presented by Lever Brothers–Lux Toilet Soap (Kathleen Fritz as "Libby Collins" in Lux commercials).

Producer, Cecil B. DeMille; director, Sanford Barnett; music, Louis Silver; writers, George Wells, Sanford Barnett, based on a screenplay by William Ludwig, Charles Lederer, and David Hertz; set decorator, George Sawley; special effects, Max Uhlig, David Light, Walter Person, Charlie Forsyth; announcer, John Milton Kennedy.

Cast: Hedy Lamarr (Susan Ireland), William Powell (Steve Ireland), Gale Gordon (Ward Willoughby), Dorothy Lovett (Isabel Kimble Grayson), Verna Felton (Mrs. Bessie Cooper), Joseph Kearns (Dr. David Klugle), Fred MacKaye ("Pinkie" Grayson), Arthur Q. Bryan (George Renny), Wally Maher (Attendant/Man #2), Eddie Marr (Joe/Cop), Griff Barnett (Judge/Janitor), Ferdinand Munier (Man/ Dr. Wuthering), James Bush (Taxi driver/Mike), Bessie Smily (Woman/Secretary), Horace Willard (Butler, Betty Hill (Girl/ Operator), Boyd Davis (Dentist), Norman Field (Man). Cecil B. DeMille (Host).

Commercials: Sandra Coles (Sally), Janet Waldo (Girl).

Based on the 1941 MGM film, *Love Crazy*.

THE LADY ESTHER SCREEN GUILD THEATER (WABC). "Come Live with Me." August 2, 1943. 30 minutes. Monday, 10:00–10:30 p.m., from Hollywood. Presented by Lady Esther Cosmetics.

Producer, Bill Lawrence; director, Bill Lawrence; writers, Bill Hampton, Harry Kronman; based on the story by Virginia Van Upp, and on the screenplay *Come Live with Me* by Patterson McNutt. Music by The Oscar Bradley Orchestra.

Cast: Truman Bradley (Host), Hedy Lamarr (Johanna Janns [Johnny Jones]), John Loder (Bill Smith), Vincent Price (Barton Kendrick).

THE EDGAR BERGEN/CHARLIE MCCARTHY SHOW (NBC). September 26, 1943. 30 minutes. Sunday, 8:00–8:30 p.m., from Hollywood. Presented by Chase and Sanborn Coffee.

Director, Earl Ebi; music, Ray Noble and His Orchestra; writers, Carroll Carroll, Dick Mack, Shirley Ward, Stanley Quinn, Joe Bigelow, Joe Connelly, Bob Mosher, Alan Smith, Zeno Klinker, Royal Foster, Roland MacLane, etc.; sound effects, John Glennon, etc.

Songs: "Ice Cold Katie," music by Arthur Schwartz, lyrics by Frank Loesser; "Put Your Arms Around Me, Honey, Hold Me Tight," music by Albert Von Tilzer, lyrics by Junie McCree.

Cast: Edgar Bergen, Charlie McCarthy, Mortimer Snerd, Victor Moore, William Gaxton, Dale Evans, The Sportsmen, Hedy Lamarr (Guest Star), Bill Goodwin (Announcer).

Skits: "Checking Account"; Victor Moore and William Gaxton in "Leading Man"; Hedy Lamarr in "Bergen Buildup."

THE BURNS AND ALLEN SHOW (CBS). October 26, 1943. 30 minutes. Tuesday, 9:00–9:30 p.m., from Hollywood. Presented by Lever Brothers–Swan Soap.

Directors, Ed Garner, Ralph Levy; writers, Paul Henning, Harvey Helm, Hal Block, Henry Garson, Keith Fowler, Aaron J. Ruben, Harmon J. Alexander, Helen Gould Harvey; music, Feliz Mills and His Orchestra; sound effects, David Light, Al Span.

Music, Felix Mills' Orchestra; Announcer, Bill Goodwin.

Theme song: "The Love Nest" by Louis Hirsch.

Songs: "My Heart Tells," music by Harry Warren, lyrics by Mack Gordon; "They're Either Too Young or Too Old," music by Arthur Schwartz, lyrics by Frank Loesser.

Cast: George Burns, Gracie Allen, Hedy Lamarr, Elvia Allman, Lawrence Nash, Mel Blanc, Hans Conried, Jimmy Cash (Vocalist), Bill Goodwin (Announcer).

Skit: "Queen of the Fleet."

THE EDGAR BERGEN/CHARLIE MCCARTHY SHOW (NBC). November 21, 1943. 30 minutes. Sunday, 8:00–8:30 p.m., from Hollywood. Presented by Chase and Sanborn Coffee.

Director, Earl Ebi; music, Ray Noble and His Orchestra; writers, Carroll Carroll, Dick Mack, Shirley Ward, Stanley Quinn, Joe Bigelow, Joe Connelly, Bob Mosher, Alan Smith, Zeno Klinker, Royal Foster, Roland MacLane, etc.; sound effects, John Glennon, etc.

Songs: "Someday My Prince Will Come," music by Frank Churchill, lyrics by Larry Morey; "You Discover You're in New York," music by Harry Warren, lyrics by Leo Robin.

Cast: Edgar Bergen, Charlie McCarthy, Jane Powell, Victor Moore, William Gaxton, The Pied Pipers, Hedy Lamarr (Guest Star), Bill Goodwin (Announcer).

Skits: "Sleepwalking"; Victor Moore and William Gaxton in "Navy"; Hedy Lamarr in "Plumbing."

Broadcast from the US Naval Air Station at Terminal Island, California.

WHAT'S NEW (WJZ). December 11, 1943. 60 minutes. Saturday, 7:00–8:00 p.m. from Hollywood.

Cast: Don Ameche (Host); Hedy Lamarr, Arthur Treacher, Nancy Walker, Captain Charles Romaine, Andrew Higgins (Guests).

SOLDIERS WITH WINGS (WEAF). December 12, 1943. 30 minutes. Sunday, 12:00–12:30 p.m., from Hollywood.

Cast: Bill Goodwin (Host), Hedy Lamarr (Guest Star).

LUX RADIO THEATRE (CBS). *Casablanca*, January 24, 1944. 60 minutes. Monday, 9:00–10:00 p.m., from Hollywood. Presented by Lever Brothers–Lux Toilet Soap (Doris Singleton as "Libby Collins" in Lux commercials).

Producer, Cecil B. DeMille; director, Sanford Barnett; music, Louis Silver; writers, George Wells, Sanford Barnett, based on a screenplay by Julius J and Philip Epstein, and Howard Koch; based on the play "Everybody Comes To Rick's" by Murray Bennett and Joan Alison; set decorator, George Sawley; special effects, Max Uhlig, David Light, Walter Person, Charlie Forsyth; announcer, John Milton Kennedy.

Cast: Hedy Lamarr (Ilsa Lund), Alan Ladd (Rick Blaine), John Loder (Victor Lazlo), Edgar Barrier (Captain Renault), Norman Field (Major Strausser), Ernest Whitman (Sam), Rene Gacaire (Casselle), Ed Emerson (Voice), Charles Seel (Carl), Jay Novello (Hans Ugarte), Leo Cleary (Ferrari), Charles Lung (Sascha). Cecil B. DeMille (Host).

Commercials: Richard C. Howell (Jim), Paula Winslowe (Peggy), Dorothy Lovett (Girl).

Based on the 1942 Warner Bros. film, *Casablanca*.

SILVER THEATRE (WABC). "She Looked Like an Angel," February 20, 1944. 30 minutes. Sunday, 6:00–6:30 p.m., from Hollywood. Presented by the International Silver Company. Director, Conrad Nagel.

Cast: Conrad Nagel (Host), Hedy Lamarr, John Loder, H. Charles (Announcer).

STARS AND THEIR STORIES (CBS). "Romance," July 23, 1944. 30 minutes. Sunday, 8:00–8:30 p.m., from Hollywood. Presented by the Goodyear Tire Company.

Cast: Walter Pidgeon (Host), Hedy Lamarr (Guest Star).

RADIO HALL OF FAME (NBC Blue). *Experiment Perilous*, February 4, 1945. 60 minutes. Sunday, 6:00–7:00 p.m. Presented by Philco.

Music: Paul Whiteman Orchestra; variety editor, Abel Green.

Cast: Al Pearce (Host), Hedy Lamarr (Allida Bedereaux), George Brent (Dr. Huntington Bailey), Andy Russell, Marjorie Main, Marlin Hurt (Beulah), Eileen Barton, Matty Melneck, Robert Maxwell, Glen Riggs (Announcer).

THE CHARLIE MCCARTHY SHOW (NBC). April 7, 1946. 30 minutes. Sunday, 8:00–8:30 p.m., from Hollywood. Presented by Chase and Sanborn Coffee.

Director, Earl Ebi; music, Ray Noble and His Orchestra; writers, Carroll Carroll, Dick Mack, Shirley Ward, Stanley Quinn, Joe Bigelow, Joe Connelly, Bob Mosher, Alan Smith, Zeno Klinker, Royal Foster, Roland MacLane, etc.; sound effects, John Glennon, etc.

Songs: "It's Anybody's Spring," music by Jimmy Van Husen, lyrics by Johnny Burke.

Cast: Edgar Bergen, Charlie McCarthy, Mortimer Snerd, Axel Swenson, Hedy Lamarr (Guest Star), Anita Gordon, Martha Wentworth (Aunt Minerva), Ken Carpenter (Announcer).

Skits: Edgar Bergen, Charlie McCarthy, Anita Gordon, Hedy Lamarr in "Build Up"; Charlie McCarthy, Martha Wentworth, Hedy Lamarr in "Plans for the New House."

THE BOB HOPE SHOW (NBC). "From Coronado Island," April 10, 1951. 30 minutes. Tuesday, 9:00–9:30 p.m. Presented by Chesterfield Cigarettes.

Music: Les Brown Orchestra.

Cast: Bob Hope, Hedy Lamarr (Guest Star), Frankie Laine, Jack Kirkwood, Marilyn Maxwell, Hi Averback (Announcer).

LUX RADIO THEATRE (CBS). *Samson and Delilah*, November 19, 1951. 60 minutes. Monday, 9:00–10:00 p.m., from Hollywood. Seventeenth Season. Presented by Lever Brothers–Lux Toilet Soap (Kathleen Fritz as "Libby Collins" in Lux commercials).

Producer, Cecil B. DeMille; director, Erle Erbi; musical director, Rudy Schrager; writer, George Wells; adapted by Sanford H. Barnett; set decorator, George Sawley; special effects, Max Uhlig, David Light, Walter Person, Charlie Forsyth; announcer, John Milton Kennedy.

Cast: Victor Mature (Samson), Hedy Lamarr (Delilah), Edgar Barrier (Saran), Leif Erickson (Ahtur), Herbert Rowlinson (Minoah), Hope Sansbury (Hisham), Norma Varden (Hazel), and Kay Stewart, Lynn Allen, Herbert Butterfield, Jeffrey Silver, Bill Bouchey, Jonathan Hole, Theodore van Eltz, Robert Griffin, Bill Johnstone, Eddie Marr. Gale Gordon (Narrator). William Keighley (Host).

Intermission guest: Nancy Hale, Paramount starlet.

Commercials: Dorothy Lovett as "Libby Collins" in Lux commercial commenting on Universal's newest comedy release of *Week-End with Father*, starring Van Heflin, Patricia Neal, and Gigi Perreau.

Rudy Schrager included portions of Camille Saint-Saëns's opus "Bacchanal" into the production.

Based on the 1948 Paramount film, *Samson and Delilah*.

NOTES

Preface

1. John Springer and Jack Hamilton, *They Had Faces Then: Annabella to Zorina—The Superstars, Stars and Starlets of the 1930s* (Secaucus, NJ: Citadel Press, 1974), 156.

2. *Merriam-Webster's Collegiate Dictionary*, 10th ed. (Springfield, MA: Merriam-Webster, Inc., 1994), 101.

3. Frank S. Nugent, "Glamour Girls: A Film Cavalcade," *New York Times*, June 25, 1939.

4. Ibid.

5. Richard Schickel, *The Stars* (New York: Bonanza Books, 1962), 212.

6. Margaret J. Bailey, *Those Glorious Glamour Years: Classic Hollywood Costume Design of the 1930s* (Secaucus, NJ: Citadel Press, 1982), 191.

7. Stephen Michael Shearer, *Beautiful: The Life of Hedy Lamarr* (New York: Thomas Dunne/St. Martin's Press-Macmillan, 2010), 357.

8. George Hurrell, *Hurrell Hollywood: The Photographs of George Hurrell, 1928–1990* (New York: St. Martin's Press, 1991), frontispiece quote.

Chapter 1: Monsters, Ogres, and Knights

1. Shearer, *Beautiful: The Life of Hedy Lamarr*, 7.

2. James Forsman, "Hedy Lamarr's Astonishing Story," *Picture Play*, February 1939.

3. Angela Lambert, *The Lost Life of Eva Braun* (New York: St. Martin's, 2007), 25.

4. George Weller, "The Ecstatic Hedy Lamarr," *Ken* magazine, January 26, 1939.

5. "Fun and Finance," *New York Times*, November 16, 1932.

6. Aribert Mog (1904–1941) was a modestly successful leading man in German cinema, as "Aryan" as one could get with his looks. Tall, masculine, and dependable, he is best remembered for his role in *Extase*, as well as in legendary auteur director Frank Wisbar's two 1936 classics, *Fahrmann Maria* (*Ferryman Maria*) for Pallas Film, and *Die Unbekannte* (*The Unknown*) for Terra Films. Both starred him opposite Sybille Schmitz. A passionate and devout Nazi, he was killed in action in Nova Trojanova inside the then Soviet Union during World War II.

7. Quoted in *Hedy Lamarr: Secrets of a Hollywood Star*, documentary film by Donatella Dubini and Fosco Dubini (Dubini Filmproduktion, 2006).

8. Shearer, *Beautiful: The Life of Hedy Lamarr*, 27.

Chapter 2: The Most Beautiful Girl in the World

1. "The Film Society," *London Times*, March 12, 1933.

2. Franz F. Planer (1894–1961) left Austria in 1937, the same year as Hedy, before the *Anschluss*. In demand by such directors as John Huston, Robert Siodmak, Stanley Kramer, and Edward Dmytryk, Planer enjoyed a long and profitable career in Hollywood as a cinematographer for such popular films as *The Caine Mutiny* (1954) and *Breakfast at Tiffany's* (1961), and received five Academy Award nominations, for *Champion* (1949), *Death of A Salesman* (1951), *Roman Holiday* (1953), *The Nun's Story* (1959), and *The Children's Hour* (1961).

3. Shearer, *Beautiful: The Life of Hedy Lamarr*, 38.

4. Ibid., 37.

5. Rob Walters, *Spread Spectrum: Hedy Lamarr and the Mobile Phone* (Charleston, SC: BookSurge, 2005), 79.

Chapter 3: Madame Mandl and the Gathering Storm

1. This first meeting with Louis B. Mayer and Hedy Kiesler has been verified in several Hollywood accounts, most notably in Otto Preminger's 1977 autobiography, *Preminger: An Autobiography* (New York: Doubleday & Co., 1977), and in Peter Hay's *MGM: When the Lion Roared* (Atlanta, GA: Turner Publishing, 1991).

2. Marian Rhea, "I Have Lived," *Movie Mirror*, February 1939.

3. " 'Ecstasy' Star to Quit Rich Mate for the Stage," New York *Daily News*, September 19, 1937.

4. Charles Higham, *Merchant of Dreams: Louis B. Mayer, M.G.M., and the Secret Hollywood* (New York: Donald I. Fine, 1993), 267.

Chapter 4: The Power of the Hollywood Studio Machine

1. Raymond Sarlot and Fred E. Basten, *Life at the Marmont: The Inside Story of Hollywood's Legendary Hotel of the Stars* (Santa Monica, CA: Roundtable, 1987), 55.

2. Ibid., 55.

3. Ibid., 56.

4. Maria Riva, *Marlene Dietrich* (New York: Alfred A. Knopf, 1992), 400–01.

5. Joseph Schmidt (1904–1942) was a gifted and brilliant Austro-Hungarian and Romanian operatic tenor. His diminutive height, however—under five feet tall—limited his appearances in staged opera. Instead, he became an extremely popular and prolific radio and recording artist in Europe throughout the 1930s. He even appeared in several films of the era. His most popular motion picture was filmed both in German in 1933 (*Ein Lied geht um die Welt*) and in English in 1934 (*My Song Goes Round the World*). In 1937 after a voyage on the *Normandie*, he toured the United States, appeared on NBC Radio, and performed at Carnegie Hall alongside coloratura soprano Grace Moore. He also performed

with Maria Jeritza, Helen Jepson, Donald Dickson, and Richard Tauber as part of the General Motors Concert Company. Welcomed back to the Netherlands and Belgium after 1937, he remained immensely popular in concerts, radio, and film. When war broke out in 1939, Schmidt attempted to flee Europe but was captured in France and interned at a refugee camp in Girenbad, near Zurich, Switzerland, where he tragically fell ill and died in November 1942.

Chapter 5: *Algiers* and the Creation of Hedy Lamarr

1. Sarlot and Basten, *Life at the Marmont*, 55.

2. Shearer, *Beautiful: The Life of Hedy Lamarr*, 58.

3. Sarlot and Basten, *Life at the Marmont*, 57.

4. Born Emmanuel Radnitzky, Man Ray (1890–1976) was an American visual artist who spent most of his life in Paris. A moderate contributor to the Dada and Surrealist movements, he was best known for his portrait and fashion photography, though he always considered himself a painter.

5. Trude Fleischmann (1895–1990) studied at *Lehr und Versuchsanstalt fur Photographie und Reproduktionsverfahren* in Vienna for three years. After the 1938 *Anschluss*, Fleischmann came to New York, opening a studio next to Carnegie Hall in 1940. There she photographed such important people as Eleanor Roosevelt, Albert Einstein, Lotte Lehmann, and Arturo Toscanini. As a fashion photographer her work was featured in such publications as *Vogue*, her photography benefiting from her ingenious use of diffused artificial lighting.

6. W. Robert LaVine, *In a Glamorous Fashion: The Fabulous Years of Hollywood Costume Design* (New York: Charles Scribner's Sons, 1980), 212.

7. Ibid., 214.

8. Jeanine Basinger, *The Star Machine* (New York: Alfred A. Knopf, 2007), 383–84.

9. Ibid., 385.

10. Mildred Adams, "Glamour Changes—Beauty Remains," *New York Times*, September 3, 1939.

11. Fred E. Basten, *Max Factor: The Man Who Changed the Faces of the World* (New York: Arcade Publishing, 2008), 129.

12. Richard Griffith and Arthur Mayer, *The Movies* (New York: Simon & Schuster, 1957), 365.

Chapter 6: Hollywood Glamour and Style

1. Gottfried Reinhardt, *The Genius: A Memoir of Max Reinhardt* (New York: Alfred A. Knopf, 1979), 290.

312

2. Anonymous, unknown magazine article.

3. Lucie Neville, "What Have They Got That You Haven't Got," *Arizona Republic*, June 18, 1939.

4. Springer and Hamilton, *They Had Faces Then*, 155.

5. Shearer, *Beautiful: The Life of Hedy Lamarr*, 61.

6. "Make-Up: The Shadows We Paint on Human Faces," *World Film News*, April 1938.

7. Neal Gabler, *An Empire of Their Own* (New York: Crown Publishers Inc., 1988), 214.

8. Ibid., 214.

9. Basinger, *The Star Machine*, 26.

10. Shearer, *Beautiful: The Life of Hedy Lamarr*, 61.

11. John Kobal, *Hollywood Glamor Portraits: 145 Photos of the Stars, 1926–1949* (New York: Dover Publications, Inc., 1976), vi.

12. Vicki Goldberg, "The Images that Gave the Stars Their Faces," *New York Times*, May 18, 1997.

13. Kobal, *Hollywood Glamor Portraits*, vi.

14. Ibid., xii.

15. John Kobal, *Movie-Star Portraits of the Forties: 163 Glamor Photos* (New York: Dover Publications, Inc., 1977), ix.

16. Kobal, *Hollywood Glamor Portraits*, xi.

17. Whitney Stine and George Hurrell, *50 Years of Photographing Hollywood: The Hurrell Style* (New York: Greenwich House, 1983), 139.

18. John Kobal, *People Will Talk* (New York: Alfred A. Knopf, 1985), 379.

19. Ibid., 371.

20. Kobal, *Hollywood Glamor Portraits*, x.

Chapter 7: The Machine at Work

1. Tracy Christensen, telephone interview, July 2, 2020.

2. Elizabeth Leese, *Costume Design in the Movies* (New York: Frederick Ungar Publishing Co., 1977), 19.

3. Laura Jacobs, "Glamour by Adrian," *Vanity Fair*, June 2000.

4. Jay Jorgenson and Donald L. Scoggins, *Creating the Illusion: A Fashionable History of Hollywood Costume Design* (Philadelphia, PA: Running Press, 2015), 151.

5. Lyn Miller, "You Wear What They Tell You," *Movie Classic*, September 1935.

6. David Chierichetti, "Star Style: Hollywood's Legendary Fashion First," *Los Angeles Times*, October 27, 1978.

7. Jorgenson and Scoggins, *Creating the Illusion*, 137–38.

8. Douglas Fairbanks Jr., *The Salad Days* (New York: Doubleday & Co., 1988), 142.

9. Jimmie Fidler, "Star Wears 25-Pound Gown," *Los Angeles Times*, September 6, 1939.

10. Thomas Schatz, *The Genius of the System: Hollywood Filmmaking in the Studio Era* (New York: Pantheon Books, 1988), 270.

11. Ibid., 270.

Chapter 8: The Indelible Image on the Silver Screen

1. Basinger, *The Star Machine*, 56.

2. Kobal, *Movie-Star Portraits of the Forties: 163 Glamor Photos*, v.

3. Unknown newspaper source, August 6, 1940.

4. Christensen interview, July 2, 2020.

5. Jacobs, "Glamour by Adrian," 205.

6. LaVine, *In a Glamorous Fashion*, 167.

Chapter 9: The Kalloch Style

1. King Vidor, *King Vidor: On Film Making* (New York: David McKay Company, Inc., 1972), 52.

2. Jorgenson and Scoggins, *Creating the Illusion*, 183.

3. Kobal, *Movie-Star Portraits of the Forties: 163 Glamor Photos*, v.

4. Christensen interview, July 2, 2020.

5. Ibid.

6. Kobal, *Movie-Star Portraits of the Forties: 163 Glamor Photos*, v.

7. James Montgomery Flagg, "Noted Artist Calls Hedy Lamarr 'The Girl with the Perfect Nose,' *Lancaster New Era*, Lancaster, PA, September 18, 1941.

8. Cinematographer Karl Freund was born on January 16, 1890. Beginning his career in Germany in 1916, Freund became an innovator of cinema film photography. He shot such classic silent features as *Variety* (UFA, 1925) and Fritz Lang's *Metropolis* (UFA, 1927). Coming to Hollywood in 1929, he mastered the camera for such films as *Dracula* (1931) and *Murders in the Rue Morgue* (1932), both for Universal, where he also directed the original 1932 Boris Karloff *The Mummy*. He moved over to MGM and lensed *Camille* (1936) and *Conquest* (1937), both with Garbo, and *The Good Earth* (1937), for which he won the Academy Award. He would earn two more Oscar nominations in 1941 for

314

black-and-white cinematography, for Metro's *The Chocolate Soldier*, and for color, the studio's *Blossoms in the Dust*. For MGM he would later film *Du Barry Was a Lady* with Lucille Ball (1942), *A Guy Named Joe* (1943), and *Without Love* (1944), and for Warner Brothers, *Key Largo* (1947) and *Bright Leaf* (1950). Beginning in 1951, Freund filmed all five seasons of the original *I Love Lucy* television series. He died on May 3, 1969.

9. Christopher Young, *The Films of Hedy Lamarr* (Secaucus, NJ: Citadel Press, 1978), 161.

10. Kobal, *Movie Star Portraits of the Forties: 163 Glamor Photos*, vi.

11. Sidney Skolsky, "Lamarr in Chiffong," *Cincinnati Enquirer*, June 18, 1942.

Chapter 10: The Lamarr Look and 1940s Style

1. Kelma Flake, "Irene," *Movieland* magazine, June 1944.

2. Ibid.

3. Irene scrapbooks, Academy of Motion Picture Arts and Sciences Library, Los Angeles, California.

4. Ibid.

5. Jorgenson and Scoggins, *Creating the Illusion*, 106.

6. Frank Westmore, *The Westmores of Hollywood* (Philadelphia, PA: J. B. Lippincott Co., 1976), 60.

7. Jorgenson and Scoggins, *Creating the Illusion*, 260.

8. Leese, *Costume Design in the Movies*, 60.

9. Jorgenson and Scoggins, *Creating the Illusion*, 127.

Chapter 11: *Samson and Delilah* and the Demise of the Studio System

1. Eric Brown, "Hedy Lamarr Complains: I Can't Get Any Privacy," *The National Enquirer*, n.d.

2. Jorgenson and Scoggins, *Creating the Illusion*, 233.

3. Edith Head in letter to Kenneth Douglas at Universal City Studios, February 5, 1971.

4. Edith Head and Paddy Calistro, *Edith Head's Hollywood* (New York: E. P. Dutton, Inc., 1983), 81–82.

5. Cecilia DeMille Presley and Mark A Vieira, *Cecil B. DeMille: The Art of the Hollywood Epic* (Philadelphia, PA: Running Press, 2014), 343.

6. Ibid.

7. Ibid.

8. Head and Calistro, *Edith Head's Hollywood*, 74.

9. Cecil B. DeMille papers, Special Collections, Brigham Young University, Provo, Utah.

10. Presley and Vieira, *Cecil B. DeMille: The Art of the Hollywood Epic*, 343.

11. Anne Edwards, *The DeMilles: An American Family* (New York: Harry N. Abrams Inc., 1988), 196.

12. Presley and Vieira, *Cecil B. DeMille: The Art of the Hollywood Epic*, 343.

13. Head and Calistro, *Edith Head's Hollywood*, 85.

14. Ibid.

15. Frank Billecci and Lauranne B. Fisher, *Irene: A Designer from the Golden Age of Hollywood—The MGM Years 1942–1949* (Atglen, PA: Schiffer Publishing Ltd., 2013), 127.

16. LaVine, *In a Glamorous Fashion*, 213.

17. Jorgenson and Scoggins, *Creating the Illusion*, 262.

18. Edwin Schallert, "Unique Deal Arranged with Dramatists: Paula Raymond in Bright Arc," *Los Angeles Times*, December 19, 1949.

19. LaVine, *In a Glamorous Fashion*, 203.

Chapter 12: The End of an Era

1. Shearer, *Beautiful: The Life of Hedy Lamarr*, 279.

2. Basinger, *The Star Machine*, 320.

3. Philip K. Scheuer, " 'Mankind' Comes Out as Vulgarized History," *Los Angeles Times*, November 14, 1959, quoted in Medved and Dreyfuss, *50 Worst Films of All Time*.

4. Harry Medved and Randy Dreyfuss, *The 50 Worst Films of All Time (And How They Got That Way)* (New York: Popular Library, 1978), 225.

5. Shearer, *Beautiful: The Life of Hedy Lamarr*, 320.

Chapter 13: Legacy: The Dichotomy of Beauty and Brains

1. Shearer, *Beautiful: The Life of Hedy Lamarr*, 108.

2. Jesse Kratz, "Pieces of History: The World War II–Era Actress Who Invented Wi-Fi: Hedy Lamarr," National Archives, May 26, 2020.

3. Alun Butler, "Brunette Sinks Battleship," *New Scientist*, December 19/26, 1998–January 2, 1999.

4. Annette Tapert, *The Power of Glamour: The Women Who Defined the Magic of Stardom* (New York: Crown Publishers, Inc., 1998), 11.

BIBLIOGRAPHY

Books

Antheil, George. *Bad Boy of Music*. Garden City, NY: Doubleday & Co., 1945.

Bailey, Margaret J. *Those Glorious Glamour Years: Classic Hollywood Costume Design of the 1930s*. Secaucus, NJ: Citadel Press, 1982.

Basinger, Jeanine. *The Star Machine*. New York: Alfred A. Knopf, 2007.

Basten, Fred E. *Max Factor: The Man Who Changed the Faces of the World*. New York: Arcade Publishing, 2008.

Billecci, Frank, and Lauranne B. Fisher. *Irene: A Designer from the Golden Age of Hollywood—The MGM Years 1942–1949*. Atglen, PA: Schiffer Publishing Ltd., 2013.

Bull, Clarence, and Raymond Lee. *The Faces of Hollywood*. Cranbury, NJ: A. S. Barnes and Company, Inc., 1968.

Chierichetti, David, and Edith Head. *Edith Head: The Life and Times of Hollywood's Celebrated Costume Designer*. New York: Perennial-HarperCollins, 2003.

Edwards, Anne. *The DeMilles: An American Family*. New York: Harry N. Abrams, Inc., 1988.

Fairbanks, Douglas, Jr. *The Salad Days*. New York: Doubleday & Co., 1988.

Finler, Joel. *The Hollywood Story*. New York: Crown Publishers, Inc., 1988.

Fleming, E. J. *The Movieland Directory*. Jefferson, NC: McFarland & Company, 2004.

Gabler, Neal. *An Empire of Their Own: How the Jews Invented Hollywood*. New York: Crown Publishers, 1988.

Griffith, Richard, and Arthur Mayer. *The Movies*. New York: Simon & Schuster, 1957.

Guilaroff, Sydney, and Cathy Griffin. *Crowning Glory: Reflections of Hollywood's Favorite Confidant*. Santa Monica, CA: General Publishing Group, Inc., 1996.

Gutner, Howard. *Gowns by Adrian: The MGM Years 1928–1941*. New York: Harry N. Abrams, Inc., 2001.

Hay, Peter. *MGM: When the Lion Roared*. Atlanta, GA: Turner Publishing, Inc., 1991.

Head, Edith, and Paddy Calistro. *Edith Head's Hollywood*. New York: E. P. Dutton, Inc., 1983.

Higham, Charles. *Merchant of Dreams: Louis B. Mayer, M.G.M., and the Secret Hollywood*. New York: Donald I. Fine, 1993.

Hurrell, George. *Hurrell Hollywood: The Photographs of George Hurrell, 1928–1990*. New York: St. Martin's Press, 1991.

Jorgensen, Jay, and Donald L. Scoggins. *Creating the Illusion: A Fashionable History of Hollywood Costume Designers*. Philadelphia, PA: Running Press, 2015.

Kobal, John. *Hollywood Glamor Portraits: 145 Photos of Stars, 1926–1949*. New York: Dover Publications, Inc., 1976.

———. *Movie-Star Portraits of the Forties: 163 Glamor Photos*. New York: Dover Publications, Inc., 1977.

———. *People Will Talk*. New York: Alfred K. Knopf, 1985.

Lambert, Angela. *The Lost Life of Eva Braun*. New York: St. Martin's Press, 2007.

LaVine, W. Robert. *In a Glamorous Fashion: The Fabulous Years of Hollywood Costume Design*. New York: Charles Scribner's Sons, 1980.

Lawton, Richard. *Grand Illusions*. London: Octopus Books, Ltd., 1974.

Leese, Elizabeth. *Costume Design in the Movies*. New York: Frederick Ungar Publishing Co., 1977.

Maltin, Leonard. *The Art of the Cinematographer: A Survey and Interviews with Five Masters*. New York: Dover Publications, Inc., 1978.

Medved, Harry, and Randy Dreyfuss. *The 50 Worst Films of All Time (And How They Got That Way)*. New York: Popular Library, 1978.

Merriam-Webster's Collegiate Dictionary, 10th ed. Springfield, MA: Merriam-Webster, Inc., 1994.

Pepper, Terence. *The Man Who Shot Garbo: The Hollywood Photographs of Clarence Sinclair Bull*. New York: Simon & Schuster, 1989.

Preminger, Otto. *Preminger: An Autobiography*. New York: Doubleday & Co., 1977.

Presley, Cecilia De Mille, and Mark A. Vieira. *Cecil B. DeMille: The Art of the Hollywood Epic*. Philadelphia, PA: Running Press, 2014.

Reinhardt, Gottfried. *The Genius: A Memoir of Max Reinhardt*. New York: Alfred K. Knopf, Inc., 1979.

Rifkind, Donna. *The Sun and Her Stars: Salka Viertel and Hitler's Exiles in the Golden Age of Hollywood*. New York: Other Press, 2020.

Rinella, Michael D. *Margaret Sullavan: The Life and Career of a Reluctant Star*. Jefferson, NC: McFarland & Company, 2019.

Riva, Maria. *Marlene Dietrich*. New York: Alfred A. Knopf, 1992.

Rose, Helen. *"Just Make Them Beautiful": The Many Worlds of a Designing Woman*. Santa Monica, CA: Dennis-Landman Publishers, 1976.

Sarlot, Raymond, and Fred E. Basten. *Life at the Marmont: The Inside Story of Hollywood's Legendary Hotel of the Stars*. Santa Monica, CA: Roundtable, 1987.

Schatz, Thomas. *The Genius of the System: Hollywood Filmmaking in the Studio Era*. New York: Pantheon Books, 1988.

Schickel, Richard. *The Stars*. New York: Bonanza Books, 1962.

Sharaff, Irene. *Broadway & Hollywood: Costumes Designed by Irene Sharaff*. New York: Von Nostrand Reinhold Company, 1976.

Shearer, Stephen Michael. *Beautiful: The Life of Hedy Lamarr*. New York: Thomas Dunne/St. Martin's Press-Macmillan, 2010.

Springer, John, and Jack Hamilton. *They Had Faces Then: Annabella to Zorina—The Superstars, Stars and Starlets of the 1930s*. Secaucus, NJ: Citadel Press, 1974.

Stallings, Penny. *Flesh and Fantasy: The Truth Behind the Fantasy, the Fantasy Behind the Truth*. New York: St. Martin's Press, 1978.

Stine, Whitney, and George Hurrell. *50 Years of Photographing Hollywood: The Hurrell Style*. New York: Greenwich House, 1983.

Tapert, Annette. *The Power of Glamour: The Women Who Defined the Magic of Stardom*. New York: Crown Publishers, Inc., 1998.

Tietjen, Jill, and Barbara Bridges. *Hollywood: Her Story, An Illustrated History of Women and the Movies*. Guilford, CT: Lyons Press, 2019.

Trent, Paul. *The Image Makers: Sixty Years of Hollywood Glamour*. New York: McGraw-Hill, 1972.

Vidor, King Wallis. *King Vidor: On Film Making*. New York: David McKay Company, Inc., 1972.

Walters, Rob. *Spread Spectrum: Hedy Lamarr and the Mobile Phone*. Charleston, SC: BookSurge, 2005.

Westmore, Frank. *The Westmores of Hollywood*. Philadelphia, PA: J. B. Lippincott Company, 1976.

Young, Christopher. *The Films of Hedy Lamarr*. Secaucus, NJ: Citadel Press, 1978.

Articles

Adams, Mildred. "Glamour Changes—Beauty Remains," *New York Times*, September 3, 1939.

Brown, Eric. "Hedy Lamarr Complains: I Can't Get Any Privacy," *The National Enquirer*, n.d.

Butler, Alun. "Brunette Sinks Battleship," *New Scientist*, December 19/26, 1998–January 2, 1999.

Chierichetti, David. "Star Style: Hollywood's Legendary Fashion First," *Los Angeles Times*, October 27, 1978.

" 'Ecstasy' Star to Quit Rich Mate for the Stage," New York *Daily News*, September 19, 1937.

Fidler, Jimmie. "Star Wears 25-Pound Gown," *Los Angeles Times*, September 6, 1939.

"The Film Society," *London Times*, March 12, 1933.

Flagg, James Montgomery. "Noted Artist Calls Hedy Lamarr 'The Girl with the Perfect Nose,'" *Lancaster New Era*, Lancaster, PA, September 18, 1941.

Flake, Kelma. "Irene," *Movieland* magazine, June 1944.

Forsman, James. "Hedy Lamarr's Astonishing Story," *Picture Play*, February 1939.

"Fun and Finance," *New York Times*, November 16, 1932.

Goldberg, Vicki. "The Images that Gave the Stars Their Faces," *New York Times*, May 18, 1997.

Jacobs, Laura. "Glamour by Adrian," *Vanity Fair*, June 2000.

Kratz, Jesse. "Pieces of History: The World War II–Era Actress Who Invented Wi-Fi: Hedy Lamarr," National Archives, May 26, 2020.

"Make-Up: The Shadows We Paint on Human Faces," *World Film News*, April 1938.

Miller, Lyn. "You Wear What They Tell You," *Movie Classic*, September 1935.

Neville, Lucie. "What Have They Got That You Haven't Got," *Arizona Republic*, June 18, 1939.

Nugent, Frank S. "Glamour Girls: A Film Cavalcade," *New York Times*, June 25, 1939.

Rhea, Marian. "I Have Lived," *Movie Mirror*, February 1939.

Schallert, Edwin. "Unique Deal Arranged with Dramatists: Paula Raymond in Bright Arc," *Los Angeles Times*, December 19, 1949.

Skolsky, Sidney. "Lamarr in Chiffong," *Cincinnati Enquirer*, June 18, 1942.

Weller, George. "The Ecstatic Hedy Lamarr," *Ken* magazine, January 26, 1939.

Miscellaneous

Cecil B. DeMille papers, Special Collections, Brigham Young University, Provo, Utah.

Christensen, Tracy. Interview, July 2, 2020.

Head, Edith. Letter to Kenneth Douglas at Universal City Studios, February 5, 1971.

Hedy Lamarr: Secrets of a Hollywood Star. Documentary film by Donatella Dubini and Fosco Dubini. Germany: Dubini Filmproduktion, 2006.

Irene scrapbooks, Academy of Motion Picture Arts and Sciences Library, Los Angeles, California.

INDEX

Note: Page numbers in *italic* refer to photographs.